CW01456184

Strategic Management in the Media

Third Edition

Strategic Management in the Media

Theory to Practice

Lucy Küng

1 Oliver's Yard
55 City Road
London EC1Y 1SP

2455 Teller Road
Thousand Oaks, California 91320

Unit No 323–333, Third Floor, F-Block
International Trade Tower Nehru Place
New Delhi 110 019

8 Marina View Suite 43–053
Asia Square Tower 1
Singapore 018960

Editor: Natalie Aguilera
Editorial Assistant: Sarah Moorhouse
Production Editor: Neelu Sahu
Copyeditor: Diana Chambers
Proofreader: Salia Nessa
Indexer: KnowledgeWorks Global Ltd
Marketing Manager: Elena Asplen
Cover Design: Victoria Bridal
Typeset by KnowledgeWorks Global Ltd
Printed in the UK

© Lucy Küng 2024

Apart from any fair dealing for the purposes of research, private study, or criticism or review, as permitted under the Copyright, Designs and Patents Act, 1988, this publication may not be reproduced, stored or transmitted in any form, or by any means, without the prior permission in writing of the publisher, or in the case of reprographic reproduction, in accordance with the terms of licences issued by the Copyright Licensing Agency. Enquiries concerning reproduction outside those terms should be sent to the publisher.

Library of Congress Control Number: 2023938645

British Library Cataloguing in Publication data

A catalogue record for this book is available from the British Library

ISBN 978-1-5297-7370-5
ISBN 978-1-5297-7369-9 (pbk)

Printed and bound by CPI Group (UK) Ltd, Croydon, CR0 4YY

At Sage we take sustainability seriously. Most of our products are printed in the UK using responsibly sourced papers and boards. When we print overseas we ensure sustainable papers are used as measured by the Paper Chain Project grading system. We undertake an annual audit to monitor our sustainability.

PRAISE FOR THIS BOOK

New praise for the third edition

Covering an industry full of hope and hype, Küng's book stands out for its focus on concepts, drivers, and dynamics. Its scope and learning are brilliant and dazzling – the ascendancy of the media tech sector, the culture of digital organizations, their creative workforce, and their strategic leadership. This greatly updated and upgraded 3rd edition, with new cases and issues, will be a source of insight for aspiring students and a tool for industry veterans who seek the perspective of academia.

Eli Noam, Professor of Finance and Economics, Columbia Business School and Director of the Columbia Institute for Tele-Information

I have learned so much from Lucy Küng's work and always look forward to her next book as a chance to learn more.

Rasmus Kleis Nielsen, Professor of Political Communication and Director of the Reuters Institute for the Study of Journalism, University of Oxford

"The strategic environment of the media industry is changing fast" is perhaps the greatest understatement in this updated edition of *Strategic Management in the Media*. Around the globe, media organizations are coping with unparalleled and accelerating technological disruption of a breadth and velocity never witnessed before. With an unjaundiced approach framed by strategic theory, including more invaluable case studies than ever before, Küng provides scholars, students, and practitioners with invaluable tools to map the impact on media industries by global platforms including the rise of creator culture, the breathtaking speed in which streaming services now dominate media production and distribution, and the threat already posed by the rise of next-gen technologies, whether coined the metaverse or generative AI.

David Craig, Clinical Professor, USC Annenberg School for Communication and Journalism, Harvard Visiting Scholar, Global Fulbright Scholar

Lucy Küng's groundbreaking book enters its 3rd edition with a bang! Updated with illustrative case studies on media trends and organizational practice, this book is a must-read for any scholar or student of media management.

John Oliver, Professor of Strategic Media Management Bournemouth University, President, European Media Management Association

The long-awaited third edition of *Strategic Management in the Media* by Lucy Kueng is once again an extraordinary contribution to the scholarly field of media management. With her unparalleled expertise and insight, Kueng demonstrates her mastery in navigating the complex landscape of media industries in the digital age. This latest edition not only builds upon the foundational principles of the previous editions, but also delves deeper into the ever-evolving challenges and opportunities faced by media organizations today. The book's comprehensive coverage of cutting-edge topics, such as shifts toward network-based platforms, data-driven decision-making, and innovative business models in a VUCA world, makes it an indispensable guide for media professionals and scholars alike.

Sabine Baumann, Professor for Digital Business, HWR Berlin

Hail to the Küng! A must-read for industry as well as academy, this is one of the best books about strategy and management in the media industries. It is written at a time where most of what is solid melts into air, but as the line between media and technology sectors increasingly blurs, no one writes about these issues with more clarity than Lucy Küng.

Aske Kammer, Associate Professor, Roskilde University

The third edition of *Strategic Management in the Media* consolidates Lucy Küng's work as one of the main references for managers and scholars in the information and entertainment industry. With the same seriousness and lucidity that characterized the previous editions, the author weaves a rich theoretical substrate about the media ecosystem in addition to showing, through real and extremely current cases, the opportunities and limits behind the business models that predominate in the sector. With the publication of this third volume that updates her body of work, Lucy Küng makes *Strategic Management in the Media* – perhaps without directly intending to do so – a brilliant trilogy that brings together the recent history of communication companies. Read consecutively, the books make it possible to see, chronologically, the profound transformations that occurred in the industry and its various stages: from the initial shock through a period of unrestrained reproduction of monetization models to a greater degree of maturity, especially in terms of business strategies, to team profiles and the relative weight of technology in this whole process. An indispensable book.

Glaucia C. Noguera, Professor, ISE Brazil

Embark on a journey to comprehend the profound impact of the digital revolution on the media industry with this essential contribution. It rediscovers the key elements of strategy and provides invaluable insights for navigating the accelerating process of transformation.

Charo Sadaba, Professor and Dean of School of Communication, University of Navarre

Praise for the second edition

Once again, Lucy Küng has produced *the* standard text in media management. Fully updated, she offers a comprehensive and accessible guide to strategic management in the media for students, lecturers and researchers. It is compulsory reading in my classes!

Ulrike Rohn, President of the European Media Management Association (EMMA)

In the age of relentless technological disruption, unlimited media distribution, artificial scarcity, content abundance, and non-professionalized creators and practices, successful media firms are more dependent than ever on strategic media management. In her first book, Lucy Küng identified the core concepts, strategic themes, and best practices in the field. In her second edition, Küng articulates the iterative dimensions of the media industries to account for an ever-increasing array of challenges and strategies.

David Craig, USC Annenberg

A landmark contribution to scholarship in the area of media management, Lucy Küng's excellent and most welcome revised *Strategic Management in the Media* provides an empirically rich and analytically sharp-sighted guide to the forces, concepts and issues governing contemporary organizational strategies in a complex and dynamic digital media environment.

Gillian Doyle, University of Glasgow

In this second edition of a book many found invaluable for research and teaching, including myself, Küng accomplishes a challenging task: to preserve all the best qualities of the first edition while both extending the scope and deepening understandings about strategic management theory in application to media industries. She has thoroughly updated an already rich assortment of case studies to ensure a much needed contemporary view of how theory informs practice, and the reverse.

Gregory Ferrell Lowe, University of Tampere

Praise for the first edition

... provides vital insights into the elements of strategy and their application to media firms. Küng relates strategic concepts to the unique settings and operating conditions of various media using contemporary examples that direct attention to core issues and challenges. Solidly grounded in theory but not pedantic, the book explores the nature of change in media markets and how strategy must be altered in response. It is essential reading for those who make or wish to comprehend choices of media companies.

Professor Robert Picard, Media Management Transformation Centre, University of Jönköping, Sweden

Insightful, contextually analytical, yet easy to comprehend, *Strategic Management in the Media* successfully applies the adaptive and interpretative areas of strategic theory in the media sectors. This book's integrative approach provides a unique perspective in which common themes linking media strategy and industry environment were thoughtfully discussed. The focus on media organizations' adaptive strategic behavior, especially in technology management, creativity and innovation offers a pragmatic approach to understanding today's changing, complex world of media.

Sylvia M. Chan-Olmsted, Professor and Associate Dean for Research, College of Journalism and Communications, University of Florida

To Gebi and Hira Maya, once more and of course.

CONTENTS

LIST OF CASES

PREFACE TO THE THIRD EDITION

'Tis all in pieces. All coherence gone.' (John Donne, 1611)

This textbook, now in its third edition, explores key elements of strategy and how they apply to the media industry and the organisations in it. This sector continues to experience unprecedented levels of change. A process of transformation that started with the digital revolution a quarter of a century ago is only accelerating.

The quotation at the head of this page was written in 1611. It fits perfectly to the emerging reality of the media industry. A challenge with previous editions of this book is that it has long been difficult to establish boundaries to the field of strategy (just about any management concept is strategic in some way). Now that problem applies to the media industry itself. The playing field has changed and continues to evolve, a degree of transformation that makes strategic analysis difficult. Critically, the various sectors within the industry are moving ahead on different trajectories, driven in many cases by different sets of environmental forces.

Further, while traditional sectors such as news publishing, television, film, radio, and so on are still discernible, adjacent sectors are encroaching on the media industry, capturing audience attention and generating revenues. Amazon, which is difficult to classify but usually categorised as an online retailer and web services provider, spent nearly three times the BBC's entire annual budget on streamed content in 2022.[1] Similarly, the creator economy has matured to a point where a vast army of online content entrepreneurs can build (and monetise) brands with audiences that equal those of mainstream media companies. The creator economy's total addressable market is currently valued at $250 billion,[2] and YouTube's advertising revenues outstripped Netflix's total revenues in 2022.[3]

Underlying all these changes is one common driver – the ascendency of the technology sector and its growing influence on the media industry. As convergence theories predicted two decades ago, the lines between the media and technology sectors are blurring. This both impacts strategic priorities and influences strategic options. At the time of writing, Hollywood writers are striking in response to how streaming content has diminished their traditional sources of income, and generative AI is disrupting activities across the entire spectrum of the media organisation, creating opportunities for growth, but also opening the door to new types of competition.

Sooner or later, everything that is old is new again

Despite this, ironically, 'the return of the old' was also a recurrent theme with this new edition, at least in terms of strategic theory. Classic approaches to strategic management, which had fallen out of fashion with the advent of digital, proved to be some of the most helpful in terms of analysing the current state of the sector and, critically, are being used by organisations once more to develop strategy. Notable examples include Porter's Five Force Model (Porter, 1980), core competencies (Prahalad and Hamel, 1990), and Kurt Lewin's 'unfreeze, change, refreeze' model for reorientating a company and its culture (Lewin, 1947).

Leadership: from hard to soft

Another marked shift between this edition and the previous two is a rise in people-centred approaches to leadership. Rather than focusing on hard skills and competencies, leaders in the sector are increasingly seeking to 'lead through culture' by instilling a set of explicit shared values throughout their organisation's strategy, design and processes. As strategic circumstances become more challenging, leadership approaches that prioritise collaboration and learning, such as shared leadership, learning leadership and transformational leadership, are becoming the default option. These prioritise the establishment of a shared vision, effective communication and continuous learning as key components of successful leadership.

More case studies, a wider range of subjects

This book's case studies serve a dual purpose: to illuminate firms' strategic situations and actions, while also enriching readers' comprehension of the book's theories. There was a clear request for more cases and for greater geographic reach in the companies included. This latest edition delivers on both fronts, featuring more and longer cases, with thanks to the company representatives who collaborated on their development. A comprehensive list of case studies can be found on page xii.

New 'Resources' and 'Questions' sections

The media field is not only evolving fast, but its various sectors are moving apart on different trajectories. New 'Resources' sections at the end of each chapter provide details of further learning resources, ranging from books and articles to podcasts, newsletters and information sites. 'Questions' have also been added to each chapter, which encourages readers to reflect on the material in each and draw links between the issues discussed throughout the book, their own media consumption, and their own media interests.

The degree of change this sector is undergoing made writing this third edition longer and far more challenging than anticipated (indeed, the process was abandoned twice). This was, however, a learning experience on a grand scale. I am grateful to have had to dig deep into new dimensions of the media field and reflect on the purpose of this industry and how it must adapt to ensure that it can continue, in the words of the BBC's first director general, Lord Reith, to inform, educate and entertain, and protect vulnerable and valuable public values.

Notes

1 Lucas Shaw, 'Amazon will spend $15bn on programming this year'. Bloomberg Newsletter, 12 September 2022. N.B. Amazon's figure includes spending on sports.
2 www.goldmansachs.com/intelligence/pages/the-creator-economy-could-approach-half-a-trillion-dollars-by-2027.html, 19 April 2023.
3 https://civicscience.com/youtube-is-a-way-of-life-for-more-than-half-of-americans, 1 December 2021.

ACKNOWLEDGEMENTS

A great many individuals contributed to the writing of this third edition, and I am grateful to each of them.

At the start of this project, I convened a group of media management academics to explore the current theoretical understanding of strategy in the sector. This group was pivotal in deciding what needed to change in this new edition. Two years on, we continue to meet regularly and thrash out developments. My thanks to Leona Achtenhagen, Sabine Bauman, Joaquín Cestino, Sven-Ove Horst, Gregory Ferrell Lowe, Päivi Maijanen-Kyläheiko, Bozena I. Mierzejewska, John Oliver, Francisco J. Pérez Latre, Robert Picard, and Ulrike Rohn for many excellent discussions.

Rasmus Nielsen, Nic Newman, and Federica Cherubini at the Reuters Institute for the Study of Journalism at Oxford University can be consistently depended upon for stimulating research and conversation on the future of the news industry. I'm particularly grateful to Rasmus for his encouragement when my energy flagged on this project.

Academic insights were generously shared too by David Craig, Francois Nel, Damian Radcliffe, Chara Sadaba, Richard Sambrook, Jane Singer, and Christian Zabel.

Finding real-life cases that can bring theories of strategic management to life in a specific sector is a complex and time-consuming task. I am grateful to the leaders in media organisations who agreed for their organisations to feature in the book and who made time for research discussions and to review the case studies as they were written. My thanks go to Ros Atkins, Styli Charalambous, Christina Johannesson, Bharat Gupta, Anne Lagerkrantz, Chris Moran and Ben Whitelaw.

The media industry is evolving fast and centrifugal forces are pushing the sectors apart at speed. These developments are challenging to track. Many individuals in media organisations were generous with their time to discuss emerging developments. I would like to thank particularly Julia Bezier (Bloomberg), David Caswell (BBC), Ezra Eeman (Mediahuis), Rhys Hancock (Epic Games), Jeremy Gilbert (Washington Post) and Judy Parnell (BBC).

For the first time, this edition includes invited external contributions on specific topics. My thanks go to Kevin Anderson for his excellent input to the

'Resources' sections in Chapters 2, 4 and 7, to Robert Brookey for co-writing the Disney case, to John Oliver for the Sky Plc case, and to David Rogers for his summary of digital leadership in Chapter 7.

Working with Natalie Aguilera, Michael Ainsley and Sarah Moorhouse at Sage has been a pleasure. My thanks to them for their professionalism and patience.

And finally, my biggest debt of gratitude is to Gebi and Hira Maya. Their unparalleled support was invaluable.

Lucy Küng, Küsnacht, May 2023
Lucy.kueng@lucykueng.com
@kuenglucy

ONE

INTRODUCTION

> Spotify Technology SA has decided it's finally time to figure out how to make money. The company owns the largest music service in the world. More than 450 million people use it, and almost 200 million people pay for it. ... And yet, it has lost money every year. ... Spotify is now resetting its strategy.[1]

The media industry is a complex moving target: a composite of a varied and broad range of sectors, shadowed by tech giants who are active in the sector but don't consider themselves as part of it and hitched to a trajectory of unceasing technological advance. This degree of perpetual motion is a real, day-to-day practical challenge; for leaders developing and implementing strategy, for researchers defining and analysing developments, and for those designing academic courses for those who want to work in the sector. Against that backdrop, this book seeks to:

- **Map the contours** of the media industry, exploring business models, value drivers and current strategic issues in the various sectors that together constitute the industry.
- **Identify the common themes** surfacing in the strategic environment and the challenges these pose, as well as aspects of media organisations that influence the activities of strategic choice and implementation.
- **Explore the strategic models, concepts and approaches** that are relevant to this strategic context and these types of organisations seeking to demonstrate their relevance through application to media industry cases and examples.

The goals, therefore, are clear. But the complexity of the media industry – a diverse set of sectors that are moving ever closer to the technology sector – and the sprawling and fragmented nature of strategic theory complicate the task. To cut through this complexity, the book has been written with three guiding principles in mind:

- In terms of the media industry, it seeks to move beyond simply describing developments to interpreting them and providing insights that will aid strategy-making in the media industry.
- In terms of strategic theory, it limits the selection covered to those that have direct relevance for the field and then attempts to move beyond simply outlining concepts to demonstrating their relevance through the application (what consultants call 'showing the "so what"'). It also deliberately seeks to work with a broader set of strategic and management theories drawn from a wider range of disciplines than is often the case in media management research.
- In terms of language, the goal has been to strip out jargon as far as possible. This is partly to ensure relevance for practitioners as well as scientists, and partly because researchers and students in the field of media management, as this chapter discusses, have entered the field from many different areas of scholarship – liberal arts, social science, economics, political economics, mass communications and journalism studies to name just a few – and have therefore not been exposed to mainstream management theory and are likely to find some of its usages confusing.

Structure of the book

There is nothing as practical as good theory. (Kurt Lewin, 1943)

At base, the field of strategy is concerned with how organisations align their internal organisations to master the demands of their external environment. There are several strategic and organisational levers they can employ to achieve this. These range from highly analytic planning approaches, based on exhaustive research and data analysis, to prescriptive and pragmatic tools, which seek to transform the inner workings of organisations through gaining a deeper understanding of intangible phenomena such as cultural beliefs and levels of motivation.

This book explains and applies concepts from each of the three core areas of strategic theory: rational approaches, adaptive approaches, and interpretative ones. Central aspects of managers' strategy 'work' in media organisations are explored sequentially, starting with understanding the strategic environment and then moving through analysing a company's competitive positioning, strategic resources and competencies, responding to technological change, options for how the organisation is structured, increasing levels of creativity and innovation, managing culture and mindset, and finally looking at the role of the leader, particularly in terms of shaping the 'social architecture' of the organisation through interpretative elements such as culture and mindset. Key concepts that are relevant for the media industries are explained and then 'embedded' in case studies that explain how these theoretical constructs 'play out' in real-life organisations. Some cases feature in a number of chapters, with each 'appearance' illustrating a different dimension of strategy in the media. This underlines the complex and multifaceted nature of strategic management and the interlinked nature of strategic phenomena in firms, and, taken together, these cases will hopefully provide a richer and more nuanced understanding of the examples presented.

What is media management?

The topic of strategy in the media industry is a subset of the broader field of media management. This field, media management, is a relatively new field of academic study. It seeks to build a bridge between the general theoretical disciplines of management and the specificities of the media industry. This goal seems relatively clear. However, the field of media management is neither clearly defined nor cohesive. A review of the many media management courses that have sprung up in previous decades all over the world exhibits an enormously diverse range of theories, topics, and core readings.

This is partly a function of its relative newness. In contrast to media economics, which since its emergence in the 1970s has acquired an established set of theoretical approaches and an extensive body of literature, media management is still young: *The International Journal of Media Management* was established in 1998, the *Journal of Media Business Studies* in Jönköping 2004, the European Media Management Association (EMMA) in 2003 and the International Media Management Academic Forum (IMMAA) in 2004.

Perhaps inevitably, it is also an under-explored and under-theorised field (Cottle, 2003). Mainstream management scholars have largely neglected the media industry. This could be because managerial practices and organisational patterns in the cultural industries are often at odds with established views of management (Lampel et al., 2000). It could also relate to the fact that 'mainstream' management researchers seldom limit their research to a particular sector, preferring to choose sectors and cases according to the phenomena they are investigating. This means that the bulk of research into management and strategy in media organisations has been carried out by researchers with scholarly roots outside the study of management and organisations. Chief among these are media economics, media studies, political economics, and mass communications and journalism studies, giving rise to a body of theory that, Albarran has observed, 'crosses interdisciplinary lines, theoretical domains, and political systems' (Albarran et al., 2006: 3). This, in turn, has generated a body of literature that applies an equally diverse range of theories from various disciplines, including economics, econometrics, sociology, anthropology, technology and innovation management, political science and artificial intelligence (AI). By looking at the key academic disciplines outside the field of management that address the issue of management and strategy within media firms, we can gain a sense of the structure of the field's literature.

Media economics

Media management has grown up in the shadow of media economics. This well-established discipline applies economic principles and concepts to the media industries and has dominated scholarly analysis of the media sector (Picard, 2002a). Media economics tends to work at the industry, sector, or market level. It looks at conditions and structures in the media industries and markets and focuses on the deployment of resources, particularly financial ones, to meet the needs of audiences, advertisers, and society (Picard, 2002a). This stream of research focuses on several key issues and explores how these impact and influence the development of media business models. These include:

- structural analysis of the sector, including market structure and share
- media ownership and concentration
- media firms' revenue and cost structures, including the economics of the key processes of production, distribution and consumption, and their effects on the behaviour of media firms
- pricing policy
- regulation
- public policy and subsidy issues
- consumer and advertiser demands, and the impact of new technologies and consumer behaviours on these.

Media economics literature addresses the behaviour of media firms in aggregate and provides valuable insights into the economic forces affecting the sector, the influence these have on strategic options, and the types of strategic choices media firms are making within these contexts and why. It therefore provides a valuable starting point for examining processes and phenomena inside media organisations and for understanding the non-rational processes that also influence strategic behaviour. In terms of strategy in the media field, media economists have looked at strategy formulation and implementation by large media organisations, in particular at the antecedents and/or consequences of change, with a focus on the environment, structure and performance, often applying rationalist models from the Industrial Organisation (IO) School.

Audience economics is an extension of the media economics literature, and addresses the economic dimensions and implications of audience behaviour and audience measurement, viewing media audiences as a product market with unique characteristics and significant points of interaction with media industries (Napoli, 2003).

Political economy approaches

When media management does not fall under the umbrella of media economics, it is often a subset of political economy scholarship. This field combines perspectives from economics, politics and sociology to analyse the structure of the media industries and regulatory and policy issues, looking particularly at the economic determinants, ownership structures and political allegiances (Cottle, 2003).

Political economy approaches involve the 'study of social relations, particularly power relations, that mutually constitute the production, distribution and consumption of resources' (Mosco, 1996: 25). In practice, the application of such theories to the media field tends to involve (often, but not exclusively, neo-Marxian) critical studies of cultural production, looking also at the public policies that shape media systems and the political debates about media and communication policies (McChesney, in Cottle, 2003). Typical examples would be Burns's seminal study of the BBC (1977), Tracey's study of how political, technological and economic forces have undermined public service broadcasting (1998), or Tunstall and Palmer's study of media moguls (1998).

Media studies

This cross-disciplinary field is less clearly defined than those described above. It's a 'broad church' that applies concepts from sociology, cultural studies, anthropology, psychology, art theory, information theory and economics to analyse the output of media organisations as a means of understanding society and its cultural discourses, and the effects of mass media upon individuals and society, as well as analysing actual media content and representations (Cottle, 2003). A typical study might analyse a film's aesthetic or narrative quality, but within the perspective of the filmmaking process and the movie industry's economic, technological and industrial contexts. Separate strands look at journalism, film, gaming, audience studies, television studies and radio studies, how corporate ownership of media production and distribution affects society, and the effects and techniques of advertising. Contemporary media studies include the analysis of new media, with an emphasis on the internet, social media, gaming and other forms of mass media which developed from the 1990s onwards.

Media management: the state of play

These, then, are the major 'host' disciplines that have made the main incursions into the field of media management. The current state of the discipline reflects this development path. Viewed from a management perspective, media organisations have been largely addressed as businesses rather than organisations, at a macro rather than micro level, and much attention has been focused on the exogenous changes (technology, policy, regulation and consumption, for example) and their impact on media firms' output.

Viewed from an historical perspective, research into management in the media can be seen as reflecting changes in its strategic environment. The 1980s and 1990s were characterised by liberalisation, deregulation and globalisation, and scholars responded by focusing particularly on issues of industry structure, the growth of the conglomerates and its implications, increases in alliances and joint ventures, and transnational management. Towards the end of the 1990s, a first and second tier of global media conglomerates became established. These were multiproduct divisional entities that presented a more complex management task, and media management scholars began to focus on the specific challenges they presented, particularly in terms of structures and processes. A focus on strategic resources emerged during this period, applying approaches such as the resource-based view (RBV). The turn of the millennium saw dramatic developments in the media industry's underlying technologies. This gave rise to research looking at the emerging distribution architecture and its ramifications for the established media industry, as well as at the concept of convergence and its ramifications. The current fast pace of technological change, the development of new boundary-spanning categories of media products and increasing competition for audience attention have led contemporary researchers to focus on business models and approaches to organisational adaptation, particularly the issue of innovation.

'Nailing mercury': the challenge of defining the media industry

Defining the media industry has always been surprisingly tricky. Now, as boundaries between media organisations, the platforms, the telecoms sector, the information technology sector and the device sector blur, it becomes increasingly difficult. 'Nailing mercury' is how media historian Michelle Hilmes describes the task (2009, cited in Cunningham and Craig, 2019: 263). Indeed, Lowe and Noam (2022) find that apart from scholarship on the marketing and PR sectors (where they are needed for planning media campaigns), taxonomies of the media industry feature less and less in literature. They note, however, that such taxonomies are needed. The media industry may be 'ubiquitous, pervasive and complex' (2022: 8), but it needs classifying, for the purposes of media policy and regulation (particularly to investigate media concentration), to understand media use, and for the field of media management and economics, to develop theory on how to manage, finance and develop organisations.

In the (simpler) pre-digital days, media firms were defined as those 'involved in the production and distribution of content intended for a mass audience' (Mierzejewska and Shaver, 2014: 48). Such an understanding is rooted in an understanding that publishers and broadcasters form the core of the industry. This 'classic' conceptualisation remains pervasive, especially for those not intimately involved in navigating the changes that have been underway for the past two decades. It is shown in Figure 1.1.

Even with this depiction, variety could be found. Europeans had tended, until the onset of convergence and the associated unifying impact of digital distribution, to view the media industries more narrowly than their US peers. They limited the sector to broadcasting (radio and television), print (newspapers, magazines, journals and books), motion picture and recording industries. US analysts often included gaming, sports and theme parks (see, for example, Vogel, 1999; Wolf, 1999), and when these are included, the name often shifted

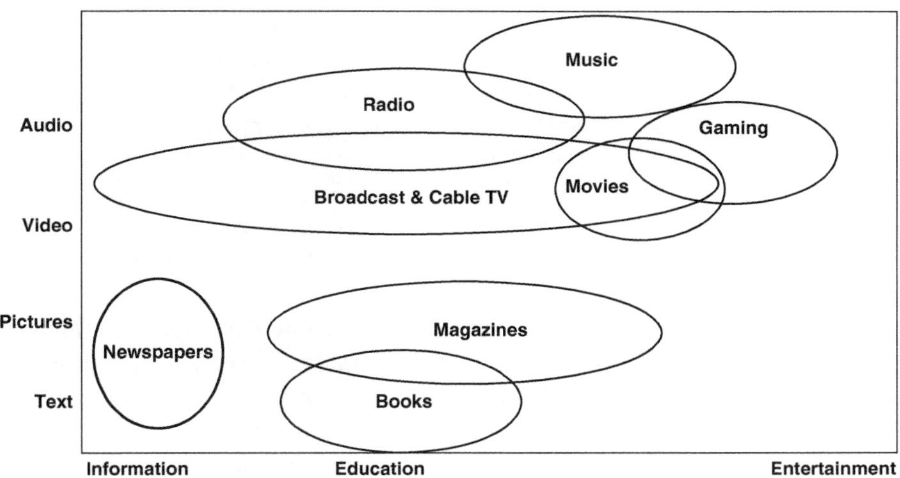

Figure 1.1 'As it was': sectors of the traditional media industry

© Lucy Küng

from the 'media' to the 'entertainment' industries. If the 'performing arts' are included, the sector can sometimes become the 'cultural industries'. An additional variation is to include advertising, marketing and public relations, which can lead to the name being altered to the 'creative industries'.

From the early 2000s onwards, software and digital technologies pushed into all industry sectors, including the mass media industry. The ongoing evolution of the digital economy started to blur the borders between the media and adjacent sectors such as technology and the social media platforms. (This shift is most apparent in advertising industry analyses, which now routinely include Alphabet, Meta, Amazon and Microsoft, alongside longstanding sellers of media advertising such as Disney, Paramount and Warner Bros. Discovery). Awareness grew that long-held assumptions about the structure of the sector may no longer capture reality. Lowe and Noam (2022) identify two definitional challenges arising from this. First, the elasticity of the sector's current boundaries (should it include only organisations primarily focused on content creation and distribution, or expand to contain any firm producing and distributing information?); and second, the risk posed by using binary distinctions – between, say, content or conduit, or between professional and user-generated content.

Hess's (2014) typology builds a bridge between a traditional understanding of the sector and the platform world, and segments the field into two sectors: organisations following a 'publishing–broadcasting approach, where professional content providers generate a one-way flow of output to specified audiences; and organisations with a 'platform approach' where user-generated content flows two-way between the platform and its users. For Voci et al. (2019), content generation remains a defining characteristic of the media sector. They propose a model of the sector comprising three concentric circles. The innermost one contains companies that are focused on content generation. The middle circle has companies that produce content but are also engaged in content aggregation and distribution. The outermost circle comprises companies active in the media in the widest sense, from network operators to infrastructure companies. Lowe and Noam (2022: 15) echo this centrality placed on content in defining the media as 'an industry or organization whose primary activity is the creation, assembly or distribution of information organized to inform, entertain, or instruct'.

Figure 1.2 shows a simple model of the consumer media industry within the digital economy. If we compare this to the pre-digital depiction in Figure 1.1, we can identify several shifts underway in the core makeup of the sector:

- The newspaper sector is shifting into a 'news publishing' sector. This renaming acknowledges that newspapers are now one product (one in structural decline) among a range of content formats stretching from text and pictures (the original content formats) to audio, video and events. Large companies, such as *the New York Times* which leads this development, are in the process of turning into platforms.

- The audiovisual sectors of television and movies have been joined (and eclipsed from a revenue perspective) by the streamed media sector. This includes video and audio content, and also (new) gaming.
- The radio sector is increasingly subsumed into the broader category of 'audio', which includes the rapidly expanding realm of podcasts.

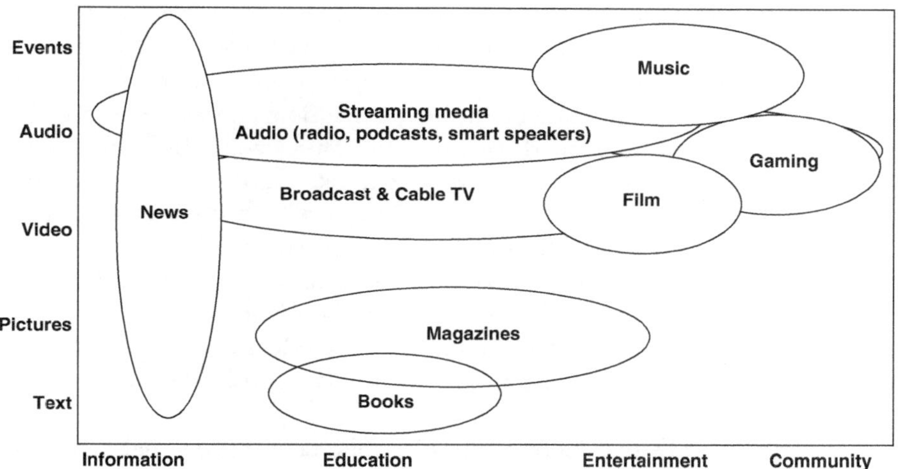

Figure 1.2 Media industry sectors shift as digital economy advances

© Lucy Küng

Characteristics of the mass media

Before delving into how the media industry is evolving, it is important to understand what came before. The structure of the classic legacy media sector is shaped by the concept of 'mass media', and while strategy is concerned with plotting a path to the future, the concept of mass media and the nature of mass media products still influence activity today. Mass media products and firms share several common and defining characteristics, many of which still influence strategic activities on the part of the media firm and the thinking of the legislators defining the regulatory architecture for the sector.

First, media products are experiential goods. Their value derives from their immaterial attributes, from their originality, from the intellectual property, messages or stories they contain, from their use of symbols to engage and manipulate perception, experience and emotion (Garnham and Locksley, in Blumler and Nossiter, 1991; Lampel et al., 2000).

Traditional mass media products are based on technologies that allow the massive duplication of material, whether physical duplication via printing and record presses or electronic duplication via broadcast systems. The production process typically involves a single cycle of product development followed by mass production. Fixed costs are high. First copy costs are also high since the content investment is front-loaded in the initial development of the product. Thereafter, production costs are low and economies of scale effects mean these reduce rapidly with volume.

Because many traditional mass media products can be reversioned into different formats (think of Hollywood blockbuster franchises, discussed on p. 31), media firms can sell and resell the same media product indefinitely with minimal additional production costs. This encourages them to maximise returns from sunk investments in content through expansion into as many product lines, outlets and geographic markets as possible. These factors influenced decisions concerning levels of content investment, marketing, distribution and pricing (Shapiro and Varian, 1999; Napoli, 2003), as well as the extent of vertical integration and scale of diversification (Chan-Olmsted, 2006).

However, media products are also heterogeneous. Each one is unique – no two newspapers, magazines, news broadcasts or books are identical, although there are standard formats (often dictated by production technologies). A substantial proportion of media products are also perishable – newspapers, for example.

This, coupled with the fickle nature of public taste, means that there has always been a high degree of product risk. (Which products will strike a chord with the market? Which content investments will pay off?) Constant product innovation is a fundamental requirement. Further, the value of media products derives from the knowledge and creative inspiration of those creating the content: the higher the level of novelty and creativity, the greater the potential for competitive advantage – thus the primacy of creativity as an organisational resource (these issues are discussed in Chapter 5).

Mass media products are also defined by the fact that they deliver an identical message to a potentially unlimited audience. Communication is one-way – the receiver of the message cannot communicate with the sender of the message using the same media, and the presentation or packaging of products is linear and fixed.

Broadcast mass media products, as historically conceived, are non-excludable and non-depletable public goods – that is, the cost of production is independent from the number of people who consume it – consumption by one individual does not limit the quantity available to other people. The cost of producing a television series or radio broadcast is independent of the number of people who will watch it. Other media products, such as books and films, have the characteristics of both private and public goods (Picard, 2002c). Their content can be classified as a public good in that the costs of its generation remain the same, irrespective of how many consume it. But the form in which they are delivered to the consumer can be identified as a private good: if consumed by one person, that product is not available to others (thus, a shop may sell out of copies of a particular book and a cinema may sell all its seats for a particular showing).

The traditional business model for media businesses (apart from public service broadcasters) is that they receive revenues from advertisers in return for 'delivering' audiences to them, those audiences having been attracted by the content that media products offer. Characteristics of this model are that it has a significant component of indirect payment (a large proportion of costs being borne by advertisers), is collective (payment models are based on aggregating the largest possible number of consumers) and is based on standardised products.

Therefore, many media organisations producing advertising-supported media – newspapers, magazines, television and radio – operate in a dual-product marketplace; in addition to producing content, they also 'produce' audiences – that is, they provide content to attract audiences, and these audiences are 'sold' to advertisers (Picard, 2002a; Napoli, 2003). This influences the content strategy. In general, the goal will be to provide content that appeals to the largest number of consumers. However, within this broad market, those demographic groups that are most attractive to advertisers will receive a disproportionate amount of attention.

Even before the onset of convergence, this model was undergoing a process of restructuring, spurred by the introduction of cable and satellite transmission technologies that allowed direct payment for specific programming through subscription-based and pay-per-view systems. The indirect, collective business model that underpinned the mass media was beginning to be undermined. The new media, however, have undermined this model even further.

Social responsibility requirements and regulation

One issue that distinguishes the media sector, and deeply influences the task of leadership in the media, is the expectation that media organisations, irrespective of their commercial goals, act in a socially responsible way and promote specific social values. It reflects an assumption that the media is a cultural force: it shapes society, and its messages are fundamental to democracy. So the media must not only seek to maximise profits and returns to shareholders, but it must also act in the public interest and promote social values such as social interaction, engagement, democratic participation, collective knowledge and cultural identities (Cottle, in Cottle, 2003; Picard, 2004). This requirement is enforced by law and, as a result, media firms contend with a slew of regulations affecting many aspects of strategic activity – for example, the scope for growth, the types of products that can be made and the prices that can be charged.

There is no uniform understanding as to what constitutes social responsibility, although a number of core societal functions have been identified:

- providing a forum for the exchange of opinions between different groups in a democratic society;
- acting as an integrative influence – especially important in countries with high levels of immigration or linguistic differences;
- protecting core values – the interests of children or a diversity of cultural expression, for example;
- furthering innovation in technological systems – for example, to encourage citizens' uptake of new technologies (Bertelsmann Foundation, 1995).

These core functions give rise to strictures designed to limit the potentially negative effects of media products and promote potentially positive ones. Negatively framed strictures limit and prevent socially undesirable elements such as the violation of human dignity, sexually explicit or violent content, content that could pose a threat to children, the violation of privacy, discrimination against minorities, and the co-option of broadcasting into the service of powerful interests. Positive ones seek to ensure independence from political or commercial influences, a plurality of opinion, promote the robust functioning of democracy through acting as a check on government, facilitate political discourse and ensure that a diversity of opinions have a platform for expression, as well as ensure that a plurality of opinions are expressed and that minority views have a platform. These requirements tend to affect generalist broadcasters more than thematic or niche ones, and the journalistic function, in particular.

The presence of regulation and its influence on the operations of media organisations is well known to scholars of political economics, mass communications and journalism theory, but can be a foreign notion to those approaching the media industry from purely business perspectives. What it means in practice for the media manager is that the regulatory framework exerts a strong influence on strategic options and by extension corporate strategies. These in turn guide programming and editorial decisions.

Overview of subsequent chapters

This book's chapters address the following issues.

This first chapter, the **Introduction** to the book, describes its goals, structure and scope.

Chapter 2, **The Strategic Context**, analyses the strategic context that influences strategy in the media and identifies several themes that are shaping the strategic agenda in the field. This set of topics includes digital platforms, streaming media and their business models, the creator economy, content 'franchises' and the metaverse. The chapter then moves from environmental phenomena to concepts that allow organisations to build an understanding of their environment, assess their position and design responses to it. These tools include VUCA, PEST analysis, the value chain and strategic adjacencies. Two cases are included: how Jagran New Media uses VUCA to navigate the complex digital media environment in India, and how PEST analysis can analyse the multifaceted challenges facing public service media organisations in Europe.

Chapter 3, **Strategic Concepts for the Media,** provides an overview of the rich and variegated nature of strategic theory. Strategic theory is an enormous, diverse and fragmented field. To reduce this complexity and variety, this chapter applies a categorisation that 'organises' strategic theory into three core schools that are situated on a continuum moving from rationalist to symbolic approaches. It explores the relevance of each school or approach for the media field, situates existing work on strategy in the media industries within this categorisation and uses it to provide an overarching framework for the subsequent chapters in the book. Three cases are featured: an analysis of the growing competition facing Netflix using Porter's Five Forces model, and exploration of Sky Plc's dynamic capabilities, and the evolution of the strategic transformation of *The New York Times*.

Chapter 4, **Strategic Responses to Technological Change**, explores the often intricate relationship between technology, technological change, strategy and the media industries. It discusses the increasing strategic significance of technology for the sector, explores the concept of convergence between sectors, looks at the challenge of distinguishing innovation from hype, untangles different variants of technological change, and highlights the importance of understanding a sector's underlying technology bundle. It moves on to explore the challenges that companies experience in responding to technology change, and the role of structure in these responses. Two cases are included, on strategic renewal via technology at *The Washington Post*, and on why *Encyclopedia Britannica* failed to respond to disruptive innovation.

Chapter 5, **Creativity and Innovation**, explores the role of creativity in the media, its strategic importance, and why this is increasing. It reviews theoretical understanding of the topic and explores the distinctions between creativity and innovation. Through discussion of one particular body of theory – theories of organisational creativity – it reviews how media organisations can raise levels of product creativity over the long term. It also examines how creativity and innovation can be applied to media organisations' wider strategy, structures, processes and business models. Two cases are included: how Home Box Office (HBO) systematically creates strategic differentiation through creativity and how Pixar builds 'reliable creativity'.

Chapter 6, **Culture and Strategy**, addresses core elements of the interpretative school of strategy, and their relevance for strategy in media firms. In particular, it looks at the roles of organisational culture and mindset – that is, cognitive structures in strategy processes and firm performance. The chapter features four cases: on how *The Guardian* uses data to change newsroom culture, how Sweden's Swedish Television (SVT) shifted cultural values in order to put audiences first and accelerate its digital transformation, how Netflix drives performance through culture, and the BBC's 50:50 initiative to change representation on gender, disability and ethnicity.

Chapter 7, **Leadership**, explores leadership in the media industries and its influence on strategy. It reviews theoretical understanding of leadership and the strands of this research that are most frequently applied to the sector. Cases in this chapter include Greg Dyke's use of transformational leadership at the BBC, Amazon's Leadership Principles, how South Africa's *Daily Maverick* secured its future by focusing on transformational leadership, and the challenges that Disney has faced in terms of finding the leader it needs.

Chapter 8, **Conclusions: Generative AI and the Disruption of Digital**, has as its main task, pattern recognition. Drawing on the analysis and discussion contained in this volume, this chapter draws conclusions about the current shape and future contours of the media industries, the implications of these for the strategic management task and for further research in the field, particularly concerning research themes and methodologies. Included here, too, is a discussion of a significant development for the sector, AI, which emerged towards the end of the writing process for this new edition and which is set to have a profound influence on the media industry's future development.

Note

1 Lucas Shaw, 'Spotify Pivots', *Screentime* Newsletter, 30 January 2023.

TWO

THE STRATEGIC CONTEXT

Strategy is concerned with how an organisation orchestrates a successful response to its environment. And the environment is never static: like all complex systems, it is in a constant state of flux. During some periods, change can involve relatively benign and easy-to-accommodate alterations to the status quo. During others, instability is rife, with high levels of change, many interrelated developments at work, a lack of clarity on how these may evolve and implications that are hard to predict.

Strategic decisions should be based on a clear analysis of the environment. An influential theorist, Michael Porter, views aligning an organisation with its strategic environment as the essence of competitive strategy (Porter, 1980). A good strategy is context-dependent and designed for that organisation's specific situation.

Until the mid-1990s the strategic context of the media sector was 'mature' (Porter, 1980), with slow growth, strong competition between a known group of players, high barriers to entry and knowledgeable customers. From the 1990s onwards, with the full-blooded advent of the internet, digitalisation and the emergence of digital platforms, the industry has been confronted by unprecedented change and has been forced to evolve strategy at an ever-faster rate.

In a constantly evolving field, it can be hard to define which issues are most critical for the media in the strategic environment. This chapter focuses on newer phenomena and ongoing developments that shape or are likely to shape strategy now and in the coming years. The environmental developments featured in this chapter are shown in Figure 2.1, where they have been mapped onto the graphic of media industry sectors included in Chapter 1. This set of topics includes digital platforms, streaming media and their business models, the creator economy, content 'franchises' and the metaverse. Each of these themes is a significant and complex issue. The analyses in this chapter provide overviews of the phenomena

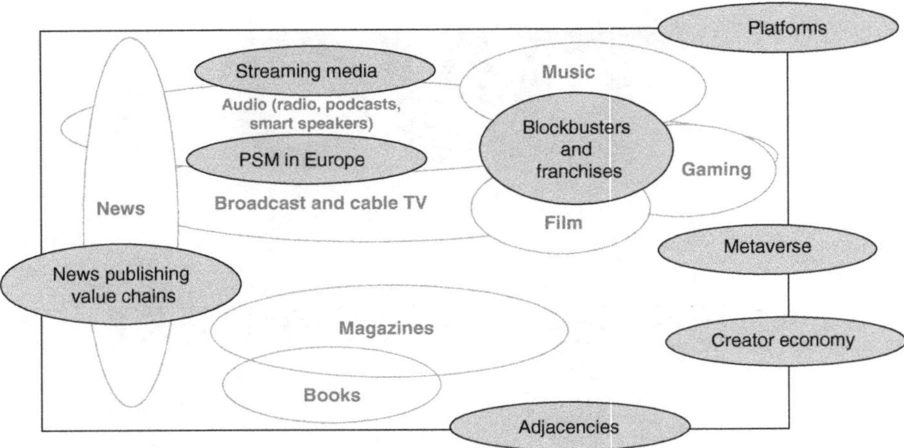

Figure 2.1 Environmental developments featured in Chapter 2
© Lucy Küng

and their strategic implications for organisations in affected sectors, but need to be understood as exactly that: if these are highly relevant for your organisation or your course of academic study, a deeper dive will be needed. The resources listed at the close of the chapter give ideas for where to start with this.

The chapter then moves from environmental phenomena to tools that allow organisations to understand their environment, assess their position and build strategies in response. These are VUCA, PEST analysis, the value chain and strategic adjacencies.

'Platform businesses require a different strategy'[1]

> They are inescapable; you may opt out of one or two of them, but together, they form a gilded mesh blanketing the entire economy. (Manjoo, 2016)

Meta, Tencent, TikTok, Alibaba and the like are digital platform businesses. This is a relatively new category of business (Facebook was founded in 2004 and TikTok in 2015), one that collectively is driving profound shifts in the global economy (Moazed and Johnson, 2016), with the media sector at the heart of some of those shifts. Platform businesses emerged from a set of interlinked technology advances, including cloud computing (which allows on-demand growth while keeping capital investments low), application programming interface (APIs) (which make interoperability, functionality, data activities and innovation by third-party app developers easier), social media (which make platform discovery and adoption easy), and the extensive global penetration of smartphones and mobile computing. It is important to note that not all platforms are the same: transactional platforms such as Airbnb connect buyers and sellers, technology platforms like Microsoft or Apple provide a core infrastructure that hosts products by third parties, and hybrid platforms, like Meta and Amazon, connect buyers and sellers and support third-party developers. This last type of platform is having the greatest impact on the media's strategic environment.

Platform businesses can grow fast and generate high profits. Where these two factors apply, a platform can develop a dominant position in its market relatively fast: Amazon, Apple, Meta and Google added greater market capitalisation between 2016 and 2020 than the largest retailers or consumer packaged goods (CPG) firms achieved over their entire history.[2] These market-leading positions in global markets generate high revenues that are invested in expanding physical, digital and intellectual assets, building economies of scale and scope (Simon, 2022). While their business models are durable, despite their size, they can adapt their strategies relatively fast if needed and are likely to continue to grow faster than the rest of other longer established sectors. Platform businesses have several defining characteristics:

- Platforms are **intermediaries,** bringing together different types of users in multi-sided markets, and providing the digital infrastructure and rules that allow transactions between user groups to take place, and it is in these transactions that value is created (Van Alstyne et al., 2016).
- Platforms are also **boundary-spanning**, meaning they don't conform to traditional industry boundaries and definitions (especially those used by regulators), which complicates both strategic analysis and regulatory intervention. Apple, from the perspective of the audiovisual media sector, is a major player in terms of investment in original productions. From the perspective of the organisation, its streamed content activities are one of a range of business units. Apple is a device manufacturer (the iPhone, the iPad, the Mac, the Apple Watch, Beats headphones, Apple TV+) and a service provider (the iTunes Store, Apple Stores, Apple Music, AppleCare and Apple Pay). These two categories are bundled (the iPhone and iTunes, for example, represent a combination of consumer devices and services providing media content).
- **The community of members** is a critical asset, and the larger the better, and the stronger the network effects at play, the faster this community can grow. Platforms, therefore, seek to facilitate more external interactions, boosting network effects and with it the value for participants.[3]

Core elements of the platform business model

Platform businesses bring communities and markets together in an eco-system of participants that interact and transact (they are also known as 'aggregators' – businesses that aggregate consumer demand by building engagement and capturing data at scale by provisioning consumer-facing services[4]). The features of a digital platform business, using Facebook as a typical example, are shown in Figure 2.2.

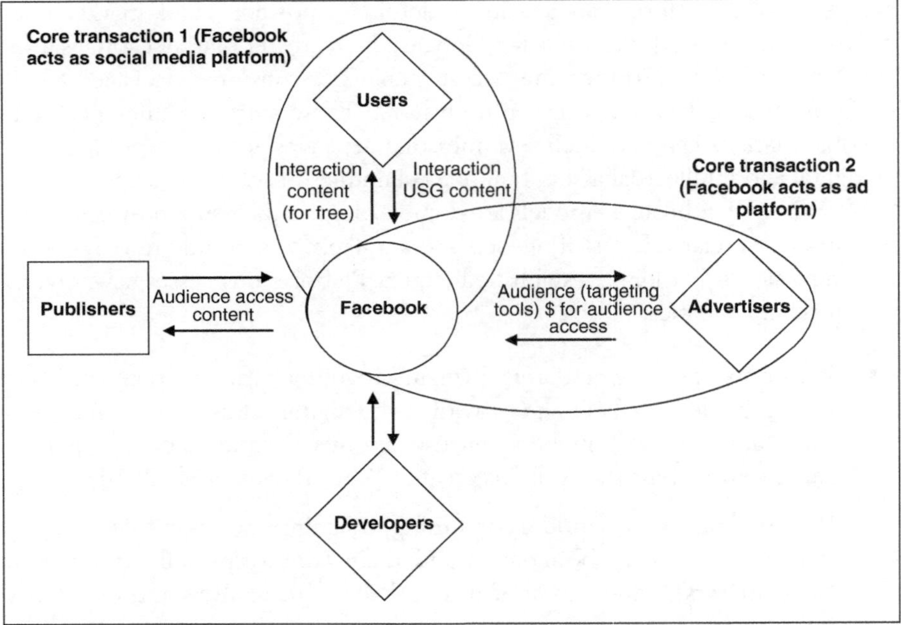

Figure 2.2 Facebook's platform business model (simplified)

The platform is the central actor. It facilitates direct interaction between users (usually of two or more types), enables a core transaction, provides functions and resources to keep users engaged and deriving value, and monetises the process (Moazed and Johnson, 2016; Rogers, 2016; Cusumano et al., 2019). It creates value by connecting 'buyers' and 'sellers' inside an eco-system.[5] They share some distinct features:

- **Network of users.** This is where the value of a platform resides, and the participants who produce and consume on the platform are the critical asset (Van Alstyne et al., 2016). Value is created by facilitating interaction and maximising users' activity on the platform. Platforms allow categories of customers to interact directly, with the platform and with other participants: they can create profiles, set pricing, and present their services and products. These interactions are not dictated by the platform, but take place through it and are facilitated by it.

- **Two or more types of users**. A platform brings different types of participants together, and these play different roles and receive different types of value from participating in the network. These different categories of participants are what differentiates a platform from a 'pure' network.
- **Users have more than one role**. They can be customers and sellers such as hosts and renters (Airbnb), celebrities and fans (Cameo), producers of content, consumers of content and advertisers (YouTube and TikTok's video creators, video viewers and advertisers wanting to reach those viewers; similarly, Google Search's website creators, search engine users and search advertisers).
- **Complementors**. These are independent businesses, often developers, that directly sell products or services that complement the products and services on the platform.[6] This brings them direct access to a large market without needing to build a platform themselves, but involves trade-offs. They pay commission fees to platforms' app stores, and to succeed, need to differentiate and market their services well.
- **Core transactions**. This is the centre of a platform's business model and the most important part of platform design, as this process will be repeated to generate and exchange value. Facebook, for example, has two core transactions:
    - **Core transaction 1:** between the platform and its users. Meta Platforms (including Facebook, Instagram and WhatsApp) provide free access to users and reported 3.74 billion global monthly users in 2023,[6] making it the largest database of people in the world. These users interact on the platform, engage with the content on the platform and upload content to the platform. Facebook captures data about these users and their activity, and can segment this by a range of criteria such as geography, demography and psychography. This transaction leads to fundamental shifts in the relationship between journalists and audiences: the relationship between news producers and news consumers becomes more fluid and interactive (Wilding et al., 2018), and the consuming audience becomes the creating audience (Meikle and Young, 2012; Bruns 2018).
    - **Core transaction 2**: between the platform and advertisers that want to address the users on the platform. Here Facebook is an advertising

> platform, and this transaction drives Facebook's revenues. This aspect of its business involves providing a range of advertising products and analytics tools that allow businesses to select which customers to address and what advertising formats for their messages (video, photo, slideshow, carousel, dynamic, etc). Facebook targeting tools are used to select which customers are addressed. Facebook gathers analytics on customer responses (attention spent on ads and clicks and impressions. The cost of entry for advertisers to use the platform is extremely low. In 2020, Facebook's global advertising revenues were $84 billion and this generated nearly 98 per cent of its total revenues.[8]

The growth of platform businesses relies on other factors too – notably cloud computing and near-universal smart mobile devices. These combine with platforms and network effects to create a 'growth flywheel', which is triggered as follows (and shown in Figure 2.3). Social media platforms offer a low-friction path for new members to join and participate in the network. This, in turn, is driven by:

- **Fast, on-demand access to a very large group of potential users**. The biggest platforms offer super-fast access from many parts of the globe.
- **Free access and free services**. Platforms need the maximum number of users to drive network effects and to attract businesses seeking to access their users, from which they can derive income. To maximise their user base, they make their services free.
- **The ability to scale fast and relatively cheaply**. Cloud computing, combined with network effects and the fact that platform businesses tend to be asset-light (see below) means that they can grow quickly at low cost.
- **Asset light.** Platform businesses in general have a lower fixed-cost base than product businesses. For example, Facebook's users or publishers create content on its platform, not paid media creators. Uber offers car rides, but drivers own the cars, not Uber.
- **Low operating costs**. Platform businesses employ few employees for the scale of revenue they generate. Users perform many tasks that employees would do in a vertically integrated business. This means that platforms can achieve high operating margins.

These characteristics are unique to the digital platforms. As the table below shows, even when publishers move to digital business models, these factors do not apply.

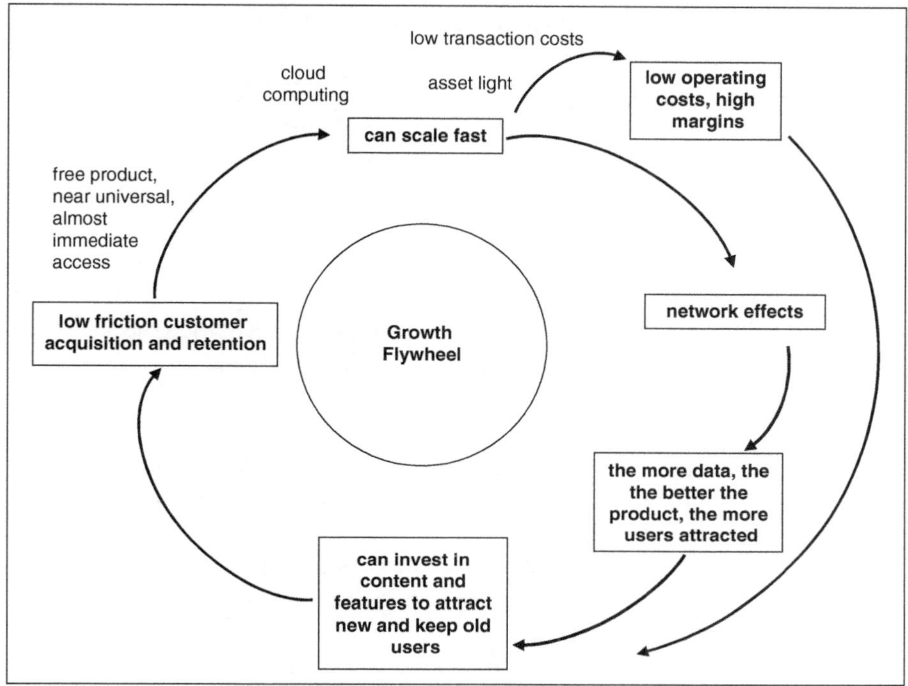

Figure 2.3 Platform model's growth flywheel
© Lucy Küng

Table 2.1 Characteristics of digital platforms and their application to publishers' digital business models

Characteristic of digital platforms	Shared by publishers' digital business model?
Low friction customer acquisition and retention.	No. Publishers' acquisition costs grow as its user base grows (and churn increases).
Free product, near-universal, almost immediate access.	No. Publishers' products increasingly not free as more adopt a subscription model.
Low operating costs, high margins.	No. Publishers' operating costs increase as the user base grows.
Strong network effects – the more users, the more attractive the product.	No. Customers are not attracted by the size of the customer base per se, but rather by the quality of content and quality of service that results from a substantial customer base and associated revenues.

Impact of platforms on the media

> There remain frustrations among publishers … about what they see as a lack of transparency from Google regarding algorithm changes and the precise way some products rank. It has a ripple effect on everything publishers do to gain and engage audiences.[9]

Media organisations are content-centric. The act of content creation lies at the heart of their activities: media professionals apply their expertise to determine what should be produced, produce it, distribute it and market it. The flow between organisation and consumer is one-directional and non-interactive. Digital platforms, probably the single most disruptive aspect of the digital revolution (certainly in terms of business viability), are user-centric. What appears on the platforms is not necessarily (indeed often not) produced by media industry professionals and is driven by user behaviours and demand. On digital platforms, content serves different functions: its purpose is to attract and retain users, and to spur interaction and transactions. As a result, different characteristics constitute what makes content 'successful'; these include programmability, popularity, connectivity and the ability to capture data associated with the content.[9] Platforms also disrupt in that they are gatekeepers in terms of connecting audiences with content, be it music (for example Spotify, Apple and Amazon Prime), video (for example, YouTube, Amazon Prime, Apple TV+) and, of course, news. Google, Meta and Apple, for example, are now dominant 'suppliers' (but not 'creators') of online news, doing that fast, to audiences that are simultaneously both large and precisely targetable, and all the while guided by algorithms that optimise the fit between content and consumer.

Digital platforms have been particularly disruptive to the news sector (Nielsen, 2018; Simon, 2022) and a complex combination of cooperation and dependency has grown up between the two (Nielsen and Ganter, 2018; Chua and Duffy, 2019) – dependency because the platforms direct the flow of attention online (Diakopolos, 2019) and are increasingly the gateways to the consumption of news online (Newman et al., 2020); cooperation because of the platforms' ability to direct online attention, and their investments in journalism projects and research (Fanta and Dachwitz, 2020).

Network effects drive platforms' fast growth

> … the larger the networks, the better the matches between supply and demand and the richer the data that can be used to find matches. Greater scale generates more value, which attracts more participants, which creates more value. (Van Alstyne et al., 2016: 4)

Triggering network effects is fundamental to the fast growth found in the platform economy. Network effects are a positive feedback loop: the more people in a network, the greater the value of that network for those people, the more attractive the network becomes, which encourages more people to join, and so on (these are also termed 'direct network effects' or 'same side network effects'). This dynamic means that growth is exponential or geometric, rather than linear. As the size of the network and its value for users increases, a secondary network effect kicks in: the success of the platform attracts investment, which allows it to invest in improving its products and services, making that platform yet more attractive to new users and existing ones.

Different factors drive network effects on different platforms. For Google, network effects stem from data: the more people using its search engine, the more data Google has to harvest and analyse, the more it can iterate its algorithm, and the better the results it delivers to its users. The more features it adds, the more value it offers to its users, and the more data it gathers. Thus, it has moved from search to maps, mobile operating systems, planning tools, virtual meeting hosting, voice recognition, and more. For Facebook, network effects derive from the number of users, and its value is dependent on the size and strength of its user base.[11]

User data is also central to triggering network effects. If a platform's functioning is contingent on gaining new users and locking them in by rolling out new features that are attractive to them, then platforms need detailed information on who those users are and what they are doing. So, data capture and analysis drive platform growth and guide the algorithm that determines key aspects of the user experience. For example, each Instagram user's feed will be designed (by the algorithm) around how that user uses the network – for example, their interests (accounts that have been interacted with, posts that have been liked and commented on) and relationships (prioritising posts from friends and family, frequency of use, who is followed and usage levels).

Indirect network effects exist, too. These are network effects that work in both directions: an increase in the number and quality of customers for one group of users increases the value to another group of users. For example, the more hosts there are on Airbnb, the more appealing it is to customers, and the more customers, the more attractive it is to the hosts. The more transactions, the more valuable the platform and the higher the revenues.

Network effects, lock-in and moats build a 'winner-takes-all' dynamic

Network effects make strong businesses stronger; taken to extremes, they create the near-monopoly positions we have seen with Google for Search and with Facebook for mobile advertising. The underlying growth dynamic functions as follows:

- the platform with the most current users will likely draw the most future users;
- the data provided by current users allows the platform to design and enhance its content and services in a way that increases the likelihood of attracting future users;
- the more content or services designed around user needs on the platforms, the more users it will attract and keep;
- the more customers it has that can be monetised, the more it can invest in providing additional features to create additional value for customers.

'Lock-in' enhances network effects. Lock-in is created by adding features that users value highly and that they would be reluctant to lose. 'Lock-in', combined with network effects, create what strategists call a **'competitive moat'** around platform businesses. (A competitive moat is something that allows a company to fend off competition and maintain profitability – the classic moats related to Porter's Five Force model that is discussed in the next chapter and are low-cost production, high switching costs for customers, intangible assets, scale efficiencies and network effects).

Several factors can create lock-in, particularly:

- The sheer number of participants in a network (you want to join a social network that most of your friends and family are most likely to be on, or if you are renting a property, you want that property to be available to the greatest number of potential renters).
- The quality of user experience (UX). If an app is overly complex to sign up for, difficult to use, crashes a lot and is unappealing as a digital product, users are likely to be irritated by it rather than attracted to it.
- Frequent launches of additional new features.

Creator economy: the 'enterprisation of individual creators'

> The Creator Economy – a fancy term for the online content creator business. (Alex Kantrowitz, 2023[12])

Until recently, those wanting to make a living from their creative output needed to work in a media organisation. Now, content creators (including influencers) and the social platforms they are active on command an increasing proportion of consumers' online behaviours. The creator economy gained serious traction in tandem with the expansion of social media during the Web 2.0 era (around 2007). Individual creators – bloggers, creators, influencers – started to amass large personal followings on platforms like YouTube and Instagram. Initially, there was no infrastructure to monetise or productise their work, nor were there the audience analytics and the social proof that brands need to justify advertising spend.

But the field matured and a 'complementor' layer developed, made up of businesses supplying the tools and services that creators needed to build businesses. The platforms, too, anxious to promote the creator economy, also launched a range of tools and services to help creators build their businesses. The result was that creators on social media now had resources to produce and promote products and build their follower base systematically. The creator economy, helped by the social media platforms, the 'King Kongs of the online world' (Cunningham and Silver, 2013[13]), a 'vast global wave of online cultural producers' that operate outside the traditional media industry (Craig, 2019[14]) emerged.

The 'creator economy', combines content entrepreneurs with online platforms such as YouTube, Instagram, Discord and Substack to build and monetise audiences in niche areas that may have been overlooked by mainstream media companies. This is a sector where 'winner-takes-all' dynamics are brutal (in 2022, of one billion Instagram accounts, over half of the top 50 accounts had over 100 million followers[15]). The lion's share of revenue goes to a fraction of a per cent of top creators. And being a creator is hard work – creators cover the entire value chain, from content creation to monetisation and marketing, although when a niche hits a nerve and scales, creators build out their businesses and hire staff.

Creators work across all genres of media. They include writers (producing blogs and newsletters), visual creators (making videos, photos, art), audio creators (creating music, podcasts), online course creators and gamers. By connecting directly with followers and building communities, they can in some cases turn this into a business and generate a living (although relatively few creators manage to generate substantial incomes).

The creator economy is an eco-system of mostly small, entrepreneurial media businesses. It is growing fast but young, with a structure and dynamics that are poorly understood (Sanyoura and Anderson, 2022) and its actual size is hard to gauge. In 2021, SignalFire[16] estimated the total number of creators, globally, to be 50 million and that the sector was worth around $104 billion[17]. In 2021,[18] Roblox claimed that over half of all US children under 16 were using the platform. In 2022, 29,000 YouTube channels had over one million subscribers.[19]

The creator economy has four elements:

1 **Creators:** the individuals who create the content – they can be influencers, bloggers, videographers, podcasters, musicians, and so on.

2 **Community** – the followers they engage with, the equivalent of the audience.

3 **Platforms** – the social and professional platforms that provide a place and the tools for creators to showcase their talents, create digital content and monetise their audiences. For example:

   - Twitch (livestream video gaming). Access is free, anyone can follow a game, but users can also subscribe to streamers. Streamers share in the advertising revenue generated by their content.
   - Substack (newsletter platform). Provides writers with a homepage, mailing list, payments and analytics to creators and takes a portion of subscription revenues.
   - Roblox (game platform and game creation system) where players can create games and play games created by other users, and buy and sell virtual items for avatars.

4 **Tools** – these are the services that allow creators to grow their community, monetise that audience, merchandise to them, and generally build professional businesses without specialist knowledge and capabilities. Some of these tools are provided by the platforms themselves, others by a growing sector of new businesses that offer affordable and accessible tools to support creators' businesses.

For creators, the range of monetisation options is wide – for example:

- **Advertising** – e.g., YouTube places ads in creators' videos, and those who upload videos to the platform earn a cut of the revenues generated when users click on them. At the time of writing, creators of long form videos received more than creators of short videos.
- **Brand deals** – e.g., a brand pays a creator to feature their product in a post or creators tag brand products in their content and earn commission on any sales driven from that content.
- **Creator funds**. Many platforms channel revenue to creators based on how their content performs. TikTok's creator fund of $1 billion was

launched in 2021. YouTube's Shorts Fund ($100 million) paid creators for short-form content in 2021 and 2022.

- **Subscription and membership fees** for higher value features, such as access to exclusive content which can range from research reports to access to events, courses and private communities.
- **'Tip jars'** that allow users to send money to creators.

Streaming media

Watching traditional TV channels has almost stopped among younger viewers, with 90 per cent of 18- to 24-year-olds heading straight to their favourite streaming service.[20]

Streamed media represents a fundamental evolution in the provision of mass media services. As Lotz (2022: 2) points out, streamed video-on-demand (SVOD) services 'deviate significantly from many of the norms upon which the television and film industries have long operated': they have different technological capabilities (enabled by internet distribution), different content strategies and different monetisation models (offering content on demand that is paid for directly by users) and are usually international in scope. While the content on a streaming video service may be the same as that shown on linear, ad-supported television, the underlying model is different, as shown in Figure 2.4. Broadcasting's fixed schedules, channels, release windows and licensing structures are absent. Streaming media platforms are a new breed of video providers and occupy a position between classic linear TV and social media platforms like YouTube. Cunningham and Craig (2019: 32–3) define them as:

> Closed platforms that distribute syndicated and original media content … prelicensed from and financed and produced by traditional media firms. Although distributed and curated differently … these platforms emulate the same genres and textual features of … professionally generated content.

The global video streaming market size was valued at US$59.14 billion in 2021 and is expected to expand at a compound annual growth rate (CAGR) of 21.3 per cent from 2022 to 2030.[21] This section focuses particularly on the streamed video market. Service providers in this sector vary according to key characteristics of geographic reach (which determines the total addressable market available to the organisation), library specificity (which can range from general, making it attractive to a broad audience, or specialist, which will attract

Figure 2.4 Streaming versus broadcasting, differences in underlying models

	Broadcasting	**Streaming**
Technology	Broadcast model/ broadcast engineering: • Cameras/microphones to playout systems to transmitters to TV sets. • One-way connection to audiences.	Platform model/software engineering: • Users request content via app, delivered over IP. • Two-way connection to users.
Funding	Indirect (via licence fee, advertising etc.). Minimal audience data (via research).	Direct payment by audiences. Granular real-time user data.
Offer	Fixed schedules, channels, windows. National (usually in Europe).	Data/AI tailor offering on individual basis in real time. Global.

© Lucy Küng

a smaller number of subscribers, but ones that may be willing to pay more), library ownership (whether the streamer owns the IP or licences content from third parties, or does both), and corporate ownership (if the streamer is part of a conglomerate, like Disney+, standalone, like Netflix, or part of a larger entity that uses the service as a loss leader to support other products (like Apple TV+ and Amazon Prime Video (Lotz, 2022).

There are three basic variants of service:

- **SVOD** – subscription-based video on demand (for example, Netflix). For companies offering a combination of services, SVOD is the 'premium tier'.
- **AVOD** – advertising-based video on demand, also known as 'free ad-supported TV' or **FAST**. Here, no subscription is paid; instead, the service is advertising-funded (examples include Hulu and Pluto TV).
- **Tiered** – where the lower priced services carry adverts, while premium packages are ad-free (Disney+ Basic, Netflix with Ads).
- **Internet-distributed video services** – including TikTok, Facebook and YouTube, are also streamed video services and sometimes are classified as examples of AVOD, but are 'open' platforms and allow users (creators) to upload and share content. Not all are revenue-generating, but those that rely on programmatic advertising and sponsor financing. YouTube pays no fees for the content it shows; rather, it splits advertising revenues with content creators.

Streamed video has a platform business model: customers request content from a streaming service via their device (smartphone, tablet, TV or PC). The streaming provider's servers send the content in data packets to the consumer's internet-connected device where they are assembled and deleted after consumption. The technological advances that enabled the streamed media sector include new devices, better storage, faster, cheaper internet connections and improvements in graphic chips. Particularly significant are cloud-based solutions that allow providers to serve domestic and international audiences efficiently, cost-effectively and reliably. AI is used at many points in the streaming business – in editing, cinematography, subtitling, voice-overs, scriptwriting and to enhance personalisation for subscribers.

The shift to streaming brings changes to the underlying industry value chain (see Figure 2.6). While content acquisition and creation remain critical (streamers, like linear players, need both large libraries of existing content and new content to attract and keep users), as the sector expands and more players compete for audiences, the investment in entertainment and sports content has risen dramatically to over $140 billion in 2022.[22] The value chain also includes a strategically critical bundle of activities concerned with running subscription activities and shaping the consumer experience, which include marketing, billing and customer service, and capturing and analysing data from its customers.[23] These newer activities are strategically critical: customer retention because there are many competing services and switching between them is easy, and marketing to ensure; discoverability because providers need to stand out from competitors to gain attention, and data analysis to match the product to market needs.

Netflix's strategy flags up the nature of the streaming sector and its fundamental differences from national broadcasting models:

- **Global** – Netflix went global early and is available in every country except China, North Korea, Syria and Crimea. In 2021, non-US streamers make up 65 per cent[24] of users and generate 56 per cent of total revenue.
- **'Glocal'** – Netflix is global but also seeks to address local preferences. It invests in original programming in 40 countries and has produced original scripted shows in 20 languages. In each country, work is commissioned from the local creative community.
- **Use of data and AI to personalise** – Netflix uses these technologies to tailor marketing and content offerings to individuals in huge numbers of viewers to new content in real time.
- **High investment in original programming** to drive subscriber uptake – Netflix relied initially on other companies' content libraries. As the media organisations who owned that content started to launch their own streamed service, it shifted to producing content itself. In 2019, Netflix launched more original content than the entire cable TV industry a decade earlier (spending $16–17 billion a year).

As streaming becomes the dominant model for content consumption, more players are entering the field and competition is increasing. Companies are fighting to have the maximum number of subscribers (which also brings inclusion in bundled offerings from telcos and prime positions on consumer interfaces). This is triggering acquisition activity, where companies are buying assets (primarily content) and acquiring capabilities and competencies along the value chain to position themselves to take a leadership position and gain scale. This is also leading to consolidation – some of the biggest media deals recently have been in this sector – for example, The Walt Disney Company and Fox, Viacom and CBS, and Time Warner and Discovery.[25]

Killer content and the rise of the blockbuster franchise

> Nobody knows anything .... Not one person in the entire motion picture field knows for a certainty what's going to work. Every time out it's a guess and, if you're lucky, an educated one.[26]

An eternal challenge in the media industry is that consumers are supremely unpredictable. Creative content involves alchemy -- informational, creative, technical and performative elements are combined in ways that may or may not strike a chord with the public. Over the years, the industry has grappled with this fundamental challenge, and developed different strategic approaches to guide their decisions on where to focus resources and investment.

As digitalisation has progressed, it has moved through three distinct strategic approaches.

'Mud against the wall'

> During their testimony, Penguin Random House executives said that just 35 per cent of books the company publishes are profitable. Among the titles that make money, a very small sliver – just 4 per cent – accounts for 60 per cent of those profits.[27]

If William Goldman is right, and 'nobody knows anything', then throwing mud against the wall to see what sticks is not unintelligent. Indeed, it was a favoured strategy in the media for decades and is still used in mature sectors with low margins that do not have the resources or infrastructure to play the blockbuster game, let alone apply the franchise model (book publishing is a classic example).

The 'strategy' is to increase the odds of success by increasing the number of attempts: generate high volumes of unique products in the hope that a number of these will strike a loud chord with the public. Publisher Bloomsbury had no idea that the first *Harry Potter* book would be a bestseller. The initial print run was around 500 copies – standard for a first novel by an unknown author. Now *Harry Potter* is at the heart of the five biggest earning multimedia franchises in the world (see below).

The underlying assumption is that 'cream rises to the top'. The market, prompted by critical acclaim and word-of-mouth recommendation, will find good products and sales will follow as positive publicity spreads. From an organisational perspective, this is a *laissez-faire* approach: all products receive limited and relatively equal time and investment until clear winners emerge, at which point marketing investment scales up rapidly. The disadvantage is that resources are spread thinly over a wide range of diverse products, and revenues and profitability overall are generally low. The advantage is that it allows many employees to work creatively, meaning that levels of intrinsic motivation tend to be high. Historical accounts of 'the golden age' of book or magazine publishing often describe media organisations operating under this product strategy.

'Go big or go home' – the lure of the blockbuster

> A Hollywood executive once told me that the marketing budget for a Will Smith movie was set to ensure that one in three Americans knew it existed: 'Spend whatever it takes to get to that one-in-three level of saturation and you'll have a blockbuster on your hands, fail to hit the tipping point and the movie will flop.'[28]

During Jeffrey Katzenberg's decade as Disney chairman, of the thousand projects he oversaw, just 10 per cent accounted for 91 per cent of the studio's operating income (Stewart, 2005: 2). These products were blockbusters, a term used throughout the media for winning books, hit films, television shows or sports fixtures – the products that generate a disproportionate proportion of revenues.

The blockbuster strategy involves identifying projects with strong hit potential, devoting the lion's share of attention and investment to these, and spurring demand by spending aggressively on marketing. If the initial bet is right, and the production and marketing deliver what they should, the products will generate disproportionate profits and compensate for poorer performance by the rest of the portfolio (Vogel, 1999; Aris and Bughin, 2005; Elberse, 2013).

This approach influences creative decisions. A project should appeal to the largest number of audience groups and eliminate the risk that specific groups might reject it. Narratives and characters need to be straightforward, plots should explore universal themes and sophisticated special effects are needed to compensate for the simplicity of other elements (Schatz, in Collins et al., 1993).

Franchises, sequels, prequels and spin-offs

> Streaming will have to mimic film in terms of turning its content into worlds, worlds that can be sequalised, prequelised, and accessorized with all sorts of different spin-offs ... people like watching iterations of what they know. (Lucas Shaw)[29]

The franchise is the blockbuster on steroids. *Harry Potter, The Lord of the Rings, Game of Thrones, Star Wars* are all franchises: 'a shared universe that features characters, occupations, or settings that overlap and maintain connective tissue via multi-platform and multi-delivery content'.[30] A franchising strategy involves the development, management and extension of intellectual properties (IP) across multiple texts and media platforms (Lomax, 2019).

In 2021, the highest-grossing film franchises at the box office[31] were:

- The Marvel Cinematic Universe. Disney ($22.59 billion).
- *Star Wars*. Disney ($10.2 billion).
- *The Wizarding World* (Harry Potter). Warner Brothers ($9.18 billion).
- *James Bond*. Wilson/Broccoli family ($6.89 billion).
- *Spider-Man*. Disney ($6.35 billion).

Disney's domination of movie franchises jumps out from this list. This has roots in its extraordinary heritage of animation franchises (think of Mickey Mouse or Donald Duck). CEO Bob Iger built on this when he recognised the current-day benefits of franchises and made them a lynchpin of Disney's strategy (and the studio's ability to create or acquire and manage franchises is a core strategic competence, as discussed in the next chapter). Iger's franchise acquisitions include Pixar (2006), Marvel Entertainment (2009), Lucasfilm, owner of the *Star Wars* franchise (2012) and 20th Century Fox in 2019. The Marvel Cinematic Universe (MCU) has been developed in 'phases'. Each phase includes a slate of new movies and new characters. Phase 6, scheduled for autumn 2024, is scheduled to mark the conclusion of the MCU.

Franchises are hard to build, but a goal for all. Netflix building *Stranger Things* into a franchise, responding to the echo it has struck in the market: it was the 'Most In-Demand Drama Series' of 2022, bringing its lifetime total of Global Demand Awards up to four, and it was the world's 'Most In-Demand Streaming Original' in both 2018 and 2019. It was 260 times more in demand than the average show worldwide, by far the highest ever global demand tracked for a streaming original series.[32]

Financially, these universes and characters are gifts 'that keep on giving' (Jeff Gomez, 2017).

- They are multiplatform: the 'shared universe' can be extended from film and television to games, stage plays and consumer products.
- They build loyal tribes of devoted fans: audiences move from one film release to the next over multiple phased movie releases.
- They are multinational: franchises appeal to viewers in all geographies.
- They are built on imaginary worlds, meaning they can be prolonged almost indefinitely with prequels, sequels and spin-offs.
- The are based on made-up figures, not real-life talent. Unlike Hollywood blockbusters, franchises usually feature supernatural beings and animated figures, meaning they are far less dependent on individual stars.
- Because they attract fans on a global basis, they are relatively recession-proof.
- They can cut through in an era of content oversupply. In the words of *The New York Times*' Chief Television Critic, James Poniewozik, 'the content boom on streaming TV makes rehashing familiar franchises more attractive. When viewers are paralyzed by choice among hundreds of series, it's easier to stand out with a brand people already know'.[33]

Metaverse

This is an emergent concept and riven by hype – a fully-fledged metaverse is still a way off, but elements already exist, and there is a growing acceptance that a global computing and network platform will emerge and shift the internet from 'something we visit' to 'something we viscerally experience'. Mathew Ball, an analyst, defines the metaverse as:

> ... a massive, interoperable 3D virtual world that is persistent (still there when you log off), synchronous (everyone experiences it the same way)

and able to support an unlimited number of users with their own identities, virtual objects, and access to payment systems.

The metaverse could impinge on the media industry from multiple directions – it combines aspects of entertainment, events, gaming, the creator economy and social media platforms. Users will be able to have virtual identities, undertake transactions and create content, and interactions with content will be more intense than with current media products. Gaming is the point of entry for the classic media industry, but the metaverse will be an enterprise phenomenon too, with both Microsoft and Meta developing metaverse products for business use. A range of development path options is likely:

- **Experiences**: the metaverse is an experiential environment, so a logical extension of concerts, film festivals and sports. Epic Games's Fortnite has held concerts where fans can interact with musicians. Disney is developing a metaverse theme park.
- **Gaming and TV**: Minecraft and Roblox are synchronous virtual online spaces and give insights into the sector's development path (and as an indication of the potential size of the sector, in 2021 gaming overtook TV as the biggest media sector). Similarly, media content formats and franchises with an appeal to younger demographic (Stranger Things, for example, has an official Roblox experience) are developing gaming experiences, which could iterate further into metaverse products.
- **Brands**: the metaverse allows companies to engage with customers in new ways, especially Gens Z and Alpha. Virtual clothing allows consumers to express their style in digital domains: H&M has launched a digital fashion collection. Meta has stores where Facebook, Instagram and Messenger users can buy digital clothing for their avatars from brands such as Balenciaga and Prada; Nike has filed patent and trademark applications for downloadable virtual goods.

Like other step changes in technology, the metaverse stands on the shoulders of other technologies. The widescale adoption of cloud computing is foundational to it, as is the real-time 3D rendering software used by game developers, publishers and platforms. They have laid a foundation, particularly Epic Games's Unreal Engine and Unity Technologies' engine, with further elements, including virtual reality (VR), augmented reality (AR), non-fungible tokens (NFGs), Web3 infrastructure and advanced haptic feedback. The development of the metaverse is dependent on these succeeding, and the complexity and investment required for each are significant. The Gartner Hype Curve (see p. 104) is relevant here, the path to adoption, if that happens, will be bumpy, but the tech majors are making significant commitments to this field. Microsoft has developed Microsoft's Mesh, a cloud-based AR/VR platform, and acquired Activision Blizzard. Facebook has rebranded as Meta, and its Meta Reality Labs invested $10 billion in the field. Epic Games raised $1 billion to accelerate the development of the metaverse.

Generative AI: digital media gets disrupted

Generative AI is a new and significant development that will change the media industry fundamentally, as did the advent of digital quarter of a century ago. This new technology emerged just at the conclusion of writing this new edition. The final chapter of this book explores predictive AI, ChatGPT and co, using the various concepts in this book to analyse its strategic impact on the sector.

Strategy in a volatile environment

> The metaverse is not yet established .... There are no best practices, playbooks, or business models. We will all get things wrong – probably often .... These leaders will be working on hypotheses, not facts.... Many companies will fail, not because of their ambition or earliness per se, but because they are too far down the road by the time they realise they made a wrong turn. (Matthew Ball[34])

This quote from Mathew Ball neatly encapsulates the challenge that high-change environments pose for strategy in the media sector. What do strategy makers know? They know that traditional revenue streams are diminishing, consumer habits are shifting and technology will continue to evolve. This type of environment is termed 'emergent'. Emergent environments are highly uncertain: industry boundaries are unclear, business models are evolving and consumer preferences along with them, and competition comes from new directions (Eisenhardt and Brown, 1999; Robins and Wiersema, 2000).

They are dangerous for incumbents because they change industry dynamics irrevocably: the basis of industry competition changes, and strategic assets (production and distribution systems, competencies and other types of expertise) lose relevance or may become liabilities because they tie the organisation to its past. Burgelman and Grove (2012) describe this situation as the 'valley of death'. To cross this valley, organisations need to make radical strategic changes while the existing business is still robust and revenues are holding up. This means creating a strategy, adapting the business model, and acquiring the competencies and other assets required to ensure success in the new environment. Building a bridge from old to new needs careful calibration – if the changes are too radical, they may undermine the existing business and revenues or be rejected by the organisation. If adjustments are too light and avoid fundamental change, there is a risk that demand or financial resources may collapse before the company makes it across. The art, therefore, is to transform the organisation, to make it across the valley of death before this happens. Figure 2.5 shows this dynamic, comparing the outcomes between a company that adapts as needed, and a company that seeks to traverse the valley without adapting sufficiently. The first sees revenues dip and then expand in the new market environment. The second does adjust, but changes are inadequate to reshape the business to the extent that it can generate solid revenues in the new environment. It then finds itself in the position of needing to put through a substantial transformation as demand or revenues for the old business are collapsing.

Having explored external phenomena shaping the strategic context, this chapter moves on to explore tools that help leaders identify and track the most critical environmental developments, assess their position with respect to these and identify the strategic priorities that result. These concepts include VUCA, PEST analysis, the value chain and strategic adjacencies.

VUCA

> 'It's not knowable' (Jerome Powell, Chair of the Federal Reserve speaking on the 2023 prognosis for recession, inflation and unemployment[35]).

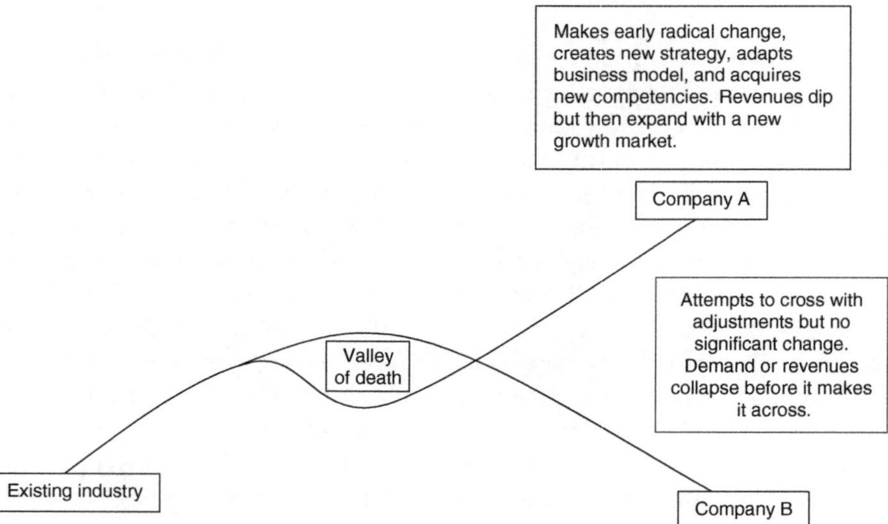

Figure 2.5 Crossing the 'valley of death' (based on Burgelman and Grove, 2012)

Of all the terms in this book, 'VUCA' will probably be one of the most familiar to leaders designing a strategy in industries that are undergoing serious disruption (a very large group). The term 'VUCA' started life in the military, standing as an acronym for volatile, uncertain, complex and ambiguous. It was coined by leadership gurus Warren Bennis and Burt Nanus in 1985 as a means of conceptualising the challenges posed by the post-Cold War global security environment. The concept has been used ever since by leaders to describe contexts that are turbulent and uncertain (Bennett and Lemoine, 2014; Mack and Khare, 2016). 'VUCA' is used now to guide strategic thinking and analyse risk across a broad range of industries, including the media (Halek and Strobl, 2016; Picard and Lowe, 2016).

As the Jagran New Media case study at the close of this chapter shows, VUCA is a useful tool to help media companies understand and navigate the complex and dynamic environment in which they operate. It can help them identify potential sources of volatility, uncertainty, complexity and ambiguity. VUCA can also help develop a framework to address these challenges.

VUCA environments have four characteristics, shown in the table below.

Volatility	• The environment is unstable. • Change is often unexpected, quick, multi-directional, and hard to predict.
Uncertainty	• Trends and patterns in the environment are opaque. • It is hard to anticipate events or estimate correctly how they may play out. • Forecasts are likely to be guesses. • Experience based on past events becomes less relevant. • Planning is difficult.
Complexity	• Strategic problems have many interrelated variables (multiplicity of competitors, markets, key decision factors, communication points, and outcomes). • There is a risk of oversimplification, and of strategy being reactive not proactive.
Ambiguity	• Situations are seldom completely clear. • There are many unknowns and 'unknown unknowns', contradictory demands and priorities. • Multiple interpretations are possible and equally valid. • Deciding on a course of action and gaining consensus from all stakeholders is hard. • Decisions are riskier. • There needs to be a tolerance for mistakes.

Analysing VUCA environments

VUCA environments are high-risk. The quandary this presents is that they must be analysed (Baaj and Reinmoeller, 2018), but their intrinsic nature makes such analysis extremely difficult to do. A recommended approach is to apply both rational and emergent strategy lenses and then to 'layer' structured organisational learning on top (Argyris and Schön, 1995; Bataci and Balci, 2017; Chawla and Lenka, 2018, in Dhir and Sushil, 2018). Edmondson and Verdin (2017) term this 'strategy as learning'. The basic stages in this process are:

1. **Classic environmental assessment** sets a baseline and establishes as far as possible what is not known and what needs to be known.
2. **Maximising learning** about the environment. Make this an ongoing process by building structured collaborative learning throughout the organisation. Feed in specialist expert information as needed.
3. **Reduce complexity by mapping the environment using systems thinking and design thinking.** Use this to create a shared understanding inside the organisation.
4. **Build hypotheses and assumptions to guide strategic responses, and test and revise these** as knowledge about the environment increases.

PEST analysis

PEST is an acronym: it stands for political, economic, social and technological – broad categories into which macro-environmental factors in the environment can be analysed as a basis for strategic analysis. Applying PEST analysis is straightforward. It involves identifying environmental factors, grouping them into these categories and then assessing them in terms of impact.

A very broad range of factors can fall into these categories, for example:

Type	Includes
Political	Regulation, tax policy, labour law, government media policy, subsidies. For example, new regulation regarding tech platforms and consumer protection rights in online environments, or government bans, such as the temporary ban on ChatGPT issued by the Italian Privacy Authority.
Economic	Competition, state of the economy including growth rate, cost of living, inflation, interest rates, average earnings, levels of household debt, labour availability, and employment trends.
Social	Demographic trends, changes in lifestyle, work habits, and media consumption patterns, and penetration of new technologies.
Technological	Technological advances, for example, the launch of cloud computing or generative AI, changes in consumer technology or utility infrastructures, levels of R&D activity, government investment policy, etc.

While extremely simple, the PEST model offers an excellent starting point from which to grasp and map critical factors in the complex environment surrounding media organisations and build an understanding of an organisation's overall strategic position vis-à-vis these. Done smartly, it throws a spotlight on the factors with a disproportionate impact on strategic outcomes and clarifies high-level priorities. The trick when using this model is to scan widely, but then to be highly selective in terms of factors included in the analysis: aim to pinpoint a smaller number of critical issues, rather than generate an exhaustive list of external elements. At the close of this chapter is a case study applying PEST analysis to public service media (PSM) organisations in Europe.

Value chain analysis

If VUCA is the second best-known term in this book, then the value chain (Porter, 1985) is number one. The media industry tends to turn to this model first when big disruption hits. It was ubiquitous as a tool to map out the potential impact of the internet at the start of the dot.com era and is being applied in this way again by the sector to explore the opportunities and challenges presented by AI.

The value chain is a tool that analyses how each of the activities that the organisation undertakes impacts on the overall value that the company creates. It views a firm as a system that is made up of various subsystems, each of which has the capacity to create additional value for customers, and also, if costs are managed well, these subsystems can also create cost advantage. Porter viewed the failure of many firms' strategies as resulting from difficulties in translating a strategy into specific action steps. The value chain was designed to create exactly those steps and build a bridge between strategy formulation and implementation, and is shown in Figure 2.6.

Breaking down an organisation's value-creating activities into strategically relevant stages allows each one to be analysed, and the behaviour of costs and potential sources of differentiation to be uncovered. In Porter's words:

> A company can outperform its rivals only if it can establish a difference that it can preserve. It must deliver greater value to customers or create comparable value at a lower cost or do both. The arithmetic of superior profitability then follows; delivering greater value allows a company to charge higher average unit prices; greater efficiency results in lower average unit costs. Ultimately, all differences between companies in cost or price derive from the hundreds of activities required to create, produce, sell, and deliver their products or services.... Overall advantage or disadvantage results from all a company's activities, not only a few. (Porter, 1996: 62)

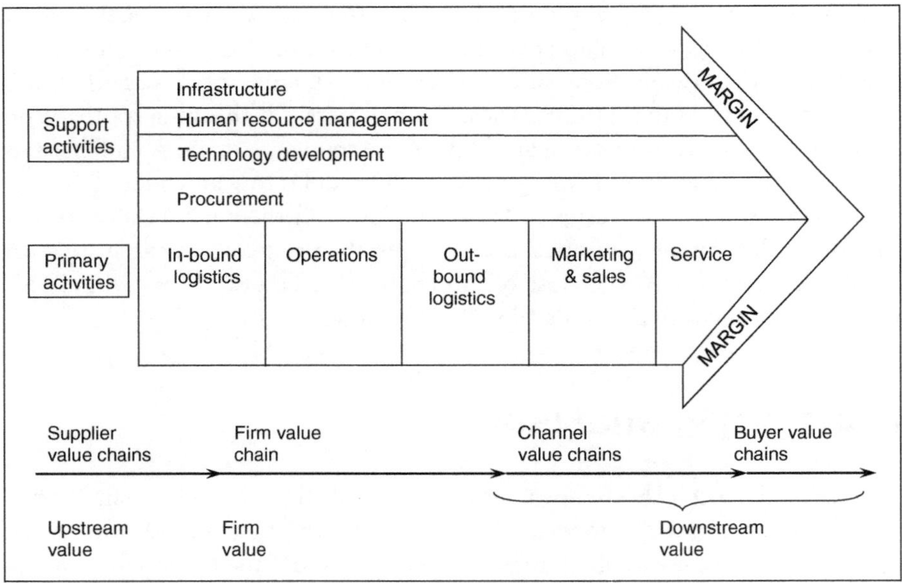

Figure 2.6 The value chain (based on Porter, 1985)

The value chain disaggregates the entire span of an organisation's operations into sequential subsystems or activities stretching from the supply side to the demand side, from inputs to outputs. These are all the internal activities the firm engages in to produce goods and services. There are **primary activities** (the central chain of elements in the diagrams in this chapter) that add value directly to the production process, and **support activities,** such as HR management, strategic management, research and development, which run the entire length of the organisation's activities and have the potential to increase overall value across the entire chain. The more competitive an organisation can make its value chain, the more the overall value of its product will exceed the sum of elements that go into that product, and the more the overall margin that can be realised as profits. There are two core approaches to gaining competitive advantage through the value you create:

- **Differentiation – e.g., Apple**: a company's products or services are superior to competitors', allowing the firm to charge more. This is Apple's strategy. Its products are more expensive than rivals', but it can charge more because it invests in aspects of those products (design, performance, materials, marketing, etc.), which make them superior to customers, who are willing to pay a premium price. In the newspaper sector, The *Financial Times* and *The Economist* follow this strategy, too. Both have invested in creating superior value for readers – in the calibre of their journalism, the size of their newsrooms and the sophistication of their digital products – and on the basis of this higher value can charge higher prices to readers.

- **Cost management – e.g., Amazon**: an organisation analyses the costs associated with each stage of its value chain and how efficiently they are carried out. If they can perform these at a lower cost than competitors can, they can create a competitive advantage by having higher margins at that stage. Amazon competes via cost advantage. In the words of its Chief Financial Officer, 'we will always be chasing the cost savings'[36]. Following this value strategy, Amazon increased its margins by reducing its packaging, shipping and labour costs (in the latter case through the increased use of automation and robotics).

Many assumed the value chain concept would lose relevance in a digital world (see, for example, Rayport and Svioka, 1995; Yoffie, 1997; Downes and Mui, 1998). The argumentation was that the assumption underlying all value chain thinking is that competitive advantage stems in part from scale and that this in turn is created by vertically integrating as much of the value chain as possible. Digitalisation would render this redundant, as value chains fragmented in response to new digital technologies and new digital businesses. Digital disruption has, however, in many cases led to an even tighter integration of value chains: vertical integration across the value chain to create strategic advantage and value is also still with us. When in 2001 Steve Jobs, CEO of Apple, opened Apple stores, he was pursuing a strategy of increasing vertical integration across Apple's value chain. Apple already controlled product design and manufacturing, and this move gave it control over distribution also.

Changing value chains in news publishing

Before digital transformation, the basic value chain for a newspaper had been unchanged for decades. This is shown in Figure 2.7: content was generated/procured, as was advertising, that content was prepared for publication, and the newspaper was produced, printed and distributed to readers. A set of company-wide activities supported these processes, including human resources (HR), technology and engineering and finance. Newspaper publishers were highly integrated exactly in the sense described by Porter: they owned all stages of their value chains or had high levels of control over them, and derived value from this degree of vertical integration. This is shown in Figure 2.7.

As the media industry went digital, newspapers launched digital editions alongside their print publications. They started with a website for desktop PCs and gradually broadened their digital products to include an app, perhaps an

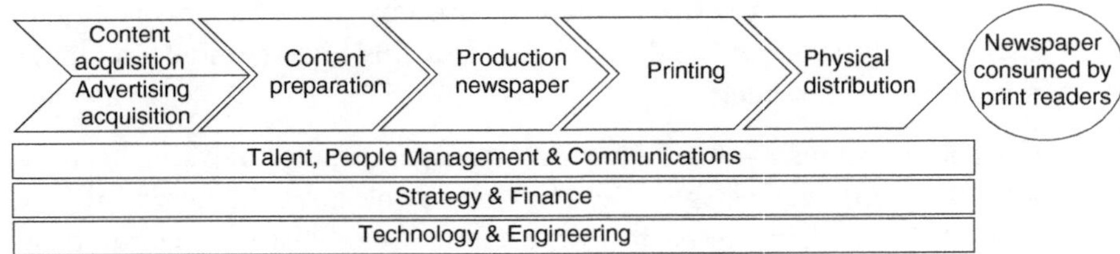

Figure 2.7 Newspaper value chain pre-digital
© Lucy Küng

e-paper, and newsletters also. For players without a paywall, this generated a value chain, as shown in Figure 2.8, where the following changes can be seen:

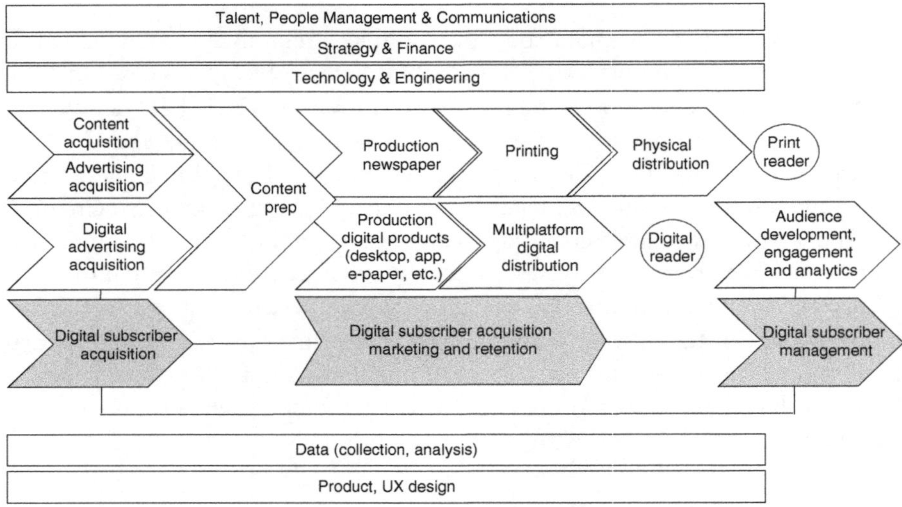

Figure 2.8 Digital news publishing value chain
© Lucy Küng

- **An additional digital value chain now runs alongside** the original print one, making an overall value chain that is more complex and contains more elements.
- A new activity has been added, 'Acquisition of digital advertising'.
- '**Content acquisition**' and '**Content preparation**' become more complex because they cater for both print and digital editions. Covering this spectrum in a single newsroom is one of the biggest challenges presented by digitalisation because digital journalism and its formats are different.

- '**Production of digital products**' is a new function that straddles journalism, technology and business activities. Frequently, there is one product team that is focused on products for the newsroom, creating CMS systems, developing content formats, graphics templates, and so on, and another larger product team that operates as a support process across the entire value chain.
- '**Distribution**' is now multiplatform. In addition to the traditional processes involved in printing and distributing digital products, there is multiplatform digital distribution taking place via an online delivery medium – over the internet or via content delivery platforms owned by the publisher. Digital distribution is also direct. The product goes direct from the news organisation to the news consumer.
- Consumption by the '**Digital reader**' is integrated into the digital value chain, rather than being the activity that happens once the publisher's value chain has ended. The product is produced, distributed via digital platforms and consumed by the reader.
- Consumption by the digital reader is now followed by a new value chain stage, '**Audience development, engagement and analytics**'. This includes audience planning and strategising social media distribution to promote the publishers' content on social media platforms like Google and Facebook, both to boost readership and also to drive traffic to the publishers' websites.
- Two new support activities have been added that run across the length of the value chain. '**Data collection and analysis**' analyses how content is consumed and feeds those insights into content creation, product design and distribution stages. '**Product and user (UX) design**' encompasses all the processes necessary to create a digital product and ensure that it reaches its audience in a digital distribution ecosystem. This can include designing apps, websites, newsletters, e-paper editions and more, as well as both customer and newsroom-facing dimensions of registration and paywalls.

As digital transformation progressed, an increasing number of publishers pivoted to a subscription-funded model and introduced a paywall. The introduction of a paywall adds an additional layer of processes connected to the management of subscribers – these are Digital subscriber acquisition planning, Digital subscriber acquisition marketing, and Digital subscriber management.

Adjacencies: growth outside the value chain

Media organisations also develop products and services outside their value chain. The 'product/market' matrix (Ansoff, 1957) provides a structured means to approach this. Its two axes, 'market' (customers) and 'product' (the goods and services sold to customers), build a two-by-two matrix with four quadrants. Each represents a different growth strategy: market penetration, product development, market development and diversification.

The concept of 'adjacencies' (Zook and Allen, 2010) is based on Ansoff's matrix. This allows organisations to explore growth options that build off existing capabilities, resources and know-how. Companies are recommended to focus either on moving existing products into adjacent markets or developing new products for existing markets but to avoid launching new products for new markets since the organisation will be unable to leverage its existing capabilities and assets. It will need to acquire entirely new competencies, thus increasing the risk of failure.

Amazon.com follows an adjacency strategy. In e-commerce, it started in a small market it felt it could take a commanding position in and expanded from there into adjacent fields (Thiel and Masters, 2014). It started with books, because this category of products possessed a set of intrinsic characteristics that were extremely well suited to online e-commerce:

1 A very wide range of products that were already categorised using a universal system.
2 Products that were similar in shape came in standard sizes and were easy to pack and ship.
3 The wide range of books published meant that bookshops could only offer a fraction of the millions published. Amazon, which didn't initially hold stock, could simply request the book from its supplier and ship it on to the customer. This meant that it could from the outset offer a greater number of books than any physical bookshop, and thus differentiate its service.

Once established in books, Amazon.com moved progressively through adjacent product categories (CDs, videos, software) and as its expertise and competence grew, it moved in an ever-wider group of product types – toys, clothes, sports equipment, and ultimately to groceries and medication. At the same time, it also expanded by turning aspects of its own internal value chain into businesses:

- **Services and the infrastructure to support e-commerce** (warehouses, private postal services, drone delivery and the Amazon Dash Button).
- **Devices** to consume content (e-readers and smartphones).
- **Streamed media content** (Amazon Prime).

- **B2B services** created by 'white-labelling' internal processes it had developed to speed up the deployment of its new applications and services (Amazon Web Services).
- **Producing original programming** – series, movies and games.

Conclusions

The media industry is in a volatile, fast-changing and emergent environment. Such contexts present a complex management challenge, particularly for incumbents encumbered by their legacy systems and processes. They need to embrace new strategic directions that will lead to corporate renewal. They need to master new products requiring different competencies. They need to strategise more rapidly (even if decisions regarding strategic priorities, technological choices and capital investments must be made with imperfect information) and make their organisations more agile. And underlying all these shifts is a need to change shared cultural assumptions and how leaders lead. The subsequent chapters of this book will explore approaches for tackling these issues.

Questions

1 Keep a diary of your personal media consumption for one day. What percentage of your time did you spend on social media platforms versus more classic media products? Did you create content?

2 Which creators do you follow? Research as far as possible their businesses? How large are these? What income streams do they have?

3 Identify two personal favourite pieces of media content and reflect on the content strategy underlying their production. Are they part of a global media franchise? Are they blockbusters? Where did you consume them? If you consumed them on a streamed media service, how much did their presence in that streamer's catalogue influence your decision to subscribe to that service?

4 Identify the value chain for an organisation you are interested in. How is this changing? How complex is it? Which activities add the most value now? Which could add the most value? On the basis of this analysis, suggest how this organisation could increase the value it creates and increase its strategic differentiation.

Resources

Books

The Business of Platforms: Strategy in the Age of Digital Competition, Innovation and Power. Michael Cusumano, Anabelle Gawer and David B. Yoffie. Harvard Business School Press, 2019.

Vaporized. Robert Tercek explores how new technologies such as mobile, cloud and AI are reconfiguring a range of industries from the media to retail. LifeTree, 2015.

The Power of Platforms. Rasmus Kleis Nielsen and Sarah Anne Ganter. Oxford University Press, 2022.

The Wealth of Networks. Yochai Benkler. Yale University Press, 2006.

The Platform Revolution: How Networked Markets are Transforming the Economy and How to Make Them Work for You. Geoffrey G. Parker, Marshall W. van Alstyne and Sangeet Paul Choudary. Norton, 2016.

Netflix and Streaming Video. Amanda D. Lotz. Polity Books, 2022.

Crossing the Chasm. Geoffrey A. Moore. HarperCollins, 1991.

Tarzan Economics. Will Page. Little Brown, 2021.

The Metaverse. Matthew Ball. Liveright, 2022.

The Attention Merchants. Tim Wu. Atlantic Books, 2016.

The Digital Mindset. Paul Leonardi and Tsedal Neeley. Harvard Business Review Press, 2022.

The Digital Transformation Playbook David L. Rogers. Columbia Business School Publishing, 2016.

Newsletters

Alex Kantrowitz's Big Technology: https://bigtechnology.substack.com

Axios Media Trends Newsletter: www.axios.com/newsletters/axios-media-trends

Ben Thompson's Stratechery: https://stratechery.com

Casey Newton's The Platformer: www.platformer.news

Mediagazer – a curated aggregator of media news with a wide-ranging mix of stories from across the industry: https://mediagazer.com

Medianama – specialises in media policy in India: www.medianama.com

nScreenMedia: https://nscreenmedia.com covers the digital video space

State of the News Media (Project) – Pew Research Center: www.pewresearch.org/topic/news-habits-media/news-media-trends/state-of-the-news-media-project

(*Continued*)

Daily Media News Briefing – Pew Research Center: www.pewresearch.org/about/follow-us
Platform Papers: https://platformpapers.substack.com
Storytelling in Virtual Worlds: https://stringfield.substack.com
SuperJoost PlayList – a free weekly review of the business of video games: https://superjoost.substack.com

Podcasts

There are a great many podcasts covering the media industry and its strategic environment. These include:

Media Voices: https://voices.media
Pivot: https://podcasts.voxmedia.com/show/pivot
Splice Pink – digital media and media start-ups in south and south-east Asia and APAC: www.splicemedia.com/pink
Recode Media with Peter Kafka: https://podcasts.apple.com/us/podcast/recode-media/id1080467174?i=1000613147792
The Rebooting Show on how to build and operate media businesses. www. https://podcasts.apple.com/us/podcast/the-rebooting-show/id1595625177

Industry research

Reuters Institute for the Study of Journalism. Oxford University.
The Digital News Report (published yearly).
Trends and Predications (published yearly).

From management consultancies:

Deloitte's *Media and Entertainment Industry Outlook*: www2.deloitte.com/us/en/pages/technology-media-and-telecommunications/articles/media-and-entertainment-industry-outlook-trends.html
PwC's Annual Global Entertainment and Media Outlook: www.pwc.com/gx/en/industries/tmt/media/outlook.html

From regulators:

Ofcom's annual communications market reports: www.ofcom.org.uk/research-and-data/multi-sector-research/cmr
Ofcom's recommendations on the future of public service media in the UK: www.smallscreenbigdebate.co.uk/statement

Case: Bharat Gupta – leading Jagran New Media in a VUCA world

For Bharat Gupta, CEO of Jagran New Media (JNM), VUCA is a fact of life. India's digital media environment is exceptionally fast-moving, reflecting that India has one of the largest internet populations in the world, with over 65 per cent of the population under 35 and consuming digitally on mobile devices, and around 70 per cent of news found via search and social channels. As publisher of nine digital platforms in genres ranging from news to entertainment, Bharat has tailored his strategy for VUCA. He focuses on building four elements inside the organisation, each one responding to a different dimension of VUCA. The table below summarises this approach.

From volatility to vision	• Use clearly articulated vision to provide orientation when it feels like everything is changing. • Make sure leadership team always keep this in mind and continue to reinforce the core message. • Create universally accessible information tools that provide everyone with up-to-date information on the business and how it's doing.
From uncertainty to understanding	• Provide transparent, speedy information – essential if you want accountability. • Create real-time data dashboards to monitor performance and define measures. • Hold quarterly townhalls to share what is happening and break down goals into quarterly targets. • Ensure constant knowledge exchange between leaders and the wider organisation, using collaborative digital tools like chat and videoconferencing. • Deal with risks early on by conducting detailed risk assessments. • Create a climate that encourages innovation and learning.
From complexity to clarity	• Ensure the entire organisation is clear on what it is trying to achieve and what action is needed to get there. • Design processes as simple as possible. • Identify champions of change who model what you need – talented individuals who are performing excellently on targets and innovation.
From ambiguity to agility	• Ensure cooperation and constant communication between participants in projects and processes. • Use agile approaches to increase responsiveness – for example, through daily Scrum meetings to keep everyone up to date.

(*Continued*)

Combatting VUCA with strategic clarity

The starting point is strategic clarity. Care has been taken to ensure that all staff understand JNM's **mission** ('to provide factual and credible content that empowers through knowledge, information and providing a point of view'), **vision** ('to increase shareholder value by creating scalable and sustainable business models in line with the Mission'), and **top objectives**; scale (be in the top five news sites in India), impact (achieve specified targets for audience, revenue and industry rankings), sustainability (be earnings before interest, taxes, depreciation, and amortization (EBITDA) positive and achieve 'Great Place to Work' status).

'The only way it can succeed is when everything is measurable'[37]

Bharat needed to build buy-in to this set of strategic objectives and a clear link between individuals' daily work and the long-term goals. He also needed an internal feedback system that would allow the organisation to naturally adjust in step with its VUCA context. This led to building a 'transparent real-time environment', which was established with three pillars:

- **Transparency** – vision, mission and objectives are clear to all.
- **Measurability** – all activities are measurable and data dashboards provide fast information on progress.
- **Accountability** – systems for performance appraisal, learning and development, and talent management mean that everyone knows their personal objectives, has the skills to achieve them, and receives constructive feedback on their performance:

> Most top websites largely offer the same kind and the same genres of news. We carried out research to understand what the online consumer is looking for ... The insights were really brilliant and now these insights are helping us to strengthen our differentiator strategy.[38]

A cascading set of goals, projects for achieving them and targets for measuring progress towards them were developed for each activity from editorial to HR. Each function identified key focus areas, and progress to achieving them was measured and fed into performance management systems.

Audience understanding is at the core of all activities: data insights guide decisions, identify opportunities, inform product development, clarify priorities,

(Continued)

track progress, and drive the basic cycle of ideate, innovate, collaborate and optimise for scale. This data-driven approach is applied to the internal organisation, too. For Bharat, this is:

> ... nothing but a scientific way not only to practice great management and people development ... to ensure true value creation both within the company and outside of the company. What we sow is what we reap, the value system remains the same.[39]

Culture – 'the difference between stagnation and growth, competitiveness and being left behind'[40]

Bharat has sought to build a high-performance, high-trust culture by implementing a range of pan-organisation measures.

To drive high performance	• Give individuals the scope to make key decisions and own those decisions. This increases engagement. • Build two-way fast feedback mechanisms – between leadership team members and between leaders and the wider organisation. • Empower people by equipping them with the skills they need through learning and development opportunities.
To drive trust	• Have strong internal communications via chat and video conferencing. Communicate as many leadership decisions as possible by individual meetings or town halls. • Recognise imperfections in the organisation and take action to correct them. • Track employee engagement to ensure that culture is aligned with values and goals. • Demonstrably care for staff and explain what you are doing. When Covid hit, JNM guaranteed zero redundancies or salary cuts. Instead, it sought to inspire concerned staff with a clear plan for navigating the new environment and linked EBITDA incentives to this.

By creating a strategy and leadership style deliberately designed to respond to VUCA, Bharat Gupta has led JNM to digital success. In 2016, 90 per cent of JNM's 30 million users came from news. Five years later, it had over 109 million users, with 60 per cent from news and 40 per cent from non-news segments.[41] In 2021, JNM was recognised as 'India's Best Place to work in Media',[42] and Bharat as one of 'India's Best Leaders in Times of Crisis' for his 'exemplary leadership' during Covid.

(Continued)

Case questions

1 What are the core elements of Bharat Gupta's strategy to respond to the challenges of VUCA?

2 Read about the factors that drive creativity in Chapter 5, p.143. How many of these are present in Jagran New Media?

3 What kind of leadership approach does Bharat Gupta follow?

4 Are you surprised by the importance of culture in creating high performance? How does Jagran New Media seek to build a high-performance culture?

Case: PEST analysis of Europe's public service media

Public service media organisations – like the BBC in the UK, PBS in the US and ARD in Germany – are a long-established element in the media industry (the UK's BBC is over a hundred years old). While these organisations vary, particularly in terms of how they are funded (options include licence fee, government funding, director public media tax, household levy and advertising), common to all is the concept of service to the public as their *raison d'être*. Indeed, the EBU, an alliance of public service media organisations, defines the nature and focus of these organisations as follows:

> Public service media is broadcasting made, financed and controlled by the public, for the public. Their output, whether it be TV, radio or digital, is designed to inform, educate and entertain all audiences.[43]

PSM emerged in an era of scarce media choices and limited spectrum availability, but now operates in a vastly different media landscape, where they must contend with new products, platforms, consumption patterns and competitors. Against this challenging backdrop, PSMs must preserve their independence and integrity while providing high-quality programming and meeting the evolving needs of their communities, as the Council of Europe explains:

> In exercising their role, public service media face a number of challenges, such as securing the right level of independence from those

(Continued)

holding economic and political power, securing appropriate funding, adapting to the digital age and maintaining high editorial standards in a competitive market.[44]

The following PEST analysis digs into the environmental challenges faced by PSM organisations. It is summarised in Figure 2.9.

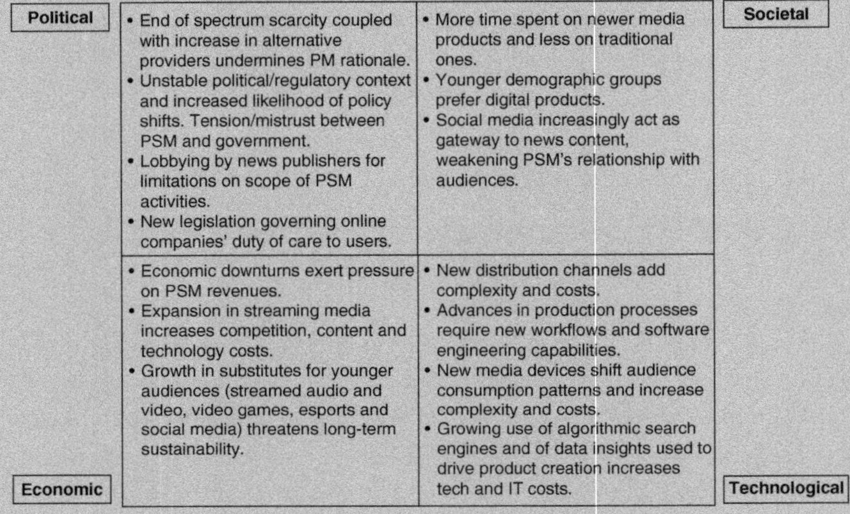

Figure 2.9 PEST analysis of publics media in Europe
© Lucy Küng

Political factors

> DR [Danish Broadcasting] today announced the imminent closure of a number of its television and radio services. The broadcaster is having to reduce its output as a result of the 20% budget cuts imposed by the Danish government ... six TV channels will be reduced to three and radio channels will drop from eight to five ... 400 positions will close.[45]

The legal standing of PSM organisations varies by country, as they are typically established through national legislation. In some countries, such as the United Kingdom, PSM organisations have a specific legal status, such as a Royal Charter, which sets out their purpose, structure and governance arrangements. In

(Continued)

other countries, such as France, PSM organisations are defined in law as entities that are separate from the government and have a specific public service mission. PSM organisations may also be subject to regulatory frameworks that govern their operations, such as codes of conduct for journalists and standards for programming. Overall, the legal standing of PSM organisations is designed to ensure their independence and to support their public service mission. This means that political factors, notably around government attitudes towards PSM and regulation, can be some of the most pressing strategic factors in their environment. For example:

- **End of spectrum scarcity coupled with rapid increase in alternative content providers undermines PSM rationale.** Spectrum scarcity was a central argument for the establishment of public service broadcasters over a hundred years ago: they should provide a 'portmanteau' programme that offered something for everyone. This was necessary because they were at that point often the only broadcasting service provider. In return, they received assured income in the shape of a universal licence fee. The increase in the supply of media content that has occurred since this model was created undermines the logic underlying this model: if consumers have a very broad range of content options, the argument for a universal service supported by the public is weaker. In response, PSM organisations need to clarify and demonstrate the value they create for national audiences (particularly in terms of the provision of high-quality and highly trusted news and current affairs), not just to the public, but also to politicians who determine PSM funding arrangements and permitted scope of services.
- **Unstable political and regulatory context and increased likelihood of policy shifts.** Changes in media consumption (away from television and radio sets towards online) mean that basic funding mechanisms (which were often based on a 'per set' fee) need to be revised, which opens the door for more fundamental reviews of how PSM is funded. As the quote at the head of this section indicates, changes in government can bring sudden changes in government policy towards PSM, especially concerning funding. Additionally, political forces may exert pressure on public service media to produce content that is more partisan or aligned with the government's agenda.

(*Continued*)

Economic factors

Economic factors in the wider environment can have significant impacts on public service media, both in terms of funding and content priorities. Public service media organisations need to be aware of and adapt to a range of factors, for example:

- **Economic downturns exert pressure on PSM revenues.** Public service media, like all media organisations, are affected by economic factors in the wider environment, particularly by economic downturns. Increases in the cost of living, levels of inflation and unemployment, and drops in disposable income all affect consumers' willingness to pay for public service media, and reduce levels of advertising activity (an important revenue for PSM organistations with a dual revenue model). The rise of alternatives, especially free sources of news and entertainment, also influences attitudes. During such periods, households may question the fees they pay, governments may seek to reduce funding levels, and advertising revenues may shrink. A 2022 report by the EBU into PSM funding found that PSM revenues had fallen in 66 per cent of markets between 2019 and 2022.[46]
- **Increased competition leads to a drop in audiences.** Streaming media, podcasts, social media creators and influencers, and other developments discussed in Chapter 2, add up to heightened competition for PSM. This poses significant challenges to PSMs. Perhaps the most critical one is the loss of audience share. The migration of viewers or listeners from public service media towards competitors can kick off a vicious circle: lower audiences precipitate reduced funding, which may negatively impact on the quality and quantity of content produced by public service media, further reducing audiences.
- **The boom in streaming media increases content and technology costs.** The boom in streamed video and audio services is increasing competition and accelerating changes in consumption patterns (PSM are active in this sector also). The calibre and range of content are critical to the uptake and retention of these services by users, and significant capital investment is needed to establish streaming services, particularly in terms of product, UX and data capabilities. Taken together, these factors have competition for content and certain categories of talent, and pushed up content costs.

(Continued)

Social factors

> Five years ago, broadcast TV reached nearly 80% of young adults a week. Today it's around 50%, and radical changes are happening across all ages. TikTok is now bigger than the BBC in video for 16–24s in the UK.[47]

Changes in social factors significantly impact on the ability of PSM to achieve their mandate of serving the public interest. PSM both reflects and is influenced by the society it operates in, and it must remain relevant and cater to the evolving needs of its audience. Changes such as those discussed in this chapter, including shifts in demographics, cultural attitudes and technological advancements, all have a profound impact on the demand for and delivery of PSM. These changes also affect the types of issues and topics that PSM cover, the way in which they are presented, and the voices that are included or excluded from the discourse. Significant changes in the social realm include:

- **The more time spent on newer media products, the less that is spent on traditional ones**. An explosion in the volume of media products is changing consumption patterns and fragmenting audiences. This, coupled with the fact that human attention is inevitably limited, means that audiences for traditional media products are shrinking.
- **Younger demographic groups prefer newer digital products**. Younger demographic groups favour the newer breeds of media products, ranging from streamed content and e-sports to TikTok and podcasts. If PSM fails to create a strong presence in these new product areas, a universal funding basis will become even harder to justify.
- **Social media are an increasingly important gateway to news and entertainment content**. Social media platforms have fundamentally transformed the way that individuals consume news and entertainment content. These platforms have become a gateway for users to access a vast array of media content, including breaking news stories, live events and viral videos. Social media not only facilitate the discovery of new and relevant content, but they also provide a space for users to engage with and share content with their social networks. The implications of this development are very significant and go far beyond the focus of this PEST analysis. The key issues for our purposes here are that PSM must have a strong presence on social media if they are to maintain a strong presence in the lives of their audiences, but also that by doing this they become dependent on a third-party and weaken their relationship with audiences.

(*Continued*)

Technological factors

The BBC can invest far less in its digital products than other media organisations, many of which are digital-only and are not constrained by the BBC's universal service commitments. In 2021, for example, Netflix spent £1.7 billion on technology and development. In consequence, the BBC has not been able to develop its product portfolio with the same pace and sophistication as that of rival media organisations.[48]

PSM operate in an environment that is heavily influenced by technological advancements (as discussed in Chapter 4). Technological changes can impact PSM media in several ways:

- **New distribution channels add complexity and costs.** Changes in technology affect the way that PSM content is distributed. For example, the rise of online streaming services has provided PSM organisations with new channels to distribute their content. On the other hand, traditional distribution channels such as broadcast television are becoming less relevant if viewers increasingly turn to online platforms. In response to these technological advances, PSMs have progressively added new services, platforms and internal functions, including online and on-demand, apps, podcasts, product development teams, and more. These are necessary to march in step with consumer behaviour, but they have added costs and complexity.
- **Advances in production processes bring changes in workflow and expand engineering capabilities from broadcast to software**. Technological advancements can also impact on the production processes used by PSM organisations. For example, the introduction of digital cameras and editing software has made it easier and cheaper for PSM to produce high-quality content.
- **New media devices change audience consumption patterns and also increase complexity and costs**. The increasing use of smartphones and social media has led to a shift in the way that audiences consume news and other forms of media. PSM organisations need to adapt to these changes to remain relevant and engaging to their audiences.
- **Data capture and analytics become critical.** Data capture and analytics are becoming increasingly important for PSM media organisations and requiring significant investment. These tools provide valuable insights into audience behaviour and preferences, enabling PSM to better understand their audience and tailor their content accordingly. This is particularly important in an era of increased competition for audience attention and the fragmentation of media consumption across multiple

(Continued)

platforms. Data capture and analytics can also help PSM organisations to measure the impact of their content and assess their performance. This includes metrics such as audience engagement, reach and satisfaction, as well as more granular insights into how audiences are interacting with specific pieces of content. By analysing this data, PSM organisations can identify areas for improvement and optimise their content to better meet the needs and expectations of their audience. Finally, data capture and analytics can also help PSM make more informed decisions about their operations, such as resource allocation and strategic planning.

Case questions

1 Using the analysis above, draw a table clarifying the key factors in PSM's strategic environment. Using your judgement, rank these. On the basis of this analysis, what strategic priorities do you see for PSM organisations?

2 Carry out a PEST analysis for an organisation or a sector. Define the firm or sector clearly first and focus on the most critical factors. Rank the factors you have identified. For each one, explore its implications. What strategic priorities emerge for you as a result?

Notes

1 'Pipelines, Platforms and the New Rules of Strategy'. Marshall W. Van Alstyne, Geoffrey G. Parker and Sangeet Paul Choudary. *Harvard Business Review*, April 2015.

2 Scott Galloway, 'Fire and Fawning', 24 July 2020.

3 'Pipelines, Platforms and the New Rules of Strategy'. Marshall W. Van Alstyne, Geoffrey G. Parker and Sangeet Paul Choudary. *Harvard Business Review*, April 2015.

4 To read further on this definition, see 'The State of the Platform Revolution 2021', Sangeet Paul Choudary. Available at: https://drive.google.com/file/d/1DcjiB3sJsdw2sdwmeyLY0gj_N1seBmiG/view

5 The term 'platform' is widely used and definitions vary. It can be used to mean an underlying product that allows modular components to be built on it, a basis upon which other things are set up.

6 Marius Deilen and Manuel Wiesche, 'The Role of Complementors in Platform Ecosystems' (2021), Wirtschaftsinformatik 2021 Proceedings, 5. Available at: https://aisel.aisnet.org/wi2021/GFuture18/Track18/5

7 Statistica.com, 8 March 2023. Available at: www.statista.com/topics/9038/meta-platforms/#topicOverview

8 'Facebook's advertising revenue worldwide from 2009 to 2020'. Available at: www.statista.com/statistics/271258/facebooks-advertising-revenue-worldwide

9 Peter Bale, 'How Newsrooms Succeed in Google Search', INMA, December 2022.

10 J. Van Dijck and T. Powell (2013) 'Understanding Social Media Logic'. *Media and Communication*, 1(1), 2–14.

11 Ben Thompson, *Stratechery*, 15 May 2018.

12 Alex Kantrowitz, 'The creator economy was way overblown', 5 January 2023. Available at: www.bigtechnology.com/p/the-creator-economy-was-way-overblown?utm_source=substack&utm_medium=email

13 Cunningham, S. and Silver, J. (2013) *Screen Distribution and the New King Kongs of the Online World*. New York: NYU Press.

14 David Craig, 'Creator management in the social media entertainment industry', in Mark Deuze and Mirjam Prenger (eds) *Making Media* (2019). Amsterdam University Press.

15 Hubspot Instagram-Report 2022. Available at: https://mention.com/en/reports/instagram/followers

16 www.cbinsights.com/research/report/what-is-the-creator-economy/#size

17 https://theinfluencermarketingfactory.com/creator-economy

18 'Roblox ramps up brand purchases', *Digiday Daily*, 9 June 2021.

19 www.tubics.com/blog/number-of-youtube-channels

20 Younger viewers shun traditional TV channels, as 90 per cent opt for streaming services. Mark Sweeney, *The Guardian*, 17 August 2022.

21 www.grandviewresearch.com/industry-analysis/video-streaming-market

22 www.parrotanalytics.com/parrot-perspective/netflix-amazon-hbo-max-svod-licence-original-content/?utm_campaign=Parrot%20Perspective&utm_medium=email&_hsmi=244230096&_hsenc=p2ANqtz-9r9k3-TziJxH6n-bO5pbrHnGIjJff1gWqG7KWcdtn7ujqfFGv7AULOEvOtphW_pb-rrkfpENE1GU8TCzpSKPpuWfMJXuw&utm_content=244229757&utm_source=hh_email

23 https://advisory.kpmg.us/articles/2020/media-industry-transformation.html

24 Wendy Lee. *Los Angeles Times*, 20 September 2021. Available at: www.latimes.com/entertainment-arts/business/story/2021-09-20/netflix-global-expansion-international-tv-bella-bajaria-lupin

25 www.bain.com/insights/in-video-scale-matters-more-than-ever-m-and-a-report-2021

26 William Goldman, *Adventures in the Screen Trade* (1989). Grand Central Publishing.

27 *New York Times* article on the 2022 case between the Department of Justice and Penguin Random House to determine whether Random House may buy Simon & Schuster. The US government sued to stop the deal on antitrust grounds. Available at: www.nytimes.com/2022/08/19/books/prh-penguin-random-house-trial.html

?action=click&pgtype=Article&state=default&module=styln-penguin-random-house&variant=show®ion=MAIN_CONTENT_1&block=storyline_top_links_recirc

28 Will Page, *Tarzan Economics*. Simon & Schuster (2021: 253).

29 Lucas Shaw interviewed on 'Plain English' podcast, 21 July 2022.

30 Parrot Perspective #4, ibid.

31 www.cnbc.com/2021/01/31/the-13-highest-grossing-film-franchises-at-the-box-office.html

32 www.parrotanalytics.com/announcements/franchise-ip-dominates-parrot-analytics-5th-annual-global-demand-awards/?utm_campaign=GTVDA&utm_medium=email&_hsmi=244065525&_hsenc=p2ANqtz-9pNrD0QP_kl2Nq0a2igAExq7yvFYTENWUGfcLg-OwVGz1_vEYNjfVZ8ldJnoiAlFZMJKO1YZRcD6CEEfYREzHOxofpRg&utm_content=244065478&utm_source=hs_email

33 'The Morning' newsletter, *The New York Times*, 10 September 2022.

34 Matthew Ball, cited in 'So you're looking for a chief metaverse officer', Meg Wilson Schaeffler and Ashling O'Connor, Spencerstuart.com, *Research and Insights*, July 2022.

35 Commenting on interest rate increases, 14 December 2022.

36 Greg Bensinger, 'Amazon posts surprise profit, while sales surge', *Wall Street Journal*, 22 October 2015.

37 https://wan-ifra.org/2020/11/harnessing-audience-data-using-data-maturity-to-drive-business-outcomes

38 www.exchange4media.com/digital-news/todaywe-stand-tall-at-40-million-usersbharat-guptajagran-new-media-90895.html

39 https://english.jagran.com/india/jagran-new-media-s-ceo-bharat-gupta-named-one-of-india-s-best-leaders-in-times-of-crisis-2021-by-gptw-india-10030662

40 https://english.jagran.com/india/jagran-new-media-s-ceo-bharat-gupta-named-one-of-india-s-best-leaders-in-times-of-crisis-2021-by-gptw-india-10030662, 13 August 2021

41 https://wan-ifra.org/2021/09/thriving-in-a-post-cookie-world-by-harnessing-data

42 www.adgully.com/jagran-new-media-has-been-recognized-as-india-s-best-place-to-work-in-media-105019.html

43 www.ebu.ch/about/public-service-media

44 Council of Europe: https://www.coe.int/en/web/freedom-expression/public-service-media

45 www.ebu.ch/news/2018/09/dr-forced-to-close-tv-and-radio-stations

46 www.ebu.ch/publications/research/membersonly/report/funding-of-public-service-media

47 BBC Director General Tim Davie, speech to Royal Television Society, 7 December 2022.

48 National Audit Office, 'A Digital BBC', 14 December 2022, p. 8.

THREE

STRATEGIC CONCEPTS FOR THE MEDIA

So far, this book has examined the strategic environment in which media organisations operate. This chapter builds on this to explore strategic approaches that can be used to understand and master that context. This means building a bridge between general theories of strategy and the specificities of the media industry and its organisations. This sounds straightforward. In practice, it is complex because of the characteristics in this body of theory.

- **Breadth.** The sheer volume of theory relating to strategy is enormous. As Starbuck (1965) pointed out over 50 years ago – since when the field only expanded – potentially everything ever written about organisations in some sense concerns strategy.
- **Fragmentation**. While the field of strategy theory started with a relatively coherent and widely accepted set of premises, tools and techniques, successive waves of research and critical reflection have generated a profusion of further concepts, approaches and schools. The field is now richer, more mature and subtler, but also fragmented.
- **Incommensurability**. The field of strategic theory is highly compartmentalised. The various concepts and research subfields are not simply diverse, but often mutually inconsistent.
- **Unclear boundaries**. If Starbuck is correct in asserting that virtually everything ever written about an organisation can theoretically be classified as concerning strategy, then where does the discipline of strategy stop and that of organisational theory start? If we accept the assertion made by some scholars that all strategy is about change, do theories of organisational change differ from strategic change and, if so, how?

One way to reduce the complexity in the field of strategy is by categorising the theories within it. Researchers have developed proposals for organising the strategic theory (see, for example, Whittington, 1993; Rajagopalan and Spreitzer, 1996; Mintzberg et al., 2003). This book uses a categorisation adapted from those of Johnson (1987) and Chaffee (1985): it places strategic models in three core schools which are situated on a continuum moving from rationalist approaches on one side to interpretative approaches on the other (see Figure 3.1). This both reduces complexity and accommodates divergent approaches.

Rationalist approaches

Just about all typologies of strategy literature start with some variant of this category. Rational or positivist approaches draw on industrial organisation (IO) economics and have a deterministic view of organisational behaviour. Concepts are based on analytical reasoning, and assume firms and individuals behave in the main rationally. They focus on the strategic behaviour of firms, the structures of markets and their interactions.

Morgan (1986) uses the metaphor of 'organisations as brains' to describe such approaches: organisations are rational systems that operate as efficiently as possible with standardised processes, mechanistic designs and clear goals. Chaffee (1985) uses the adjective 'linear', denoting the methodical, directed, sequential approach they entail. Rationalist approaches have also been termed

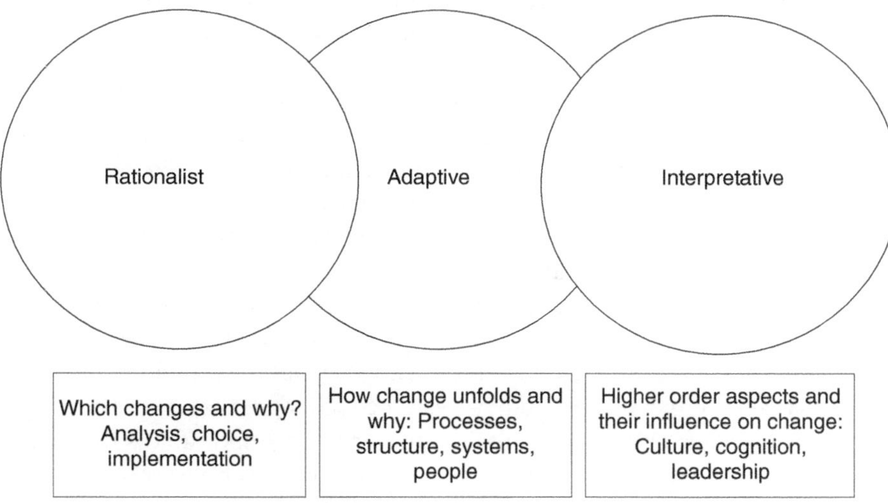

Figure 3.1 'Organising' strategic theory (adapted from Chaffee, 1985; Johnson, 1987)

the 'external environment school' because of their focus on the external factors that provide competitive and comparative advantages and limitations.

The strong influence of this school reflects the development of the discipline of management in general. In the 1960s, formal business education grew dramatically in the US, and business strategy emerged as a field of study, as did the strategic planning function in firms. The business environment in the US at that time was stable: US companies faced relatively little competition from abroad and the economy was growing strongly (Fulmer, 2000). During this period, the foundation stones of rational approaches to strategy were laid. They were to be extended and enhanced in future years and still provide the cornerstone of undergraduate and MBA management courses, as well as of the activities of management consultants (who have created some well-known models in the field, such as the Boston Consulting Group's growth/share matrix or Bain's Structure–Conduct–Performance (SCP) paradigm).

According to the rationalist school, strategy is essentially a plan, formed through the methodical, sequential analysis of the environment and the evaluation of the extent to which organisational resources can be utilised to take advantage of environmental opportunities or to address environmental threats (Minzberg et al., 1998). Some of the strongest and most enduring theoretical influences are Chandler's (1969) work in the distinction between strategy and structure, and Porter's (1980, 1985) work on competitive strategy and competitive advantage. According to Chandler (1969: 383), strategy is 'the determination of the basic long-term goals and objectives of an enterprise, and the adoption of courses of action and the allocation of resources necessary for carrying out these goals'. The underlying assumption is that competitive forces in the marketplace determine the success and long-term viability of the firm.

Thus, the external environment is the starting place for strategy, and the uncertainty and complexity present in the strategic environment can be reduced through comprehensive analysis. The models within the rational school focus on the content of strategy, and on how plans should be formulated in a way that provides a clear basis for strategic decisions and action. The school is extensive, and some of the best-known concepts include Porter's Five Forces Model (explained below), Porter's value chain (explained in Chapter 2) and the resource-based view (also discussed below).

A large proportion of research into strategy in the media applies rationalist approaches (see, for example, Croteau and Hoynes, 2001; Doyle, 2002b; Hesmondhalgh, 2002; Sanchez-Tabernero and Carvajal, 2002). In broad terms, these studies tend to explore whether a variance (change in state) has occurred in the media sector and which causal factors may be responsible – for example, whether the number of joint ventures and alliances by media firms has increased and if the search for specific strategically relevant resources can explain this. This research has provided fine-grained insights into shifts in the media landscape and into the drivers of firm behaviour. However, it has meant that the processes of management within the media organisation and the complex interplay of organisational phenomena at play have received less attention.

Further, rationalist models lose validity in rapidly changing industries where structural boundaries are breaking down. Well before convergence had really taken hold, Fulmer (2000) discussed the challenges of applying Porter's Five Forces Model to organisations such as Sony or Microsoft, since it was even then almost impossible to define which industries they compete in. The core problem Fulmer identifies is that some of the most significant competitors straddle many sectors and contain many different businesses, and are, as a result, too large and complex to analyse using the strategic models at hand. This problem is even more pertinent today when even sector specialists are challenged by the breadth and complexity of companies such as Alphabet or Amazon. As discussed in the previous chapter, these technology giants are a new competitive set for the media industry, hard to categorise and therefore analyse. If we take Google (leaving aside, for the purposes of simplicity, the businesses contained in its Alphabet division), it combines internet-related businesses including search (where it has a virtual monopoly position), advertising, cloud storage (where it is, at the time of writing, overshadowed by Amazon, which has a dominant market share of that market), mobile operating systems (Android – and here it is competing with Apple's iOS), and video (YouTube – a dominant business globally).

Many classic approaches to strategy involve exploring the logical consequences of various strategic options within a given set of circumstances and therefore do not adapt well to fast-changing environments (Morgan, 1986). Increasing dynamism and complexity of the media industry's environment, the fact that markets become increasingly 'fuzzy' – that is, key aspects of the market structure, such as the probability of substitution, the number of firms in a market and barriers to entry, are difficult to identify, describe and define (Lacy and Simon, 1993) – mean that it is difficult to make the assumptions necessary to apply these models, although it should be noted that key architects of the school have disputed this conclusion (see, for example, Porter, 1996).

This chapter explores two key models from the rational school and applies them to the media sector. A third model from this school, the value chain, is discussed in Chapter 2. Concepts from the adaptive and interpretative schools are explained and applied to the media industries in Chapters 5 and 6.

Porter's Five Forces Model

According to this model, five forces determine the competitive environment and provide a baseline for sizing up a company's strengths and weaknesses.

Where does the company stand versus buyers, suppliers, entrants, rivals and substitutes? Most importantly, an understanding of industry structure guides managers towards fruitful possibilities for strategic action (Porter, 1980: 12).

Porter's Five Forces Model (Porter, 1980) argues that a firm should design strategies that allow it to exercise bargaining power over suppliers and customers while preventing new entrants and rivals from entering its market. Along with the value chain (also from Porter), this is probably the single best-known model from the 'rational' school. The base assumption is that above-average performance requires determining an optimal strategic position through a close analysis of the competitive dynamics in the industry concerned. This model not only helps firms understand their competition better, but also gain a deeper understanding of factors that drive overall profitability in the sector, and insights into how to address constraints on profitability. Porter's Five Forces Model is useful at an early stage of strategic analysis to build a sense of an organisation's overall position and the prospects of the sector it occupies. Note, however, that it focuses on how the external environment affects competitiveness. It does not address the ability of an organisation to design and implement internal processes that will allow it to act on this analysis.

The state of competition depends on five competitive 'forces', and the collective strength of these determines the ultimate profit potential in and attractiveness of, the industry. These forces influence the costs, prices and the investment levels that are needed to compete. The forces are as follows.

Bargaining power of suppliers

Suppliers provide the raw materials or services necessary to create the product or service. Powerful suppliers can reduce industry profitability. The bargaining power resides in the pressure that suppliers can put on companies by raising their prices, lowering their quality or reducing the availability of their products. Any organisation is dependent on a range of external suppliers – of components, expert services or raw materials. As news organisations pivot to subscriptions, they are dependent on experts with skills in data analytics and propensity modelling. A global shortage in semiconductor chips in 2021 led to a major disruption in the gaming industry.

Bargaining power of buyers

Buyers are customers of the organisation. Their bargaining power is the pressure they can exert to force down prices or drive up costs (by demanding better quality). Consumers can force a business to improve product quality, service quality or lower prices. If a company's product is undifferentiated, this increases buyer power, as customers do not suffer if they switch products. *The New York Times* signed up a slew of leading journalists with deep expertise in specific areas (and often large social media followings also) during 2020 and 2021 to ensure that the journalism in their publication was highly differentiated from competitors: readers ceasing to subscribe to the publication would lose access to these journalists' output.

Threat of new entrants

This means the risk posed by new direct competitors entering your sector. It is determined by how easy a market is to enter (see list of questions below) and how attractive a market is in terms of how profitable it may be. The likelihood of new players entering a market depends on two things: how easy this is and how attractive the market is. Several factors can affect the threat level – how much capital must be invested to set up a business, the existence of scale economies (meaning the market only makes sense if you can operate at scale), how easy it is for customers to switch between competing products, and whether there are national restrictions on market entry. New entrants are a constant threat in digital media. Podcasts have created a gateway into the radio sector allowing publishers to move into audio. Podcast listeners skew younger than radio listeners, so this is a long-term threat to radio's viability.

Companies minimise the risk of new entrants by digging 'moats' around their business to make it harder for new competitors to enter a field. When Amazon launched Prime Membership (which originally offered unlimited delivery in two days to members, and which later expanded to include Amazon Prime Video and other services), this permanently raised the bar for convenience on online shopping and set Amazon far ahead of its competitors. When discussing this concept, Jeff Bezos explained: 'I want to draw a moat around our best customers.'[1] Many of the intrinsic characteristics of platform business create moats to new players. These include network effects, large quantities of customer intelligence in the form of data, a business model that triggers repeat engagement by customers with a product eco-system (Amazon Prime can be viewed as a moat). The cumulative size of Facebook, WhatsApp and Instagram's networks, combined with the granular real-time user data they have on the networks' users are powerful barriers that deter new players from entering the social networking space.

Barriers limiting the risk of competition can be intangible too, notably brand and culture. A strong brand encapsulates a unique value proposition that customers are prepared to pay a premium for and will keep them coming back for repeat purchases (think of Disney). An organisation's culture can also be a moat, particularly in terms of attracting and keeping talent. Top calibre creatives will be attracted to a content creator with a reputation for quality and prizewinning output. The BBC in the UK and HBO in the US have always been seen as some of the most attractive places to work, even though compensation levels are not exceptional by industry standards.

Threat of substitutes

Substitutes are alternatives that can replace a product or service, rendering that product less economically viable, or in worst cases, putting it out of business. A substitute product performs a similar function but uses different means, and can render the existing one less attractive, or in the worst case, redundant. Companies scan the competitive environment looking for substitutes that threaten their business and seek ways to mitigate this threat. News publishers' intensive lobbying to restrict the power of the platforms derives from the fact that these players offer free substitutes to their (paid) news products. A wide range of substitutes in a market will create downward pressure on prices for all players. The last two decades are studded with examples of new substitutes weakening established media products. Online streaming was a substitute for rental DVDs, cable television and public service media products. Streamed music is a substitute for music downloads. Podcasts are a substitute for radio.

'Lock-in' is a route to reducing the threat of substitution. Lock-in can be created by adding new features that create value for customers (a streamer continually adding new shows to keep subscribers, an app adding new functionalities), or making it hard for customers to leave a service (for example, requiring customers to call personally to cancel a subscription).

Extent of competitive rivalry

This means the extent of competition between players. Several factors determine how strong competition is likely to be in a sector. Many equal-sized players fighting for the same customer group, high sunk investments meaning that companies are reluctant to retreat from the market, and low growth are all factors that can lead to intense rivalry.

Strong rivalry will constrain profitability for all players, and competitive rivalry in the media sector is traditionally intense. For many products, the market is growing slowly, players are entrenched with high fixed costs and products are relatively undifferentiated. In situations like these, where rivalry is high, companies seek to increase profit by winning market share from competitors. News publishing and streamed video are both sectors with strong competitive rivalry, where new players are competing with established media companies, which see this sector as critical for their strategic future.

Using the Five Forces Model

These five forces influence the dynamics of its sector and the performance of the firms in it. The better they are understood, the greater the scope to increase profits and reduce vulnerability, for example by:

- Positioning the company where the forces are weakest – for example, by focusing on customers who are less price sensitive or more emotionally attached to products.
- Exploiting changes in the forces – for example, when Apple launched its iTunes music store, it exploited the vacuum created by the lack of a common platform for purchasing online music.
- Reshaping the forces in your favour – for example, weakening supplier power by standardising formats (allowing a firm to switch easily between vendors) or reducing buyer power conversely by differentiating your product more so that customers are less inclined to switch providers.

These questions can help assess the power of each force.

Force	Questions to establish how strong that force is
Bargaining power of suppliers	How many suppliers are there? Are there substitutes for their products and services? How important are the costs of suppliers' products to the organisation's total costs? Can suppliers forward integrate and compete with you?
Bargaining power of buyers	Are they concentrated? How many are there? How differentiated is your product? Can a customer backward integrate into your business?
Threat of new entrants	Is your product highly differentiated? Are there economies of scale? Do new players need to come in at a large scale to operate efficiently? How much do you have to invest to enter this market? How easy is it for a new entrant to access distribution channels? Are there government policies to protect markets and limit new entrants?
Threat of substitutes	How easy is it for customers to switch to a competing service? How easy is it to add new functions and features that will lock in customers? How significantly would increased competitive pressure affect your prices?
Strength of competitive rivalry	Are there several equally sized competitors? Is the market growing or stagnating? How high are fixed costs? How strong is brand loyalty? How high are exit costs?

Resource-based view (RBV)

The 'resource-based view' (RBV) looks at how an organisation's combination of resources confers competitive advantage: firms can achieve sustained superior returns only when they possess resources that other firms do not have (Peteraf, 1993; Miller and Shamsie, 1996). While the resource-based view can be tracked back to the late 1950s (Penrose, 1959), it developed into a substantial stream of research during the 1980s, when several theorists explored how the resources and capabilities a firm possesses create performance advantages in a particular strategic environment (Wernerfelt, 1984; Prahalad and Hamel, 1990; Barney, 1991; Hitt et al., 2001). Strategically relevant resources meet the 'VRIN' criteria:

- **Valuable**: it is rent-generating and makes a substantial difference to a firm's cost base or provides a source of differentiation.
- **Rare**: it is exceptional rather than standard. A standard resource is a 'threshold resource' – not strategic but necessary to compete in an industry.
- **Inimitable**: it is difficult for others to acquire or copy.
- **Non-substitutable**: there is no freely available substitutes for this resource.

A number of alternative categorisation systems have been proposed for classifying strategically relevant resources that fit the VRIN criteria (see Chan-Olmsted, 2006 for discussion). Miller and Shamsie (1996) divide resources into two categories: **property-based resources** and **knowledge-based resources**, either of which can stand alone (discrete) or as part of a network of resources (systemic). Property-based resources are inimitable because they are protected by property rights. Discrete property-based resources include legally protected 'scarce and valuable inputs, facilities, locations, or patents' (Miller and Shamsie, 1996: 524). The rights to broadcast key international sporting events such as the Olympic Games or the FIFA World Cup Soccer Championship qualify as examples. Systemic property-based resources include unique constellations of facilities, processes and systems that are too complex for competitors to imitate – for example, Sky Digital's marketing infrastructure, which encompasses a call centre, retail sales team and customer sales team.

Knowledge-based resources – tacit, implicit know-how and skills – cannot be imitated because they are protected by knowledge barriers. A creative team's network of freelance suppliers and a relationship built up over decades of collaboration and reinforced by market success is an example of a discrete knowledge-based resource. Systemic knowledge-based resources, on the other hand, involve knowledge-based resources that are integrated throughout an organisation and would therefore also qualify as core competencies – for example, Disney's ability to leverage the value of one content source across the company's many divisions.

The RBV research stream has been applied frequently to the media sector. Chan-Olmsted (2006) proposes that because competitive advantage in the media industry derives so heavily from unique properties (exclusive content) and expert knowledge (the intangible 'know-how' concerning audience appetites and creative processes), the property/knowledge-based typology is valuable for classifying and analysing media firms' resources, and, by extension, understanding performance differences.

Resources can be created in four ways (Bowman and Collier, 2006):

- **Acquisition.** A favoured route for legacy players to acquire digital resources and new digital products. Axel Springer has acquired over 190 companies since 2001, including *Business Insider*, Politico and Morning Brew, and between 2016 and 2023 Future Plc spent around £1.5 billion on over 18 companies and brands.
- **Resource picking.** To do this, a firm must have a view of the future that is not shared by other firms, which in turn relies on skills in analysing the external environment and firm information (Makadok, 2001). BSkyB's recognition in the 1980s of how 'killer content' could drive uptake of pay-television offers, which led to early moves in acquiring exclusive rights to key sporting fixtures, is an example of resource picking.
- **Internal development.** This is a path-dependent process by which, over the course of its unique history, a firm builds rare and valuable resources and can exploit these in unique ways. Disney's library of animated films and characters, which provide a basis for content re-exploitation in many formats, is an example of path-dependent resource creation.

While the RBV has become an enduring and valuable addition to strategic theory, definitions can prove imprecise when operationalised in in-company research. Barney (1991: 101), for example, defines resources very broadly indeed as 'all assets, capabilities, organisational processes, firm attributes, information, knowledge, etc. controlled by a firm that enable the firm to conceive of and implement strategies that improve its efficiency and effectiveness', a categorisation that could stretch to include just about any aspect of an organisation. The RBV can also be difficult to test empirically because idiosyncratic resources are hard to measure (Hitt, 1997). It has also been suggested that the approach is inappropriate for dynamic and volatile environments (D'Aveni, 1994; Eisenhardt and Martin, 2000) and fails to accommodate the influence of firm evolution over time (Wang and Ahmed, 2007). Finally, some criticise the lack of prescriptive guidelines arising from the theory (Bowman and Collier, 2006).

As convergence marches on, technology has moved to the heart of strategically significant resources. For example, both Meta and TikTok are social platforms with strategically relevant resources around building social networks, building communities on those platforms, and allowing individuals to create and share content on those platforms. Yet Facebook's platform has algorithms built on a social graph, while TikTok is an entertainment platform with an algorithm that seeks to bring out social trends and create unique user experiences.[2]

Netflix's data analytics capabilities

> Taste clusters … are groupings of titles based on what subscribers like … "Netflix assigns each subscriber three to five of these clusters, weighted by the degree to which each matches their taste".[3]

A strategically critical resource in data analytics capacity lies at the heart of Netflix's business model. Netflix's approach combines the human and the computational: teams of people analyse and tag Netflix content with metadata to create a database of over 70,000 data points – product attributes ranging from the obvious (plot, actors, genres, period, and so on) to the subjective (the moral status of characters or degree of plot resolution). These detailed tags are combined with machine-generated customer intelligence derived from analysis of viewing habits to develop personalised micro-genres, which resonate closely with members' viewing preferences (Fritz, 2012). This allows Netflix to improve member loyalty and acquisition, since the better Netflix knows what its members want and can provide such content, the more likely it is to retain those subscribers. This finely grained information on members' preferences also serves as a bridge to content creation, by highlighting the genres, plot twists, actors, contexts, directors, etc. that members find most compelling or appealing. This type of data-driven commissioning was a significant departure from the development and piloting process that had long been standard for the television industry. Being able to create successful original content is strategically important for Netflix. Exclusive content strengthens the brand, drives up viewing hours and allows it to differentiate itself in an increasingly competitive market. Netflix's data mastery thus fits the VRIN criteria. It is valuable (it underpins the creation of content that differentiates Netflix from competitors and attracts new subscribers, keeps those subscribers loyal, and generates additional revenues from the sales of that content in other markets and formats), rare (none of its competitors has comparable analytic database), non-substitutable (there are no freely available substitutes for this on sale on the market) and inimitable – as of 2014, Netflix invested $150 million a year in developing its recommendation engine (Filloux, 2014).

Inimitability (meaning a resource cannot be replicated) can arise because a strategically relevant resource is acquired in a path-dependent way. Disney's capability in acquisitions is an example here. Disney acquired Pixar, Marvel and Lucasfilm. These acquisitions brought valuable media properties (the Marvel superhero universe, the *Star Wars* franchise and Pixar's animated movies), to which Disney applied its expertise in merchandising and licensing to increase revenues from them. These acquisitions also brought Disney a range of cutting-edge technological capabilities (special effects from Industrial Light & Magic that was acquired as part of Lucasfilm and digital animation from Pixar) that allowed it to maintain the 'Disney magic' through an era of digital disruption and growing competition. Staying with audio-visual media, HBO's ability to 'create a creative environment ... where talented people did their best work'[4] also fits the VRIN criteria. This is valuable (it allows HBO to create hits), is rare, has no substitutes and is hard for competitors to imitate.

Core competencies

> After years during which magazine publishers everywhere had come to believe that systems were (almost) a waste of time and money and best left to others, the new CEO [of Future Plc] developed what has become a world-beating strategy with a tech stack that includes: Vanilla (a single modular web platform and content management system); Hawk (eCommerce); Hybrid (advertising system including an open auction marketplace to manage yields); Aperture (customer audience data platform); Falcon (lead gen); and Kiosq (monetising paywalled editorial content) ... The tech has been crucial to its success, not least in integrating acquisitions quickly and cost-effectively.[5]

When two companies in the same environment with similar strategies achieve very different performance outcomes, that differentiation can stem from the organisations' respective **core competence** and **dynamic capability** profile. These are more complex phenomena that are enmeshed in the wider organisational system, and harder to identify, analyse and build.

The core competence is a somewhat more pragmatic 'sister' to the RBV and has achieved greater resonance with practising managers. A core competence is also imprecisely defined, but is generally understood as a distinctive organisational attribute that creates sustainable competitive advantage and provides a platform for future growth – a 'gateway to tomorrow's opportunities' (Prahalad and Hamel, 1994). A competency is understood as a 'bundle' of skills and technologies that is integrated and company-wide, is unique to the organisation concerned, cannot be easily reproduced by competitors, delivers real and meaningful customer benefit, is extendable, is sustainable and is appropriable (that is, the added value created by the competence is retained by the organisation; if this value accrues to the individual who possesses the competence, then the competence concerned is not 'core') (Prahalad and Hamel, 1990; Quinn, 1992; Leonard-Barton, 1992; Kay, 1993).

The distinction between a strategic resource and a core competence is not easy to draw – competencies, capabilities and strategic resources all fall into resource-based theory. Competencies, however, have three differentiating characteristics: they create potential access to a broad variety of markets; they make a significant contribution to perceived customer benefits; and they are difficult for competitors to imitate. More generally, a capability or competence is a more complex phenomenon that is embedded in the wider organisational system. It involves organisational routines that have been built or acquired over time and enmeshed in the culture and structure (Teece et al., 1997) and has a high knowledge component. Further, the roots of distinctive capabilities often extend back to the organisation's founding circumstances, emerging in the first place as a means by which an organisation can fulfil its primary mission. They are thus intrinsic to a company's identity, deeply rooted in its culture, and contribute not only to competitiveness but also to the psychosocial 'glue' that creates identity, differentiation and cohesion (Schein, 1992), and they form part of an organisation's personality (Drucker, 1994).

Competencies, capabilities and resource-based analysis are powerful strategic analysis lenses. While many classic tools from the rational school are difficult to apply in the current environment, they accommodate dynamic changes in the strategic landscape, can help identify emerging strategic priorities, and allow differences in performance between competitors to be identified and explained. For example, across the media sector, these competencies are increasingly becoming fundamental to the ability to compete:

- **Data collection and analysis**, giving insights into how users interact with platforms, and content allows providers to drive engagement, market share and monetisation.
- **Personalisation** combined with data analytics tools, which allows content providers to learn what motivates audiences. This allows targeted recommendations, curated content and personalised ad strategies.

Dynamic capabilities

Core competencies and the resource-based view are static concepts – they involve analysing sources of competitive advantage at a specific point in time. However, when the external environment is changing continually, firms need to be able to adapt strategy to master that context, to maintain competitiveness and deliver superior market performance. The ability to do this confers strategic advantage. Thus, some capabilities or resources need to be dynamic – companies need to be able to build, integrate and reconfigure them as needed (Teece et al., 1997; Brown and Eisenhardt, 1997; Oliver, 2018).

Dynamic capabilities have been defined as the capacity of an organisation to purposefully create, extend and modify its resource base (Helfat et al., 2007). The concept of organisation renewal is central to the concept (Oliver, 2014). They build a bridge between the organisation and its context (Lawton and Rajwani, 2011). The research explores the capabilities and processes by which organisations adapt in response to the external environment and the factors that contribute to superior outcomes from this transformation (Di Stefano et al., 2010).

In his study of dynamic capabilities and their impact on performance in the UK media industry, Oliver (2014) summarises the four tangible resource-based approaches that underlie the development of dynamic capabilities:

- investment in new organisational processes and routines;
- product innovation and development;
- forming strategic alliances;
- acquisitions and mergers.

Dynamic capabilities are understood to have an intangible, cognitive dimension (Zollo and Winter, 2002; Tripsas and Gavetti, 2000) and involve 'managed learning' (Oliver, 2018: 2). They are higher-order capabilities rooted in learned and patterned organisational activities focused on ensuring ongoing change; they enable strategic renewal, organisational learning and change to support the firm's attempts to address a changing business environment and meet strategic targets (Maijanen, in Baumann, 2022). Dynamic capabilities therefore have both content and process characteristics (Eisenhardt and Martin, 2000). They require a balance between structural elements (robust financial control systems) and dynamic ones (ensuring managers have the scope to explore and innovate).

Three processes underlie the creation of dynamic capabilities (Teece, 2007; Lynch 2021):

- **Sensing.** Scanning the environment for potentially important changes, both threats and opportunities. They need to track technology and knowledge developments in the wider environment and learn from suppliers, customers and competitors.
- **Seizing.** Responding to the changes and opportunities identified by mobilising resources as necessary. This includes making acquisitions and investments,

changing business models, entering new sectors and building processes to assess, experiment with and develop opportunities in an ongoing way.

- **Transforming.** This means continually reconfiguring and renewing resources to respond to changes, meet strategic goals and position the organisation for the future. This involves reviewing regularly the asset and resource base, knowledge and innovation activities, and continually reconsider where value is added, and whether and how the business model needs to change, and the implications of this for resources and capabilities.

From rationalist to adaptive approaches

Innovation in tech is rarely, if ever, short-term (Mann, 2015).

Rationalist approaches have obvious limitations in an environment as dynamic and volatile as that of the media industry, where change happens fast and sector boundaries are eroding. In this context, strategy work in many media companies has become reactive and fragmented, defined on the one hand by firefighting in response to specific challenges and on the other by a large number of individual strategic projects responding to specific developments that only, if at all, coalesce into a coherent strategy in retrospect (Kueng, 2015).[5]

The global players that media companies contend with do engage in long-term, big-picture strategic planning. In 2021, Mark Zuckerberg, founder and CEO of Facebook, rebranded the company to 'Meta' to underline a long-term transition from a social media company to a metaverse company, a shift that he recognised could take at least a decade.[6] Apple's strategy today still reflects Steve Jobs's long-term strategic goal of shaping the global post-PC world. The iPod and iPad were elements in this plan and both were poorly understood when launched because they did not conform to prevailing market/product categories. Both products later established themselves as new categories. Similarly, the iPhone was both a new product in the mobile phone market and a disrupter to the PC market.

A core distinction in strategy literature is between strategy content and strategy process (Chakravarthy and Doz, 1992; Pettigrew, 1992). Rationalist approaches focus on the content of strategy, crudely put, on the contents of the strategic plan. They seek to find a strategic position that will lead to optimal performance under varying environmental conditions (Chakravarthy and Doz, 1992). They argue that the growth and survival of organisations are influenced by the structure and dynamics of an industry and the quality of response to environmental factors, particularly the economics of business cycles. Strategy involves maximising returns from resources and establishing equilibrium within this context.

An alternative perspective is that equilibrium is rare. Change is endemic to organisational environments and, echoing Schumpeter's concept of 'creative destruction' (1934), is an ultimately positive force. Researchers sharing this viewpoint began to study the interplay between the structure and dynamics of an industry and the structures, strategies and processes inside organisations. They recognised that the interrelationship between these elements needed to be explored, and that an important aspect of strategic activity involved reconciling and integrating these external and internal elements. They also recognised that environmental change, particularly technological change, can erode the strategic value of an attractive product-market position or of distinctive resources or capabilities.

Such considerations lie at the heart of the 'adaptive' school. This views strategy as 'a process not a state' (Pettigrew, 1992) and is concerned with 'how effective strategies are shaped ... validated and implemented effectively' (Chakravarthy and Doz, 1992: 5) to ensure that organisations master complex and uncertain environments. An important emphasis is on adaptation and self-renewal: 'strategies must change in keeping with both new opportunities and threats in its environment and changes in ... strategies and strategic intent' (Rajagopalan and Spreizer, 1996). Thus, strategy is not primarily about planning. Rather, it is about trying to see the world as it really is and preparing the organisation so that it has a chance of a successful future (Fulmer, 2000), and the reality of strategy lies in strategic actions, rather than strategic statements (Burgelman, 2002).

So, change (or adaptation) is intrinsic to strategy, and, by extension, strategy is intimately involved with the organisation. A shift in the content of strategy must mean shifts in the organisation – in structure, people and processes. Indeed, for Mintzberg and colleagues the field of strategy is subsumed within the broader one of strategic change, thus 'to manage strategy is to manage change – to recognise when a shift of a strategic nature is possible, desirable, and necessary, and then to act – possibly putting in place mechanisms for continuous change' (Mintzberg et al., 2003: 166).

If rationalist approaches see strategy as a plan, then adaptive ones see strategy as an evolutionary process where change takes place progressively as firms undertake a series of strategic readjustments in response to a changing environment. While the devising of the content of a strategy can be structured and formal, the actual process of strategy is gradual and messy, triggered by learning taking place in various parts of the organisation. Strategy can sometimes be visible only in hindsight as a 'pattern in a stream of decisions', as Mintzberg (1987) famously described it.

Critically, strategy is not decided, then carried out, but emerges in the process of being implemented. Monitoring the environment, analysing developments and making changes are continuous and contiguous activities. The boundary between the organisation and its environment is highly permeable, and the environment is a major focus of attention in determining organisational action.

If the frameworks in the rational school seek to support organisations in their search for a strategic position that will guarantee sustainable advantage, the concepts in this school seek to enable dynamic strategic positioning – for example, in the design and redesign of the structures and processes by which an organisation can respond to changes in the environment.

Concepts particularly relevant to the media sector from this school are those concerning responses to technological advance. For example, those that allow organisations to distinguish between different types of technological change and understand their respective implications for different types of organisation, or models that provide insight into which technology will dominate after a technology transition, and explain why an 'inferior' technology may become an industry standard, or concepts that help incumbent organisations resist inertia and establish new ventures based on new technological platforms (these are discussed in Chapter 4).

A further distinction in this field is between incremental change and transformational change. The pace and velocity of environmental change are not constant. Organisations need to be capable of both incremental and transformational change (Tushman and Anderson, 1986). Transformational change itself has more than one incarnation and can involve a quick dramatic revolution or renewal – a more gradual process. Transformational strategic change, such as is currently required in many sectors of the media in response to the internet and digitalisation, is recognised as one of the most challenging for leaders and uncomfortable for those inside organisations, since it involves moving from the known to the unknown and requires existing success formulas to be abandoned and new competencies and attitudes to be developed (Mintzberg et al., 2003). These aspects of adaptive approaches to strategy are discussed in Chapter 6.

Interpretative approaches

Rationalist approaches to strategy have been criticised for failing to accommodate the diversity and disorder of organisational life – Mintzberg once famously claimed that 90 per cent of rational strategies are never implemented successfully – and also for failing to address the habits of mind that so often prevent strong players from making a bridge between one type of environment and another.

The interpretative school of strategy focuses on exactly those elements that often prevent strategic plans being implemented – namely, the deeper 'hidden' aspects of the organisation, such as mindset, belief systems, values, motivation and emotions. These elements are often underplayed or even ignored in strategic planning, partly because they are highly subjective and somewhat ethereal, and partly because they concern subjective and unconscious phenomena that are difficult to access and interpret. Researchers in the field, however, argue that interpretative elements can both help and hinder strategic change, and that successful strategic initiatives have found a way to take these powerful but hard-to-manage forces into consideration.

The interpretative approach seeks to understand organisations from the perspective of those working in them with a focus on how meaning is constructed out of events and phenomena, the influence this meaning has on the behaviour of the firm and the outcomes of that behaviour. A basic assumption is that organisational members actively create or enact the reality they inhabit (Weick, 1979); thus, reality is understood as 'socially constructed'.

The adaptive and interpretative schools are closely linked. If all strategic activity is ultimately about change, the adaptive school looks at the changes that need to be made in routines, systems and technology. But congruent changes also need to be made in the organisation's overt and covert cultural and social systems; its interpretative phenomena. These issues form the focal point of the interpretative school.

Several levers can be pulled to achieve strategic change. While rational approaches tend to focus on tools such as analysis, education and communication, the interpretative school looks at how sociocultural, symbolic, cognitive and political processes can be employed to speed processes of transformation and signal the types of changes required from organisation members. Thus, interpretative approaches focus not only on how an organisation might need to be reshaped (a focus of the adaptive school), but also on the meaning created by the events staged to publicise the change, by the choice of individuals to head up the new structure, by the individuals marginalised through these actions, and how these flag up the changes that are required on an individual level (Johnson and Scholes, 1989).

Of all the schools outlined here, the interpretative school is the least cohesive – indeed, some would question that it even constitutes a school. However, the concepts in this approach have a common starting point – the 'higher order', or deeper psychological and often unconscious, aspects of organisations such as underlying beliefs, mindset, mental models and motivation.

Interpretative approaches also consider how the emotions expressed by the change leader allow those in the organisation to frame and 'make sense' of the changes (Gioia and Chittipeddi, 1991). Academic understanding of the role of emotions in strategic change is still in its infancy, but the emotional capability of an organisation has been identified as important in processes of radical change in that it affects its ability to acknowledge, recognise, monitor, discriminate and attend to emotions at both individual and collective levels (Huy, 1999).

Symbolic, cognitive and cultural elements are particularly important in media organisations, partly because the individuals who choose to work in the sector are often motivated to do so because of their own 'higher order' needs, and partly because of the tremendous influence that the media industries exert over our lives and societies. And there is ample evidence of the strategic relevance of concepts from this school to the media industries. Culture is an important factor in established firms' ability to respond to new technology.

Many observers have attributed the demise of the print newspaper to cultural rigidity. Meyer (2004), for instance, found that the high levels of cash traditionally generated by the newspaper industry generated a complacent culture that slowed its ability to respond to the threat of new technology, and noted that the new content forms that seize the potential of new technologies are being created by non-journalists who have worked outside the journalism culture. And in the entertainment sector, past decades have shown how mental models influenced the sector's ability to respond to not just the internet, but to a raft of earlier advances, including compact cassettes, VCRs, CDs, and so on.

Conclusions

A central tenet of this book is that strategy is contextual: different strategic conditions mandate different strategic approaches. Media organisations often start their strategy journeys with the plan-based approaches of the rational school, and these often continue to serve as the basis for subsequent strategy work by companies. This chapter has explored a number of such classic models and applied them to the media sector.

However, as discussed in Chapter 2, the strategic environment of the media industry is changing fast. In unpredictable contexts companies also need to be able to adapt dynamically to an evolving environment. Here approaches from the adaptive and interpretative schools come into play, and the next chapters of this book draw heavily on models from the adaptive and interpretative schools. In addition, the concept from the adaptive school are to be found in Chapter 4 (on technology), Chapter 5 (on creativity and innovation), and Chapter 7 (on leadership). Interpretative models feature in Chapter 6 (on culture and strategy), Chapter 5 (on creativity and innovation) and Chapter 7 (on leadership).

Resources

Books and articles

Hamel, G. and Prahalad, C.K. (1994) *Competing for the Future*. Harvard Business School Press.

Kay, J. (1993) *Foundations of Corporate Success*. Oxford University Press.

Porter, M.E. (2008) 'The five competitive forces that shape strategy', *Harvard Business Review*, January.

Rogers, D.L. (2023) *The Digital Transformation Playbook*. Columbia University Press.

Podcasts and newsletters

Ben Thompson's newsletter, *Stratechery*, analyses strategic shifts in the technology and media industry (https://stratechery.com/).

Company information

Publicly listed companies report their earnings and financial performance quarterly. Some (Netflix and Disney) also publish webcasts of these events, which are accessible via the corporate website.

Case: Netflix: Five Forces analysis

> First-mover advantages matter a lot, scale matters a lot ... product and technology investments matter a lot. Reed [Hastings] saw the future for global content services and scale that span every market, every genre, and every person, truly years before any competitor did.[7]

Netflix was founded in 1997 as an online DVD mail-order rental service. In 2007, it moved into SVOD (streamed video on demand), splitting into two businesses (DVD rental and streaming) in 2011, the same year that Reed Hastings was named CEO of the Year by *Fortune* magazine. Netflix entered the SVOD market with a simple value proposition: for a flat fee, subscribers would receive on-demand, unlimited and advertising-free content, and cancellation would be no hassle.

The service enjoyed tremendous first-mover advantages. As a new organisation in a new sector, it had all the advantages of starting with a 'clean sheet of

(*Continued*)

paper' – it could design its organisation, product, technology stack and business model from scratch, and with it, build an organisation shaped for a digital economy. As a one-of-a-kind service that was not yet viewed as a competitor by other players, it was able to strike deals to license hit series and films it knew would strike a chord with audiences. As interest rates were historically low, it could take on a high level of debt to finance the significant investments needed to establish a global streaming service and grow fast.

And for many years the financial markets were positive about Netflix, classifying it as part of the thriving tech sector (rather than the media). For many years its stock traded a tech multiple (around 30 times earnings) rather than a lower-rated media multiple.[8] However, during 2022, as competition increased, interest levels rose along with worries about recession, investor sentiment turned against the streaming sector and Netflix started to hit headwinds in the financial markets:

> Netflix produced nearly 60% of its most in-demand premieres in 2022, and … saw its market cap fall more than $120 billion as Wall Street changed the fundamentals for measuring streaming success.[9]

As a digital 'pureplay' it did not have to wrestle with the challenges that its legacy players faced as they tried to build a streaming business while still running their legacy ones (Disney and Warner had both faced strong headwinds when they put new movies on streaming services, bypassing movie theatres, and HBO found it hard to put new content on its new streaming platform ahead of cable, disadvantaging the cable companies who had been key elements in their distribution chain for a decade).

Netflix capitalised on its advantages and built a global digital video streaming platform that competed head-on with legacy broadcasters around the world. Netflix's content offering is huge – an aggregated bundle including all genres and all styles that its excellent technology stack ensured could be enjoyed by a growing number of households in over 190 countries. It invested its borrowings in developing original content, and in 2019 Netflix launched more original programming than the entire US cable TV industry had a decade earlier (spending $16–17 billion a year).[10] Its advanced analytics engine meant that it could curate personalised offerings to viewers and direct huge numbers of viewers to high-profile new content in real time.

However, the competition in its sector is also increasing. Analysis using Porter's Five Forces Model, as discussed in the case below and shown in Figure 3.2, allows Netflix's competitive position *vis-à-vis* its competitors in the streaming media space to be explored.

(*Continued*)

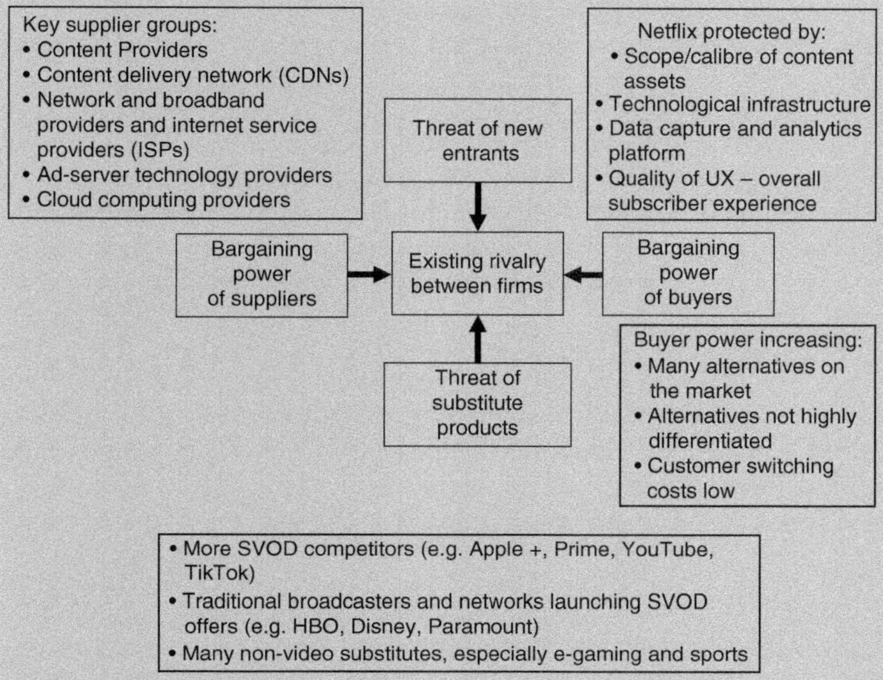

Figure 3.2 Netflix: Five Forces analysis
© Lucy Küng

Bargaining power of suppliers

> People have more choice of films and TV shows than ever so we need to ensure that there's always something great for them to watch on Netflix, regardless of their taste, mood, or who they're watching.[11]

Content providers. Netflix's competitiveness depends in part on the range and calibre of content it provides. This can create both strategic differentiation and lock-in, where subscribers become fans of particular content, which reduces their propensity to cancel their subscription. Content providers are therefore a key supplier group. Netflix started life by acquiring TV and movie content externally. It needed to gain a subscriber base and generate revenues fast (creating its own content would have been risky and expensive). Netflix still licenses content from multiple suppliers in all the markets it operates in. It bids for exclusive rights to SVOD rights against cable and broadcast networks and online suppliers, typically buying multi-year exclusive SVOD licences.

(Continued)

But as the service grew, Netflix's access to dependence on third-party content providers became a strategic risk (it was vulnerable to them increasing prices or withdrawing content, as happened when WarnerMedia withdrew *Friends* and Disney stopped licensing its movies). To reduce this set of suppliers' bargaining power (as well as to strengthen the brand and drive-up viewing hours), Netflix expanded into content production in 2012 (starting with *House of Cards*) and investments have grown progressively. This move also allowed Netflix to ensure that its content matches the taste preferences it was identifying. Exclusive content also created lock-in for subscribers (Lotz, 2022). (In a similar move, Amazon bought MGM in 2021 for $8.45 billion, which provided movies and TV shows for its Prime Video, as well as properties such as *Pink Panther* and *Rocky*, which it could potentially develop into franchises). In 2015, Netflix was the primary content acquirer in Hollywood and had a library of around 11,000 licensed titles. In 2023, it offered only 6,000 licensed titles.[12]

CDNs. Content Delivery Networks are responsible for 'primary distribution' and are the backbone of all streaming services. A CDN is a massive network running in parallel with the internet, which ensures that popular content is cached in servers in cities on every continent. By using a network of CDNs, Netflix can ensure the scale, quality and availability of its streaming. Netflix, like Apple and Amazon, has built its own CDN delivery infrastructures. The majority of streaming providers utilise a combination of CDNs to ensure that their content is delivered in the best possible way to viewers.

Network and broadband providers and ISPs. These suppliers deliver 'secondary distribution' of Netflix's services, the so-called 'last mile'. This final delivery to 'service households' involves a range of distribution technologies: optical fibre, television cable, mobile telephone network, and so on. Netflix relies on a range of network and broadband providers and ISPs in all the markets it operates in to distribute content to its audiences (and conversely, these suppliers rely on Netflix and other streamers to increase the demand for connectivity). Netflix therefore has a cooperative relationship with this category of suppliers. It has created a CDN 'Open Connect Program' by which Netflix installs its own servers at no cost in ISPs' data centres, which are directly connected to the Netflix network. Netflix (like other streaming services) does not charge ISPs, and the majority of ISPs do not charge Netflix and other streamers.[13] But the power balance is unstable. Some ISPs have tried to charge Netflix interconnection fees for 'prioritised access' to their networks, but the company is vulnerable to changes in government regulations, perhaps introducing taxes or fees on Netflix's service or limiting access.

(*Continued*)

Ad-server technology providers. Microsoft's advertising-delivery technology 'serves ads' for the Netflix advertising-funded product. (Disney has built its own proprietary technology for digital advertising to reduce its dependence on a third-party provider and allows it to gather first-party data on its audiences.)

Cloud computing services. Netflix uses Amazon's Web Services (AWS) for nearly all its computing and storage needs, including databases, analytics, recommendation engines and video transcoding.

Bargaining power of buyers

> The streamers that have been around the longest—Netflix, Amazon Prime Video, Hulu—also have strong brands, good evidence that it takes time to grow customer affinity. But with the exception of Netflix and Disney+, it's hard even for subscribers to a service to recall where to find this stuff.[14]

Buyer power increases if there are many alternatives for buyers to choose between; those alternatives are similar, there is transparency about the cost of competing offers and the switching costs for customers are low. When Netflix launched its streaming service, the bargaining power of its buyers was low – there were few alternatives. Now there are many similar offers in the market, switching costs are low (it is easy to cancel a subscription) and the bargaining power of buyers has increased. This limits Netflix's options to raise prices. In response, Netflix has turned to other routes to increase revenues, including a new advertising-funded, lower-priced service, and introducing fees for password sharing.

Threat of new entrants

Legacy players rapidly realised that a shift from linear to streaming was inevitable and launched competitors. However, the Netflix model was not as replicable as it might have looked on the surface. It had a number of barriers to entry that reduced the threat of new entrants to all but the best capitalised:

- **Technological infrastructure.** A global streaming service needs to work with a high degree of reliability on a range of devices across a range of geographic territories.
- **Data capture and analytics platform.** This is a core competence for Netflix and something that potential competitors need to build. Netflix has invested heavily in this and is well positioned to compete in this dimension (see p. 70).

(*Continued*)

- **UX – the overall customer experience.** From how the service is accessed to how easy it is to subscribe and pay for it. This is also a core competence for Netflix, and new competitors have struggled to match the ease, simplicity and reliability of the Netflix product.

Threat of substitutes

> Audiences have more options available to them than ever … Disney, Comcast, WBD, Amazon, Netflix, Paramount Global, Fox, Apple, Lionsgate and AMC Networks are estimated to spend $140 billion across entertainment and sports content in 2022. But the plethora of enticing titles are no longer enough to properly monetize large audiences in a way that consistently builds profit.[15]

Competition in the streaming sector is intense. Netflix competes against a growing number of alternative providers, as well as traditional broadcast competitors. The quality and range of the content it offers has traditionally been a basis of its differentiation strategy, but the increase in players in the sectors, all similarly seeking to differentiate through content, has restricted the amount of library content that Netflix has access to. Movie franchises are increasingly important. Netflix has few franchises that lock in subscribers, unlike Disney, which has acquired a series of global franchises during the past decade (see p. 32).

The threat of non-video substitutes is also high, especially gaming and eSports. Netflix faces competition from substitutes that look very different from the classic product. Reed Hastings, Netflix CEO, once famously named sleep as the most important competing 'product' to Netflix. Companies scan the competitive environment looking for substitutes that threaten their business and seek ways to mitigate this threat.

Competitive rivalry

> Competition for viewing with linear TV as well as YouTube, Amazon, and Hulu has been robust for the last 15 years. However, over the last three years, as traditional entertainment companies realized streaming is the future, many new streaming services have also launched.[16]

(*Continued*)

> We continue to operate in a highly competitive market as consumers have a vast number of entertainment choices. Beyond our direct streaming competitors, we also vie for consumers' time against linear TV, YouTube, short form entertainment like TikTok, and gaming, to name just a few. The silver lining is that the market for entertainment is huge and Netflix is still very small by comparison.[17]

Netflix is now an incumbent player. It faces very different challenges today than when it was building its business. Its domestic audience is nearly at saturation point, so it needs to look for growth abroad. It no longer has the streaming field to itself. Disney, Amazon, Warner Bros. Discovery and more have entered the field. As the industry consolidates, this increases competition for talent, studio space and production resources. In addition, Netflix faces competition too from gaming, esports and social media.[18] Social media platforms like TikTok or YouTube are free alternatives. The increase in competition raises both buyer and supplier power, and the scale of competition mandates continued high spending on content and on marketing. New competitors Apple and Amazon use streaming as loss leaders to boost other parts of the business. They can and are investing billions to their streamed services to grow audiences, without worrying about immediate returns.

Strategic response

Despite the stock markets souring on streaming services, Netflix is in a strong position. Unlike competitors, it is profitable and generates significant free cash flow. Its debt level is low and its debt was acquired at fixed rates. Its churn rates are among the lowest in the sector, but they are rising. The best response is a strong slate of original programming that keeps customers engaged, and there is strong demand for its original productions, but these are expensive. Netflix must continue to grow the number of subscribers globally, but also recognise that growth is flattening and that the US is approaching saturation. In this context, the cost of acquiring new subscribers rises, so maximising revenue per user also becomes important.

In response to this deterioration in its competitive environment, Netflix has made several strategic moves to ensure that growth continues:

- Launching a cheaper service with advertising. This aims to attract new subscribers in lower-income countries and retain subscribers at risk of churning.

(*Continued*)

- Reducing the subscription price in markets where Netflix is seeking to accelerate growth, including the Middle East, parts of Africa, Latin America and parts of Asia Pacific.
- Expanding into gaming, setting up a new content category that will be included in the subscription with no extra cost.
- Increasing non-US original content. Netflix has commissioned new content from 44 countries since 2020. This includes drama, movies and anime, including *Lupin* (France), *Parasite* (South Korea, which won Best Picture at Oscars 2020), and *Squid Games* (also South Korea). This strategy helps open new markets, attracts new subscribers and differentiates its content from its rivals.[19] In 2023, Netflix's local content investment will represent 47 per cent of revenues.
- Cracking down on password sharing. In spring 2023, Netflix estimated that around 100 million users were not paying subscriptions (30 million in the US and 70 million internationally[20]). This was initially seen as the means for new customers to discover the service, but slow growth coupled with price reductions in some markets mean this approach has changed.

Case questions

1 Select a competitor of Netflix'. Indentify their buyers, suppliers and competitors, the most strategically critical substitutes for their products and any potential entrants to their field.

2 Compare your analysis of this organisation to the analysis of Netflix above. Which has the strongest positon competitively? Why?

3 Based on this analysis, what strategic advice would you offer to the management of the company you have analysed? What could they do to improve their strategic positioning?

4 Netflix has traditionally made all episodes of its series available at once to allow binge viewing and has never licensed its content to other streaming services. As it explores news ways to generate revenues, would you recommend either or both of these moves?

(*Continued*)

Case: Dynamic capabilities at Sky Plc

John Oliver

In the 1990s, Sky Plc (Sky) was a UK-based pay-TV provider. Twenty years later, it had grown into a leading European, multi-product, multi-platform entertainment and communications firm. While many legacy media firms complained about the high-velocity environmental conditions and the profound impact of digitalisation and new media technologies on their business models and revenues, Sky sensed an opportunity for market leadership and appeared to thrive on high levels of turbulence.

An ambitious corporate strategy

From the outset, Sky focused on one primary corporate objective: 'profitable growth'. Initially, Sky focused on the UK pay-TV market by growing subscriber numbers and revenues through a strategic recipe of negotiating the rights to premium content (sports, film and TV) developing new conditional access technologies and delivering high-quality customer service.

Sky adopted corporate strategies that were opportunistic, flexible and adaptable. This approach, coupled with deregulation in many media markets, meant that it was able to develop into a challenger brand in a much broader category of services, including fixed line and mobile telephony, and online gaming in the UK. With the harmonisation of digital platforms and regulation across Europe, it became possible for single providers to offer consumers a far broader 'value proposition', an integrated package of entertainment and telecommunications services. Sky followed this approach and extended its corporate perimeter geographically with the acquisitions of Sky Italia and Sky Deutschland (2014). These in turn repositioned the company from a 'UK-based pay-TV provider' into a 'European, multi-product, multi-platform entertainment and communications firm'.

Sky's dynamic capabilities

Dynamic capabilities theory argues that dynamic competitive environments drive firms to renew and reconfigure resources, capabilities and competencies to deliver a sustainable competitive advantage and superior performance. Developing dynamic capabilities entails managing both intangible (knowledge-based) and tangible (resource-based) resources. The more dynamic the market conditions, the faster firms need to take strategic action to adapt and transform

(*Continued*)

their business to the demands of the competitive environment (Oliver, 2018; Oliver and Picard, 2020).

Sky's **intangible** resources, skills and capabilities included:

- **Aspirational and flexible corporate strategies** that allowed it to extend its corporate perimeter in terms of new media markets and geographic scope.
- **Persistent communication** of ambitious strategies by a succession of Chairmen and Chief Executives to stakeholders in a way that mobilised and empowered it to proactively respond and embrace changes in an uncertain competitive environment.
- **Managerial cognition and sensing skills** to identify the opportunities provided by new digital media technologies and anticipate the potential disruption of mature media markets.

Tangible resources, skills and capabilities included investment in and reconfiguration of:

- **New organisational processes and routines** to produce new operational capabilities in digital distribution and programming, customer relationship management and interactive broadcasting services.
- **Product innovation and development** where they created numerous industry-leading products and services including: Sky+ the UK's first fully integrated personal television recorder and the Sky Guide, an advanced electronic programme guide (2001); Sky Multi-room subscription (2004); Sky Gnome, a portable device to listen to audio content (2005); Sky HDTV, Sky Broadband and Sky Talk, Sky + access from customer mobile phones (2006); Sky Anytime, an on-demand service (2007); 3D television (2010) and Sky Go (2011); the streaming service, NOW TV (2014); and Sky Q (2016), which merges live TV with catch-up, on-demand and video streaming.
- **Forming strategic alliances, corporate acquisitions and mergers** that provided a more expedient route to expand into new markets and access to new resources and capabilities than organic growth. Sky consistently made strategic investments and acquisitions to access new online and interactive broadcast and communication capabilities, including: British Interactive Broadcasting Holdings Limited for digital interactive broadcast (1997); KirchPayTV (2000) for pay-TV services; Sports Internet Group for internet content infrastructure and on-line gaming (2000); WAP TV Limited for interactive TV applications (2001); Artsworld Channels Limited for

(*Continued*)

arts and music channels (2005); My Kind of Place Ltd for website development and e-commerce functionality (2006); Easynet for broadband delivery (2007); 365 Media Group for sports and gaming capabilities (2007); Amstrad for high definition PVR and set-top boxes (2008); Virgin Media Television for their channel portfolio (2010); Shine TV for content production (2011); The Cloud for Wi-Fi network capabilities across the UK (2011); O2 for consumer broadband and fixed-line telephony (2013); Parthenon Media Group for international distribution and multi-media rights management (2013); Sky Italia and Sky Deutschland (2014).

Divestment as a dynamic capability

While the dynamic capabilities literature tends to focus on the role of investment in reconfiguring and renewing resources and capabilities, divestment (the disposal of strategic resources) is also a dynamic capability. Between 1997 and 2017, Sky disposed of equity holdings in assets that did not fit its strategic focus (Granada Sky Broadcasting, BSKYB Ltd and BSKYB GmbH, 2005) or were draining corporate resources (closure of analogue TV, 2001; KirchPayTV, 2002; OpenTV, 2003). They also made tactical divestments in non-core products and services that included TV channels, entertainment and gaming services, and communication platforms due to poor performance in the marketplace.

A consolidated view of Sky's acquisition and divestment activity is presented in the table below. Most of its acquisitions and divestments are media related and led to an overall consolidation of its market-leading position. However, the most significant expansion of Sky's corporate perimeter occurred with the acquisitions of telecoms firms from 2006 onwards.

	Media	Entertainment	Telecoms
Acquisition	10	3	3
Divestment	15	8	2

Conclusion

Sky's consistent strategic goal has been profitable growth. Despite high-velocity market conditions, it has delivered superior financial performance over a sustained period. Its management of intangible and tangible resources has been 'dynamic' and this has transformed the firm during a time of significant change in the competitive environment, resulting in a step change in business capabilities and providing it with a degree of flexibility during a time of unprecedented change in the media industry. It has also allowed it to extend its perimeter of

(*Continued*)

activities to take advantage of the opportunities provided by the digital environment and the harmonisation of technology and regulation across Europe. Notably, its focus on strategic acquisitions to generate new capabilities and divestments has also repositioned the firm from a UK, single-product TV firm into a European, multi-product, multi-platform entertainment and communications firm. This product and geographic expansion of its corporate perimeter has also yielded impressive results, with corporate revenues growing from £777 million in 1995 to £12,920 million by 2017.

Case questions

1. How do you interpret Sky's corporate objective of 'profitable growth'? Is it vague, flexible or opportunistic?
2. Did Sky's acquisition of a broad range of media businesses help it overcome uncertainty in the media environment?
3. In high-velocity markets, core competencies need to be refreshed, adapted or disinvested, otherwise they will become core rigidities and barriers to strategic change. Do you agree?
4. Identify a core competitor of Sky. Analyse its resources according to the VRIN criteria. Identify its critical core competencies (understood as 'bundles' of skills, technologies and practices that are unique, competitively important and hard for competitors to copy).
5. Has Sky developed any dynamic competencies? Does the company have distinct capabilities and processes in place that allow it to respond to its environment faster or better than its competitors? How well is this company positioned? What advice would you offer its leadership team to improve its resources, core competencies and dynamic capabilities?

Sources

Oliver, J.J. (2012) Winning in high velocity markets: the case of BSkyB. *Strategic Direction*, 28(10): 3–5.

Oliver, J.J. (2014) Dynamic capabilities and superior firm performance in the UK media industry. *Journal of Media Business Studies*, 11(2): 55–77.

Oliver, J.J. (2017) Exploring industry level capabilities in the UK creative industries. *Creative Industries Journal*, 10(1): 75–88.

Oliver, J.J. (2018) Strategic transformations in the media. *Journal of Media Business Studies*, 15(4): 278–99.

Oliver, J.J. and Picard, R.G. (2020) Shaping the corporate perimeter in a changing media industry. *International Journal on Media Management*, 22(2): 67–82.

(*Continued*)

Case: *The New York Times*'s strategic transformation

> *The Times* today is a place of ambition. We're no longer trying to climb our way out of an economic crisis.[21]

> Over time, the number of [print] subscribers will decline, advertisers will decline, and ultimately the economics of that platform will fail ... The old ship is going to sink in the end.[22]

Founded in 1851, *The New York Times* (NYT) is one of the best-known news organisations in the world. Its successful digital transformation has made it a role model, but this success is relatively recent. In 2008, the company was in crisis. The financial crisis led to a steep fall in advertising revenues. The share price fell from the mid-$30s to under $8, and the company was in debt and carried high pension liabilities. CEO Janet Robinson pulled the organisation out of a dire financial situation. She launched a painful turnaround strategy, which included a loan at punitive interest levels from Mexican telecoms millionaire Carlos Slim, the sale and lease-back of its offices in New York and 'shrank to grow', involving a sell-off of non-core assets such as *The Boston Redsox* and *The Boston Globe* (which was acquired in 1993 for $1.3 billion and sold in 2013 for $70 million).

Those days are long gone. In the intervening years, the NYT's strategic adaptation and renewal process is one of the most impressive responses to digital transformation in the media. The business model has been reinvented. It has expanded its product portfolio across platforms, stretching from podcasts to events. It has created new formats for journalism and made several high-profile acquisitions. This success is rooted in an early commitment to digital, and an iterative, adaptive approach based on the sequential acquisition of the resources, competencies and capabilities necessary to thrive in digital markets, and an acceptance that the print product is one of the many NYT platforms – loved but with a limited lifespan.

From a 'leaky paywall' to a full-on subscriptions business

The New York Times introduced its paywall in the spring of 2011, 15 years after the paper first went online. They were not the first to charge online readers – *The Wall Street Journal* and *Financial Times* had already had paywalls – but they were one of the first consumer newspapers to do so (the

(*Continued*)

Financial Times and *The Wall Street Journal* are both business as well as consumer purchases, which makes a percentage of their customers less price-sensitive). This was a 'leaky paywall' – readers could access 20 articles a month for free. The strategy was to hold on to the traffic from 'occasional readers' and through exposure to the *Financial Times*'s journalism, convert some into subscribers. Expectations were not ambitious. They hoped there might be a couple of hundred potential subscribers and the company remained focused on stopping the decline in print business.[23]

Gradually, however, their centre of gravity shifted towards digital subscribers. It became clear that direct payment by readers for digital products would become the core revenue stream.

> We figured out ... we should be a subscription service first. The biggest thing we had to sell was our content and the quality of what *The Times* journalism can do. We should ... think of ourselves ... like a quality subscription service ... an HBO or Netflix.[24]

By the end of 2020, earnings from digital subscribers outweighed those from print for the first time.[25] By 2021, it was earning three times as much revenue from readers as from advertisers, and by the end of 2020 had over seven million paid subscribers, print and digital, and, for the first time, earnings from digital subscribers outweighed those from print[26] (Scholes, 2021).

'Making sure we're providing journalism worth paying for'[27]

With the pivot to digital subscriptions, readers become the core customer (with the print model, a newspaper had two sets of customers, advertisers and readers). Journalism is at the centre of the relationship between *The Times* and its subscribers. The reader revenue model's success rests on the core product's appeal to readers. This meant doubling down on news: invest in journalism and ensure consistently high standards. *The Times* would differentiate through the calibre of its coverage and build this strength while competitors were shrinking their newsrooms.

'You need scale'

> What we're going for, perhaps more than any other newspaper in the world, is real scale ... Getting the sheer number of people to pool together to pay for the journalism to make a great company means you need to scale. You need an international business.[28]

(*Continued*)

> *The Times*, perhaps alone, has doubled down on the basic business of news delivery, perfecting the productization and monetization of it in better ways than others.[29]

With digital subscribers as the key revenue stream of the future, *The Times* needed to scale the digital readers – digital subscriptions are far cheaper than print ones and churn rates are higher, so the company needed to scale the number of digital readers fast. This meant optimising the subscription engine – pouring expertise, resources and focus into the parts of the business designing, running and building the digital subscriptions business. Subscription business models have an intrinsic trade-off between volume and long-term revenue – the more subscribers you have, the higher the likelihood that these customers will churn. This makes decisions on pricing delicate. As *The Times*'s core competence in subscriptions grew, the focus evolved from increasing the overall number of subscribers to boosting retention rates and lifetime customer value (the total value of services sold to a subscriber).

Each stage of 'subscriber lifecycle' was analysed, with over a hundred consumer marketing and retention experts exploring when customers are most likely to subscribe, what offer would work best, and how to intervene when customers look like cancelling. There was permanent experimentation too, with various aspects of their offer – from pricing introductory offers to designing upsell products like games and cooking – that could function as add-ons to the basic digital package and create subscription bundles (Scholes, 2021). In the words of media analyst Ken Doctor:

> *The Times* needed to build engagement habits, to make products 'addictive' and in that way reduce churn and bring them back consistently. Audience and engagement metrics were built around what subscribers read, how often they returned and how healthy their relationship with the company and these were transmitted to the newsroom.

Underlying all these changes was an emphasis on changing the culture and work processes in the heart of the organisation. The *Innovation Report*, which the newsroom produced in 2015, was an inflection point – this highlighted the challenges *The Times* faced with digital transformation and the need to shift towards product thinking, to transforming the organisation to a digital product and technology company with journalism at its heart. Internally, the report 'was a clay breaker'[30] in that it publicly articulated the deeper challenges of digital transition. From there, *The Times* established a set of priorities for how it approached its strategic challenges. These include increasing

(*Continued*)

agility – increasing the speed from idea to implementation, limiting internal bureaucracy, establishing cross-functional teams, and creating a culture where people aren't scared to voice ideas. Part of this is a commitment to 'successful autopsy', of deliberately learning from things that don't pan out as desired. This started at the top. In the words of then CEO Mark Thomson:

> I've been more lucky with success than some of predecessors because I've made more mistakes.[31]

Successive innovations have benefited from predecessor projects that didn't work. NYT Cooking was built on the shoulders of learning from the NYT Now app. NYT Espanol showed the organisation that there was no monetisable market for pan-regional content, but it learned that readers do appreciate some articles being translated.

It is important to note, however, that advertising remains an important revenue stream, but strategy here has shifted, too. *The Times*'s focus is bigger but less – large-scale, interactive brand marketing campaigns with high production values. This allows advertisers to benefit from the suite of products the NYT has and allows the organisation to sidestep the Facebook/Google ad duopoly. (In December 2022, in a first for the paper, General Electric, as exclusive advertiser, took over all *The Times*'s print advertising inventory. In digital, there were desktop, mobile and audio 'takeovers' (including 'The Daily' podcast) and sponsorship of the AM and PM newsletters).

Move into audio – 'The Daily'

In 2017, *The Times* launched 'The Daily', a weekday news podcast based on *The Times* reporting of the day. In Q3 2022, it was the third most listened to podcast in the US.[32] Audio was an experiment, an entry point for *The Times* journalism, an on-ramp for younger subscribers, a means of deepening engagement and a means to generate advertising. This strategy worked: listeners engaged – some listening for over 20 minutes a day and over three-quarters of its audience were under 40. Podcasts were cash-positive from day one. Each podcast had two advertising slots and brought in tens of millions of dollars' advertising revenue.

From there, audio became a strategic focus. Additional podcasts were launched and the audio business was expanded via acquisitions. In 2020, it acquired Serial Productions (*This American Life* spin-off) and set up strategic and creative alliance with *This American Life.* In the same year, 2020, it bought Audm (produces high-quality performed reads from longform journalism such as magazine articles).

(*Continued*)

A 'lifestyle media company with a heavy emphasis on news'[33]

> We see even bigger market opportunities for Games and Cooking, and we expect to invest more in content, product development and marketing in these products than we have in previous years.[34]

Scale remains a 'north star' goal, and one route to scale is via the quantity of quality content: volume in content is needed to capture market share, and that content needs to be differentiated. This kicks off a virtuous circle: the more unique content, the more subscriptions, the more subscriptions it sells, the more it can invest in content.

But content doesn't just have to be news. Under first COO and now CEO Meredith Kopit Levien, President and CEO (the youngest CEO in the paper's history), *The New York Times* has broadened and diversified the business portfolio. The paper is one element of a growing multiproduct media company. Since 2017, *The New York Times* has built out a content ecosystem, with growth increasingly coming from a range of softer, 'news adjacent' products – notably, NYT Games and NYT Cooking (in Q4 2021, 54 per cent of new subscribers were non-news subscribers). These are so-called 'verticals' – mini-businesses, stand-alone subscription products that additionally provide a means to build the subscription funnel and create new opportunities for brand partnership and advertising inventory. NYT Cooking offers recipes, but is expanding in different directions to connect directly with its community[35] – for example, with at-home cooking kits curated by guest chefs, and staff will tour to offer workshops and tasting experiences.

Growth through acquisition

The Times' fortunes have been transformed since the low point in 2008. Now solidly profitable, it is investing in acquisitions, but rather than invest in property or trophy assets, it has bought properties that support the core business or allow it to grow into adjacent fields. Acquisitions have played a big part in the *New York Times*'s recent subscriber growth and the creation of its bundle of subscription products. In 2022, it made two major purchases. First was *The Athletic*, a sports media platform, reputedly with 1.2 million subscribers – the addition of these paying readers meant that *The Times* reached its goal of 10 million digital subscribers well in advance of the 2025 target date. Second was the acquisition of the word game *Wordle* which also added subscribers, with visits to the *Wordle* page in its first 24 hours under *Times* ownership equivalent to the entire monthly audience for *The Times* website.[36]

(*Continued*)

Towards the future

A decade and a half after the great recession, *The New York Times* is a world-class journalism company, but now it aspires to be a world-class digital and product company too. Step by step, through internal transformation and acquisition, it seeks to be a lifestyle brand with technology at its core – engineering is now the second largest function behind journalism and the largest on the business side.

Case questions

1. Analyse *The New York Times*'s resources, core competencies and dynamic capability profile. How did these shift over time? How were new ones created or acquired?
2. *The Times* has ambitious plans to become a global digital and lifestyle product company. How might its resource, competence and capability profile need to change to achieve this?

Notes

1. Jason Del Ray, 'The making of Amazon Prime, the internet's most successful and devastating membership programme', *Recode*, 3 May 2019. Available at: www.vox.com/recode/2019/5/3/18511544/amazon-prime-oral-history-jeff-bezos-one-day-shipping
2. Alex Sherman, cnbc.com, 16 June 2022, 'TikTok exec: We're not a social network like Facebook, we're an entertainment platform'.
3. Brian Barrett, cited in Lotz, 2022: 124–5.
4. John Lopez, 'What's the key to HBO's Emmy Success?', *Vanity Fair*, 23 August 2010.
5. Colin Morrison, 'How Zillah transformed Future', *Flashes and Flames*, 10 February 2023.
6. www.theverge.com/22588022/mark-zuckerberg-facebook-ceo-metaverse-interview
7. Matthew Ball interviewed by Ben Thomson, www.stratechery.com, 30 June 2022.
8. Alex Sherman speaking with Peter Kafka, *Recode Media* podcast, 23 June 2022.
9. Julia Alexander, *Parrot Perspective*, 5 January 2023. Available at: www.parrotanalytics.com/parrot-perspective/biggest-lessons-trends-streaming-theatrical-2022-predictions-2023-julia-alexander

10 Wendy Lee. *Los Angeles Times*, 20 September 2021. Available at: www.latimes.com/entertainment-arts/business/story/2021-09-20/netflix-global-expansion-international-tv-bella-bajaria-lupin

11 Netflix Q4, 2022. Shareholder letter.

12 www.parrotanalytics.com/parrot-perspective/netflix-amazon-hbo-max-svod-licence-original-content/?utm_campaign=Parrot%20Perspective&utm_medium=email&_hsmi=244230096&_hsenc=p2ANqtz-9r9k3-TziJxH6n-bO5pbrHnGIjJff1gWqG7KWcdtn7ujqfFGv7AULOEvOtphW_pb-rrkfpENE1GU8TCzpSKPpuWfMJXuw&utm_content=244229757&utm_source=hs_email

13 'A cooperative approach to content delivery': a Netflix briefing paper, 2021.

14 Matthew Belloni. 'Puck's official streaming service hierarchy', 19 January 2023. Available at: https://puck.news/pucks-official-streaming-service-hierarchy

15 Brandon Katz, *Parrot Perspective*, 5 January 2023. Available at: www.parrotanalytics.com/parrot-perspective/biggest-lessons-trends-streaming-theatrical-2022-predictions-2023-brandon-katz

16 Netflix Q1, 2022. Shareholder Letter.

17 Netflix Q4, 2022. Shareholder letter.

18 Edmund Lee, 'Disney is chipping away at Netflix's dominance', *New York Times*, 20 July 2021.

19 https://advanced-television.com/2022/08/15/analysis-international-commissions-key-for-netflix-growth

20 Julia Alexander. WIH+: 'Succession' questions, Netflix price cuts & Zaz's growth, *Puck*, 'What I'm hearing, 1 March 2023.

21 CEO Meredith Kopit Levien, cited in puck.news/succession-nyt-and-cnn-edition, 25 February 2022.

22 CEO Mark Thompson, cited in *The New York Times*, 'CEO shares his guide to thriving in the next decade'. Imna.org.blogs, 19 January 2020.

23 '*New York Times* CEO shares his guide to thriving in the next decade'. Imna.org.blogs. 19 January 2020.

24 Then CEO Mark Thompson, cited in *The New York Times*. 'CEO shares his guide to thriving in the next decade'. Imna.org.blogs, 19 January 2020.

25 www.nytimes.com/2020/11/05/business/media/new-york-times-q3-2020-earnings-nyt.html

26 www.nytimes.com/2020/11/05/business/media/new-york-times-q3-2020-earnings-nyt.html

27 Cited in 'How the *New York Times* maximizes customer lifetime value'. Laura Scholes, subscribed.com, 31 March 2021 (www.subscribed.com).

28 CEO Mark Thompson, cited in The New York Times, 'Times CEO shares his guide to thriving in the next decade'. Imna.org.blogs. 19 January 2020.

29 www.niemanlab.org/2020/07/newsonomics-the-new-york-times-new-ceo-meredith-levien-on-building-a-world-class-digital-media-business-and-a-tech-company

30 Interview with Stephen Dunbar Johnson, 19 January 2021.
31 Then CEO Mark Thompson, cited in *The New York Times*, 'Times CEO shares his guide to thriving in the next decade'. Imna.org.blogs. 19 January 2020.
32 www.edisonresearch.com/top-50-most-listened-to-podcasts-in-the-u-s-q2-2022
33 Dylan Byers, 'Succession watch: NYT and CNN edition'. *Puck News.* 25 February 2022.
34 NYT statement on non-core products in 2020 results.
35 hollywoodreporter.com/business/business-news/new-york-times-cooking-kits-1235220211
36 Dylan Byers, 'Succession watch: NYT and CNN edition'. *Puck News*. 25 February 2022.

FOUR

STRATEGIC RESPONSES TO TECHNOLOGICAL CHANGE

> A critical pattern in the dynamics of technological innovation … is the disturbing regularity with which industrial leaders follow their core technologies into obsolescence and obscurity. (Utterback, 1994: 162)

The media industry is symbiotically linked to technology. Each of the core dimensions that constitute the sector – content, distribution systems and platforms, and the devices that display content (Wildman, 2006; Noam, 2018) – came into existence because of technological invention and continues to be subject to technologically induced change.

Technology is a permanently moving carpet under the media industry's feet. Technological change is a growth driver, spurring firms to enter new markets or create new business areas. Walt Disney and his animators exploited new technologies to make animated films more striking (Bennis and Biederman, 1997; Catmull, 2014). The Disney Studio synchronised sound with movement in 1928, applied a new three-colour Technicolor process in 1932 and produced the first feature-length animated film, *Snow White and the Seven Dwarfs* (1938). Many decades later, Netflix combined a host of technological advances, including cloud computing, data analytics, internet service providers, mobile service providers, apps and mobile devices, to help create a new media sector, streaming media.

Advances in technology trigger the need to renew old and create new products and services (Tushman and Nelson, 1990; Nelson, 1995) and the need to adapt to technological change is a long-standing strategic requirement (D'Aveni, 1994; Bettis and Hitt, 1995; Christensen and Overdorf, 2000). That process of adaptation is invariably messy, unpredictable and interactive, with causal relationships flowing in both directions: technical change affects organisations, institutions and society, while organisations, their markets and society influence the path of technological advance (Tushman and Nelson, 1990).

This chapter explores the intricate relationship between technology, technological change, organisational strategy and the media industry. It examines the industry's synergistic relationship with technology and reviews theoretical understanding of the relationship between firm strategy and technology. It explores different types of technological change, examines the differing requirements these place on firms, and considers the factors that help or hinder effective responses.

Fear of the new: a constant drumbeat

> Technological advancements will eventually make older business models obsolete. You can either ... try ... to protect the status quo, or you can work hard to understand and embrace it with more enthusiasm and creativity than your competitors. (Disney CEO Robert Iger, 2019: 230)

The past last 100 years show a persistent pattern: technology gives and technology takes away, but it seldom takes everything away. Technological advances create new products and sectors of the industry, fuel increases in usage and spending on media products, but also erode existing markets, segments and business models.

This process of innovation and change was, until the late twentieth century, relatively measured. In recent decades, the pace of evolution has picked up markedly and the scope of impact on the sector has been far wider. The media has been buffeted by ever more frequent waves of innovation in the technologies that make up the fabric of their consumers' lives – think of the successive impact of the PC, the internet, the smartphone and social media. A permanent need for firms to adapt and innovate has been the result, and this has generated deep uncertainty about what these developments may mean for the sustainability of their businesses.

'Fear of the new' has historically characterised incumbents' response to technological advances, even though it was clear that these shifts ultimately led to growth and renewal. Hollywood was hostile to television. Both the television industry and Hollywood feared the VCR. However, these advances led to new markets and increased revenues: the consecutive introduction of video, cable/satellite, video on demand, DVD and home cinema technology led to growth for the film industry.

In even earlier times, microphones, radio and sound recording led to the emergence of radio broadcasting and recorded music, but reduced audiences for music concerts. The emergence of television created a new sector in the media, but contributed to the demise of Hollywood's studio system, spelt the end of the traditional printed comic as a major leisure product for children, and caused newspapers' share of total advertising revenues in the UK to fall from 90 per cent in the 1940s to 20 per cent by the 1960s.

Back in 1913, Riepl (1913), chief editor of Nuremberg's biggest newspaper, identified a dynamic by which established media never die; rather, they adjust to a new technological environment, often being used in different ways and with different formats. This observation became known as 'Riepl's Law', which holds that technological innovations tend to supplement, rather than replace, previous technologies. The previous medium is not destroyed, but progressively undermined, usually slipping down the food chain with lower revenues and smaller market share. Nearly a hundred years later, Mathias Döpfner, then head of Axel Springer Publishing, now CEO of the German publishing giant, held that this law still applies:

> I believe in 'Riepl's Law' ... new media do not replace existing media. Media progress is culmulative, not substitutive. New media are constantly added, but the old ones remain. This law has yet to be disproved.[1]

Convergence kickstarts 21st-century tech transitions

> Traditional media were separated by delivery technology ... Similar specializations separated the provision of content from the conduit. In the 1980s and accelerating into the 1990s, however, a technical convergence of media began gradually to blur the clear lines between segments ... The major technological trend behind this is well-known: the increased use of digital electronics to generate, store, transmit and display information.... This fundamentally affects media, the borders between them, and the market structures in which they operate. (Noam, 2018: 108)

Convergence is a meta term for the major shift in the tectonic plates underlying the media, and it has been underway since the advent of the internet and the World Wide Web. It was clear from the start that these developments, combined with advances in adjacent fields, including connectivity, storage technologies, communications hardware and software, and consumer devices would lead to fundamental changes in media production and consumption, and in the structure of the industry. Observers predicted a new industrial era – 'The Era of Networked Intelligence' (Tapscott, 1996), 'The Network Economy' (Kelly, 1997) and 'The Age of Digital Convergence' (Yoffie, 1997). While many interpreted the dotcom bubble burst of 2000 as a welcome indication that the media industries could return to business as usual, this was far from the case. The tech industry has continued to innovate, and has grown in size and strategic significance for the media secctor (as discussed in Chapter 2). The advent of the social-mobile era has brought new categories of media content and new consumer behaviour. The blending of the information technology, media and communications sectors is continuing and accelerating, and inside this broader phenomenon are nested 'sub-layers' of convergence between sectors of the 'old' mass media industry, and between content formats. And, as Riepl predicted, new formats and products are competing with 'old' ones. The result is unheralded levels of competition and decline for those unable to adapt adequately:

> Thirty years ago, each new book ... in English was competing with 500,000 ... That was the total number of books 'in print' in English in the world. Today that number [including print-on-demand titles] ... has grown to more than nineteen million. Up until twenty years ago, bookstores sold the lion's share of the books.... Now bookstores account for as little as 20 per cent of the sales. Most sales are made through online promotion and availability that give ... publishers no particular edge.[2]

Around three decades ago, the media industry anticipated convergence as a technologically driven fusing of the content (i.e., media), computing (i.e., information technology, particularly software) and communications (i.e., telecoms and broadcast distribution) industries into a mammoth new 'media and communication sector' (Bradley and Nolan, 1998), commonly expressed in the so-called '3-C Model of Convergence'. Nicholas Negroponte of the MIT media lab originated this view, predicting that communications technologies would undergo a joint metamorphosis whereby the broadcast and motion picture industry, the computer industry, and the print and publishing industry would come together to create a new sector and new forms of communications (Fidler, 1997). These shifts are indeed underway, although the emerging result is far more blurred and complex than Negropontt's original prediction. As we saw in Chapter 1, the boundaries between sectors are now porous and in places hard to define, technology companies are now very significant players in the field – a process that started with books (Amazon), and now covers all fields, with filmed entertainment (Amazon, Apple, Netflix), gaming (Amazon,

Netflix, Roblox) and music (Spotify, Apple, Google). Tech-driven content creators like TikTok, Snapchat and YouTube are new breeds of media organisations providing media content (among other services) for global mass audiences.

Noam (2018) identifies six subsets in the convergence process of the media sector: computers, communications, consumer electronics, content, connectivity cloud and cognition. He notes, for example, that the computer sector as we know now it grew from the convergence of technologies including calculating devices, electronic components and control codes, and continued to converge with consumer electronics, leading to the development of multipurpose devices, which when combined with communications capabilities, gave rise to video game hardware and software, and handheld computing devices such as smartphones. Media firms need to adjust their strategies to reflect these new competitive realities and retain brand presence and market relevance in the teeth of these organisations' scale and growth ambitions. This involves not only understanding disruptive products and their appeal for consumers but also mastering elements of the technological competencies that underpin them.

Hollywood and gaming converge

> Every generation plays games more than the one that preceded it.[3] (Matthew Ball)

Digital worlds can be watched passively (movies) or experienced interactively (as games), and a gradual blurring of boundaries between sectors of video games and Hollywood (Brookey, 2010) is one of the clearest current examples of convergence. Major studios have long licensed products related to their most successful films, and video game spin-offs have been central to these licensing arrangements, and there has long been a cross-over between the sectors: high-profile actors have always featured in video game production (Samuel L. Jackson in Grand Theft Auto, for example). Yet with the gaming industry predicted to overtake the film industry in revenues by 2024, convergence between the filmed entertainment and gaming sectors is gathering pace.

For both sectors, this is a way of generating more value from intellectual property (IP). Franchises with proven success in one sector can be expanded into another at reduced risk and lower marketing costs, and in this way, new consumer groups can be targeted and markets expanded. The studios and networks are mining gaming for hits that can transfer to the screen and game creators are extending their product range into movies. High-budget live action films and television series are being created based on video games – both Sega (*Sonic the Hedgehog* movie) and Nintendo (*Super Mario* and *Pokémon* movies) have created animated movies. These are global box office successes (*The Super Mario Bros. Movie* earned $1 billion just 26 days after its release), but also market extensions, serving as an introduction to gaming for film consumers.

Conversely, studios including Sony, Paramount+, Disney and Amazon are extending successful franchises into video gaming, often involving acquisitions. For Hollywood in particular, moving into the world of gaming is important as a response to generational changes. Gaming is becoming the default leisure activity for Generations X, Y and Z in the way that TV was for previous generations, and there is a natural affinity between the two leisure sectors. Netflix CEO Reed Hastings once named *Fortnite* as a more worrying competitor than HBO,[3] and 2021 Netflix acquired Night School Studio and appointed a vice president (VP) of gaming.

Innovation or hype?

> First, you're a joke, and nobody believes in you. Then you're a threat, and everybody's scared of you. And then you're obvious, and everybody assumes that what you're going to do is going to work. (Technology industry mantra)

New technologies evolve, and the process by which they establish themselves (or fail to, and fade into obsolescence) is rife with uncertainty and hype. The staggered and unpredictable nature of new technologies' evolution brings a risk that companies over-estimate the impact of a new technology in the near term (when use cases are unclear), but then underestimate its long-term impact.

The Gartner hype cycle is a favoured representation of the development journey taken by new technologies, and the challenges businesses face in assessing technological shifts and their potential impact. This simplifies the journey that 'breakthrough' technologies make from launch to maturity and has five stages:

- **Technology trigger** – a potential technological breakthrough triggers significant attention. At this point, however, there are few products using the technology and the commercial case is unproven.
- **Peak of inflated expectations** – early publicity generates a few successes in terms of products on the market, but more failures. Majority of players in a sector wait to see how the technology develops.

- **Trough of disillusionment** – the early experiments fail to meet expectations, which have been stoked by high levels of press and industry interest. Entrepreneurs and financial markets start to lose faith in the technology. A shakeout takes place of companies active in the emergent field.
- **Slope of enlightenment** – the second growth phase, where experiments continue, the technology continues to advance, more products are launched and refined, and evidence of the technology's benefit emerges.
- **Plateau of productivity** – growth slows down and hits a phase of maturity, mainstream adoption occurs as the technology's relevance and benefits become clear, abundant revenue is generated.

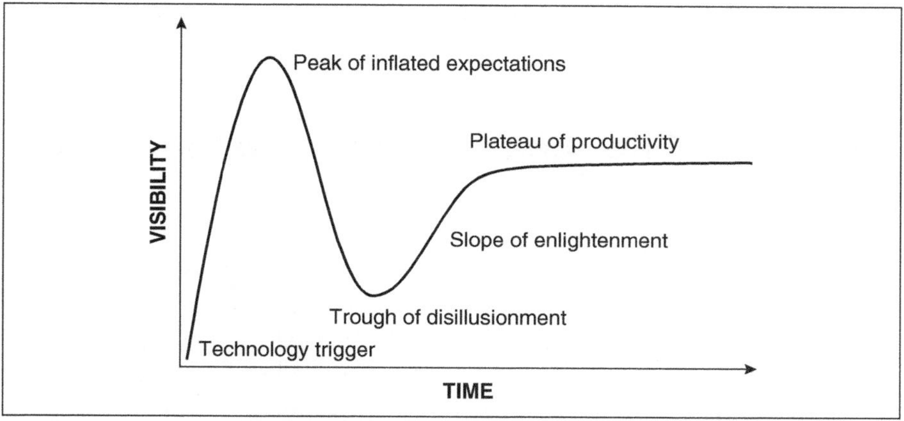

Figure 4.1 Gartner hype cycle
© Gartner.com

Steamroller or steamrolled? The challenge of technology transitions

> Once a new technology rolls over you, if you're not part of the steamroller, you're part of the road. (Steward Brand)

Change in the underlying basis technologies is always present in the media and the need to adapt to this a permanent strategic requirement. However, the volume, scope and speed of changes that have been happening for the past two decades and are set to continue – think of the fundamental changes arising from the internet, social media, cloud computing, virtual reality, augmented reality, generative AI – are contributing to an environment where existing business models are ageing but not exiting completely, and where the process of convergence has brought organisations outside the classic sector boundaries into the industry. This makes competition asymmetric, outcomes non-linear and unpredictable, and strategy development difficult.

This chapter explores strategic and organisational responses and presents several models that can be used to analyse these changes and shape responses to them. Technological change can be analysed from a rational strategy perspective – for its ability to lower entry barriers, create substitutes, alter value chains and affect competitive positioning. But as an ongoing phenomenon, an emergent one and a complex one, it can also be viewed through an adaptive lens, which would highlight the iterative processes by which an organisation aligns itself with its environment (Drazin and Schoonhoven, 1996) and the ways in which organisations alter structures, processes and systems (see, for example, Kanter, 1983, 1992).

Understanding the underlying 'technology bundle'

> What makes technological transformation difficult to predict is ... that it is caused not by any one invention, innovation or individual, but instead requires many changes to come together. After a new technology is created, society and individual investors respond to it, which leads to new behaviors and new products, which in turn lead to new use cases for the underlying technology, thereby inspiring additional behaviors and creations. And so on.[4] (Matthew Ball)

Major advances in media technologies often result from the synthesis of several independent inventions (Drucker, 1985). The mass market newspaper resulted from two technological advances: the telegraph and high-speed printing. These allowed James Gordon Bennett to found and produce the *New York Herald* at a fraction of the usual costs. Twenty years later, the concept of mass advertising was added to this model by Joseph Pulitzer, Adolf Achs and William Randolph Hearst, triggering the emergence of the national newspaper chain. More recently, the mobile internet, while long predicted and possible in the early 1990s, only really gained traction when the 'bundle' of wireless speeds, wireless devices and wireless applications had reached a point of penetration that most adults in the developed world could have a smartphone and a broadband service (Ball, 2022).

This may feel like an arcane issue, but shifts in basic technologies have big implications for how sectors grow. To take the gaming industry, this sector has expanded to become the largest in the media industry, partly because it moved on to mobile devices, and this move, in turn, was possible because of the emergence of more powerful silicon chips able to render graphics in real time. Similarly, Netflix's shift into gaming was possible because the servers that provide streaming content have become much more powerful.

Understanding the bundle of core technologies underlying a business is important because it allows organisations to judge the scope of any new advance that may impact their core activities and gives a sense of the potential scope of the opportunities and risks that may result. And this 'underlying bundle' will inevitably change, and the sector and its core technologies evolve. Figure 4.2 below shows how underlying technologies changed as the television industry moved from broadcast to on-demand to connected television.

Figure 4.2 Technologies underlying different stages in the evolution of television

Broadcast television	On-demand television (via set-top box)	Connected television
• TV cameras and microphones – convert picture and sound into signal. • Playout systems – combine individual programmes to make a broadcast channel. • TV transmitters, cable and satellites – send the signal through the air. • TV set – captures signal and converts back into picture and sound.	• Internet delivery of television (this is key innovation). • Television programmes are delivered separately and not part of a channel. • Traditional internet technologies used. • Set-top box has internet browser incorporated.	• Seamless connection between broadcast television and on-demand television as part of viewer experience. • Apps (e.g., Hulu, Twitch) which allow viewers to access digital content. • OTT/CTV devices (e.g., Chromecast) connect to TV and allow continuous stream of content. • Smart TV with built-in two-way connection to internet and other platforms (e.g., Netflix) (are display and control terminals for home-based computer networks). • Digital flat and large screen (LCD) monitors to display video content.

© Lucy Küng

The evolution of television into the realm of streamed video provision over the internet brings other actors – players that might normally be considered competitors – into an organisation's core technology bundle and value chain. This is shown in Figure 4.3. Convergence between sectors will accelerate this. For example, as Netflix diversifies into new areas such as gaming, it will need to expand its technology bundle to include player account systems, anti-cheat systems, live talk and texting.

The risk of 'technological determinism' (Williams, 1974) or 'technological reductionism' (Hesmondhalgh, 2002) – that is, the oversimplifying of the relationship between the development of an industry and technology change – is always present when seeking to decode technological change and project its likely impact. In his classic book *Diffusion of Innovations*, Rogers (2003) highlights the role of sociological factors in influencing patterns of technological adoption. A complex interplay between innovation, government policy, competitive behaviour and organisational strategies and social influences is at work. A classic example is Rupert Murdoch's introduction of electronic newspaper systems in the UK in the 1980s, which was a result of technological advances (the creation of electronic newspaper systems), but also of government initiatives to stimulate the adoption of new technologies and desire to constrain the power of the trade unions. Technological change must be viewed in relation to other contingent factors in the cultural and social environment, and, as Mathew Ball observes in the quote above, there is a complex iterative path between technological advances and the successful implementation of these developments by organisations. The very complexity of this path can lead to suboptimal outcomes: later in this chapter, we explore why a new technology can become a 'dominant design' even though it is not technologically superior due to factors such as first-mover advantages, network effects or superior marketing.

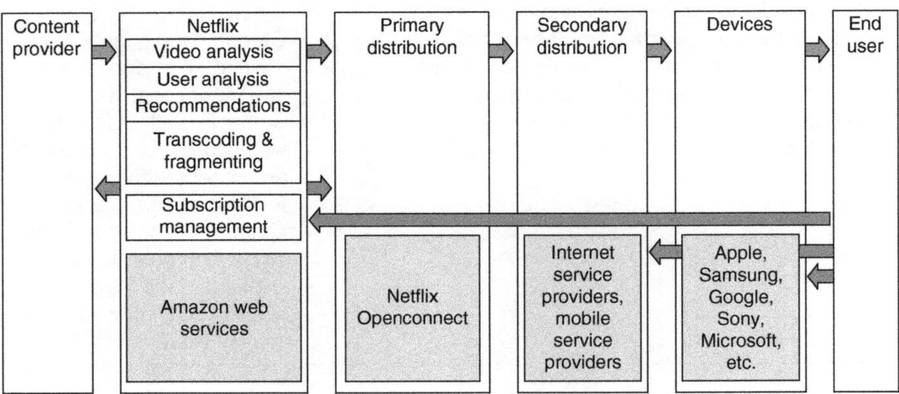

Figure 4.3 External technology providers active in Netflix's value chain
© Lucy Küng and Anders Fagerjord

'Dominant designs': why the best product doesn't always win

The path from technological discovery to economic growth runs through organisations: new technologies require an effective organisational response if they are to realise their potential. These issues underlie the substantial attention researchers pay to understand the path of technology development. A strand of this theory of considerable relevance to the media industry is known as 'organisational technology'. It concerns the interrelationship between technology, organisations and innovation. The field itself has a long pedigree with roots stretching back to Marx and Schumpeter (1934, 1942), both of whom viewed new technology as an underlying driver of organisational and political dynamics, and therefore a critical determinant of societal and institutional outcomes.

According to organisational technology researchers, the technological evolution of industries follows a cyclical pattern where long periods of relatively minor change are punctuated by much rarer instances of technological discontinuity, which disrupt entire product classes and require a response from virtually all companies in a sector (Abernathy and Utterback, 1978; Tushman and Anderson, 1986; Tushman and Smith, 2002).

These periods are confusing, uncertain and expensive for the firms involved. They trigger a period of ferment where rival new technologies compete intensively between themselves and with the existing technological regime (Henderson and Clark, 1990). They are also of tremendous strategic significance because they close with the emergence of a 'dominant design' (Tushman and Smith, 2002). This normally synthesises aspects of prior technological innovations and provides a basis for standardisation that allows scale economies to be established (Utterback, 1994).

The new dominant design has a profound impact on the industry and the structure of competition. Its emergence represents a 'technology transition'. Once it has been established, other paths of product innovation are in the main abandoned and competitors must adopt the standard or risk exclusion (Abernathy and Utterback, 1978; Tushman and Anderson, 1986; Tushman and Smith, 2002). It is followed by a period of incremental as well as architectural technological innovation (for a discussion of these terms, see below). This cycle by which organisations evolve through periods of stability during which incremental changes occur that are punctuated by irregularly occurring discontinuous transformations is also known as the 'punctuated-equilibrium model' (Gersick, 1991).

But, either way, the strategic import is the same: technologies evolve through a clearly distinguishable life cycle, starting with an early fluid state characterised

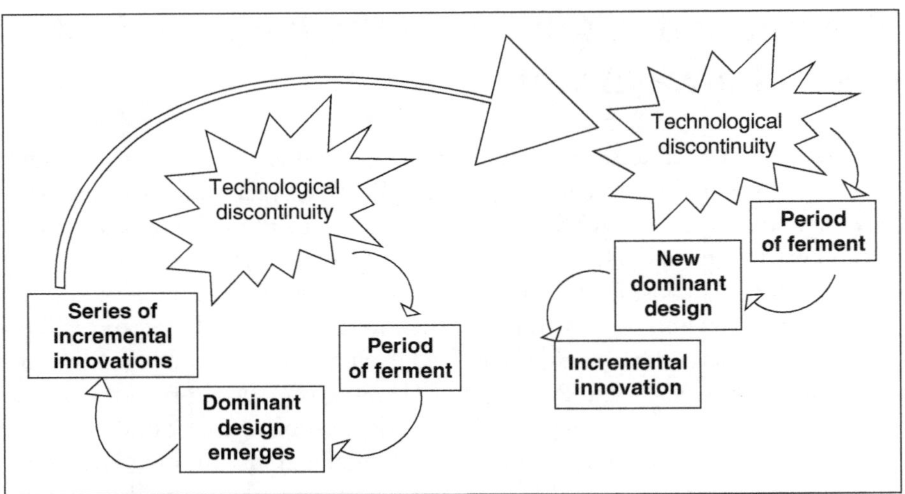

Figure 4.4 Technology transitions and dominant designs (based on Tushman and Smith, 2002)
© Lucy Küng

by relatively easy entry opportunities (and also the difficulty of evaluating the long-term significance of the development, as described in the Gartner hype cycle), moving to a highly rigid one where entry is more complex and expensive.

A technology that gets enthroned as the 'dominant design' may not automatically be the best in terms of the sophistication of the technology. Nor does the firm that pioneers a dominant design automatically retain control of it. Indeed, history shows again and again that technological superiority does not automatically bring market success. Scholars have offered many explanations for the triumph of inferior solutions, ranging from a combination of an early lead in the market and a dynamic of increasing returns to adoption (Arthur, 1994), a superior match with consumers' needs as expressed in terms of the best 'bundle' of features (Utterback, 1994), or non-technological, 'socio-political' dynamics (Tushman and Rosenkopf, 1992). However, while the best technology doesn't always win, that technology has to be good – it is not possible to 'market' an inferior product through sheer force of marketing.

Untangling types of technological change

The messy and unpredictable impact of technological change results in part from challenges in distinguishing between different types that change can take and understanding their various respective implications. The nomenclature in this area is particularly confusing. Technological change can be radical, disruptive, discontinuous, and more. Some view these terms as distinct definitions carrying precise meanings; others see these as interchangeable, and these semantic issues impede scientific understanding and managerial application (Tushman and Smith, 2002).

Clarification can be achieved by applying a typology that classifies technological change according to two dimensions: proximity to the current technological trajectory, and proximity to the existing customer/market segment (Abernathy and Clark, cited in Tushman and Smith, 2002).

Incremental innovations

These innovations are about gradually improving existing products. New features on a smartphone like new colours, different sizes or better functionalities are classic examples. Incremental innovations may feel less exciting – they do not create new products and markets, but they ensure that key products keep up with evolving market needs, and they can generate valuable revenue. And they also require less complex decision making.

Incremental innovations extend the technologies currently used and create improvements in products and increased customer satisfaction (Hill and Rothaermel, 2003). Incremental innovations are so termed because they build upon and extend the established knowledge base and current technological capabilities, and thus the organisational response involves extending existing core capabilities and engaging in continuous improvement of production processes. A subcategorisation of incremental innovations is between 'small' changes that are refinements of existing product attributes – for example, improvements to screen quality or sound systems, and 'modular' ones – those that are still incremental but more significant – for example, the shift from black and white to colour television (Dawson and Andriopoulus, 2021).

Architectural innovations

These are relatively simple technological or process innovations in the subsystems and/or linking mechanisms that allow products to be modified and directed at new markets. Personal video recorders that allowed television viewers to record programmes and blend out advertising were architectural innovations. They did not represent spectacular technological advances (VCRs had been around since the 1980s), but because they were bundled with on-demand television services, they accelerated the decline of the commercial free-to-air television model by reducing advertising income and speeding the shift to interactive television.

Incremental innovations	Extend existing technology trajectory e.g., shift from black and white to colour television.
Architectural innovations	Simple innovations in subsystems or linking mechanisms that transform a product class e.g., small, inexpensive home printers.
Discontinuous innovations	Discontinuous change to core subsystem that cascades through all processes e.g., computerised newspaper production systems.
Market-based 'disruptive innovations'	Simpler technological products that address down-market segments initially, but allow new players to gain a foothold and then move upmarket e.g., streaming video services.

Figure 4.5 Untangling categories of technological change

Although they may represent unspectacular technological advances, architectural innovations have the potential to transform a product class or fundamentally change a business because they can render existing capabilities obsolete, require the organisation to develop new competencies and make substantial internal changes – say, in manufacturing, marketing and sales (Henderson and Clark, 1990; Dawson and Andriopoulus, 2021). The launch of smaller, cheaper printers, which expanded the market for computer printers from businesses to private households, required printer manufacturers to set up entirely new product ranges, and marketing and distribution infrastructures.

The challenge of architectural innovations lies in the combination of apparent simplicity and the potential to disrupt fundamental aspects of the established business. There is a risk that incumbents 'mislabel' these as incremental rather than architectural changes and fail to understand the scope of their disruptive potential – that is, the need they may engender to restructure their organisations, seek new markets or alter core processes such as production and marketing (Henderson and Clark, 1990).

Discontinuous innovations

These are 'transformational' developments that represent a break with existing systems and processes because they 'sweep away much … existing investment in technical skills and knowledge, designs, production technique, plant, and equipment' (Utterback, 1994: 200), bringing 'discontinuous change to a core subsystem causing cascading changes in other subsystems and linking mechanisms' (Tushman and Murmann, 1998). They involve methods and materials that are novel to incumbents and are derived either from an entirely different knowledge base or from the recombination of parts of incumbents' established knowledge base with a new stream of knowledge (Freeman and Soete, 1997;

Hill and Rothaermel, 2003). These developments are dangerous for incumbents because they are 'competence destroying' (Tushman and Anderson, 1986). They make competencies that have hitherto made a source of competitive advantage obsolete and require firms to develop entirely new ones (Cohen and Levinthal, 1990).

The history of the print media industry is rife with examples of discontinuous innovation. The computerised newspaper production systems that emerged in the 1980s allowed newspaper pages to be assembled onscreen and transmitted electronically to printing plates. This made print workers' specialist competencies of setting hot metal linotype and composing text obsolete and required journalists to master desktop publishing skills (Marjoribanks, in Cottle, 2003). Similarly, the launch of satellite television in Europe was a discontinuous innovation. It expanded distribution capacity, 'decoupled' the cost of transmission for the distance involved and provoked a set of second-order changes, relieving spectrum scarcity, 'de-legitimising' political interference in broadcasting markets and weakening the philosophical foundations of public service broadcasters (Collins, 1998).

Disruptive innovations and the 'innovators' dilemma'

> The dilemma is that the criteria managers use to make decisions that keep their present businesses healthy make it impossible for them to do the right thing for the future. What's best for your current business could ruin you for the long term. (Christensen, cited in Hamm, 1999)

During the first internet era, the adjective 'disruptive', usually used in connection with 'technology' or 'innovation', felt omnipresent. This could stem from the enormous resonance of one particular concept – Clayton Christensen's theory of incumbent failure in the face of 'disruptive innovation' (Christensen and Bower, 1996; Christensen, 1997; Christensen and Overdorf, 2000). The concept of disruptive innovation has become a foundational theory for the technology industry, and Christensen's 1997 book, *The Innovator's Dilemma,* reputedly the only business book ever read by Steve Jobs, is mandatory reading for wannabe entrepreneurs and new recruits at Amazon, and was described by *The Economist* as one of the six most important books about business ever written.

Christensen sought to understand how small companies with limited resources could at times unseat dominant players in a sector. In his theory, the term 'disruption' applies to their impact on established market structures, not to the technology itself. Indeed, disruptive innovations often involve relatively simple technological developments, but these have the capacity to upset the structure of markets and undermine the attractiveness of existing products. They 'disrupt' because they trigger new and usually simpler product categories; their simplicity means that incumbents disregard such innovations because they doubt their potential market appeal.

Disruptive innovations start off at the bottom of the market by offering a very basic value proposition (BuzzFeed's early listicles and cat videos, or Netflix's mailing out of DVDs in padded bags are examples). These simple – simplistic even – new products or services are based on a different business model, carry much lower cost bases and allow new players to establish a toehold in the market. Over time, their offers become more sophisticated, and the new players offering them gradually move up the value chain, eventually challenging and 'disrupting' established players in their home territory. BuzzFeed moved on from listicles to establishing large-scale newsrooms and undertaking prize-winning investigative journalism. Netflix moved from putting DVDs in the post to streaming movies and commissioning Oscar-winning movies. However, disruptor status does not last forever – Netflix is now an established incumbent player, with a high cost-base and growth challenges in its core markets, and is now itself vulnerable to disruptors like TikTok, which offer a simpler variant of streamed video content based on an entirely different business model.

Central to Christensen's work is the difference between 'sustaining' technologies and 'disruptive' ones. Sustaining technologies improve the performance of established products along dimensions that mainstream customers in major markets have traditionally prized. Disruptive technologies are technologies that, initially at least, offer little visible benefit to incumbents. They generate simpler, cheaper products that don't meet the needs of an organisation's current key customers, appealing instead to less sophisticated lower-margin niche markets. Thus, products based on disruptive technologies are in the main unattractive initially to incumbent players with established product-market offerings because they offer less financial and market potential than current ones. Over time, however, ugly ducklings grow into swans. Applications of the disruptive technology become more sophisticated, their market appeal grows, and a new market is established, one that incumbents may need to enter late and at a considerable cost.

The dilemma is that 'doing the right thing' by existing markets can cause companies to fail in new ones. Established companies tend, not unintelligently, to focus on meeting the needs of and retaining their most valuable customers, rather than expanding product ranges to acquire new customer groups. Disruptive new players find a foothold by focusing on those overlooked customers and then expand upmarket. They are not burdened with their legacy competitors' expensive overheads, are profitable on lower margins, and have the luxury of focusing on the new emerging markets.

Disruptive innovations, therefore, disrupt two elements of incumbents' activities. First, they disrupt incumbents' markets by introducing new segments and/or product categories (Tushman and Smith, 2002). Second, and this point receives far less attention than the market disruption, they disrupt the architecture of the incumbent firm because the firm will need to revise its strategy, markets, product portfolio and business model. An organisation's ability to do this depends on its resources, processes and, critically, values (Christensen and Overdorf, 2000). Values effectively mean culture, a subject covered in depth in a subsequent chapter. Cultural values are decisive because they determine how resources are allocated and thus which new activities will be supported by the organisation. At base, therefore, the innovator's dilemma is caused by a maladaptive resource allocation process that concentrates resource commitments on markets and products that match existing business priorities and ignores 'downmarket' customer groups or less sophisticated products (Christensen and Bower, 1996).

'Disruption' as defined by Christensen is a process, not a one-off event. Netflix gradually moved upmarket to challenge HBO in its core market. Easyjet started off catering for budget-conscious flyers and moved upmarket to cater for business travellers. These definitions show that all instances of technological innovation are not the same and, critically, there are no universally applicable strategic or organisational responses. Different innovations affect different firms in different ways, and responses depend on the nature of the innovation involved and its specific implications on the firm's products. Figure 4.6 summarises theoretical recommendations on how organisations should respond to the different types of technological change discussed above.

<table>
<tr><td>Incremental</td><td>Extend existing core capabilities.
Continuous improvement of production processes.</td></tr>
<tr><td>Architectural</td><td>Recognise threat.
Alter production processes.
Address new markets.
Restructure organisation.</td></tr>
<tr><td>Discontinuous</td><td rowspan="2">Develop new competencies and perhaps abandon existing ones.
Ensure that core competencies don't become 'core rigidities'.
Create 'new organisational space' with a new value system.</td></tr>
<tr><td>Market-based</td></tr>
</table>

Figure 4.6 Different types of technological change require different organisational responses

Continuous innovation and permanent renewal

As the pace of technological innovation continues to accelerate, and as the competitive environment continues to shift, organisations face a permanent need for renewal – to renew existing products and services, and create new ones. Tidd and Bessant's (2018) model looks at how organisations can systematically develop ideas and turn these into products and services. It comprises a sequence of four activities:

Stage	Subtasks required
1. Search and assess.	• Scan environment to identify changes that offer opportunities for innovation. • Assess options that emerge.
2. Select (decide what is to be done and why).	• Ensure the options identified will fit with the business (especially its resources, competencies and culture). • Acquire the knowledge (internal and external) that is needed to proceed with the innovation.
3. Implement (develop a strategy to make innovation happen and resolve problems that occur).	• Execute the strategy internally. This is the core of the process. It usually involves a series of problem-solving loops to solve emerging challenges. This stage is further complicated by the need for different functions in the organisation to collaborate. • Launch and sustain the innovation. This stage is closely informed by insights about consumer need – for example, by bringing users into the design process.
4. Capture value.	• Realise intended benefits. These can be commercial (new revenues) but also organisational (the acquisition of new competences or new knowledge).

How inertia undermines technology transitions

> Complex societies collapse because when some stress comes they have simply become too inflexible to respond to. … In such systems there is no way to make things a little bit simpler – the whole edifice becomes a huge interlocking system not readily amenable to change. (Aitkenhead, 2010)

Firms often struggle to transform sufficiently in response to technological shifts. The pattern by which dominant incumbents, which apparently have all the strategically appropriate resources needed to master technological advances, nonetheless fail to do so, is well documented. Historical analysis of the largest US firms shows repeatedly that some of the largest, best resourced and best managed firms declined and were superseded by smaller players or newcomers that exploit new technologies (Utterback, 1994). IBM lost out to Microsoft when software became more important than hardware. Microsoft in turn lost out to Google in the field of online search. Google failed to dominate social networking; the leading position in that sector was taken by Facebook.

This 'pathology of sustained success' (Tushman and Smith, 2002: 387) has been observed in a wide range of different national and industry contexts (Tushman and Nelson, 1990; Leonard-Barton, 1992; Prahalad and Hamel, 1994; Christensen, 1997). Examples of incumbents who do manage to extend their leadership positions across technology transitions are rare rather than the rule. The cause lies not in strategies but inside the firm, in the structures, routines, systems and processes that ensure survival in stable environments, coupled with the culture and self-identity that successful incumbents develop over time, which can stifle attempts to respond to a changed environment (Burgelman, 1983, 1994; Hannan and Freeman, 1984; Tushman and Anderson, 1986; Tushman and O'Reilly, 1997; Christensen and Tuttle, 1999; Christensen and Overdorf, 2000).

Incumbents are hampered by inbuilt impediments – the routines, systems and processes that all organisations develop over time, ironically to ensure predictability and quality. These are not malign in themselves, but at the same time as they ensure reliability, reduce the risk of error, reduce costs and simplify decisions, their sophistication makes the organisations too inflexible to respond to the demands of their environments. This inflexibility is termed 'inertia': forces that stop an object from moving. Inertia is what stops successful existing organisations from benefiting from the opportunities presented by new technologies. Ironically, inertia is the inevitable by-product of running complicated organisations well, and just about any aspect of an organisation's everyday ways of doing business can give rise to it.

How success creates inertia

Success is, ironically, closely correlated with inertia. This happens in the following way. Successful organisations seek to strengthen their position still further by extending their existing core competencies and making incremental improvements to their products and processes. However, when a technology transition occurs and a new dominant design emerges, the incumbent is required to dismantle some aspect of these structures, even if they are functioning well. This is counterintuitive and normally hard to do, so the organisation is effectively trapped by its success (Tushman and Anderson, 1986; Tushman and Smith, 2002).

Inertial factors can be tangible or intangible. They can range from buildings, equipment, individuals and how their roles are designed, to the semi-tangible, say, workflow processes, competencies, performance metrics and pension arrangements, to the intangible, shared beliefs and cultural assumptions.

Inertia from infrastructure, systems and processes

Newspapers' expensive printing presses (which were essential to the emergence of the entire news publishing sector, in that they allowed mass printing at low costs), were strategic assets in the pre-digital era as they created huge barriers to anyone else seeking to enter the market and allowed those inside the industry to make healthy profits. As the industry turned digital, those investments became fixed-cost burdens that digital-only competitors did not carry and reduced their owners' competitiveness.

Processes and systems create inertia too. These elements came into being for constructive reasons – to ensure that strategies are implemented and investments are made wisely, to eliminate waste and maintain quality standards, and so on. However, they also serve to focus attention on the current business and on existing products; quality control systems can enshrine particular constellations of product attributes, and investment criteria can channel company resources into safe fields for the current business, which can preclude moves into new technologies and emerging markets that may be important for the future.

Inertia from culture and mindset

Some of the most intractable sources of inertia stem from ephemeral aspects of an organisation, particularly, as noted above, from success. When a company is generating solid returns and is respected by the markets and the media, this can reinforce confidence in the current business and can blinker the organisation to the potentially destructive impact of new technologies. Examples of the media industry failing to see the risk posed by technological advances are plentiful (see Wolf, 1999; Picard, 2004). The US television networks were slow to respond to cable television and ceded a new market to new players as a result (Auletta, 1991), and a similar phenomenon is playing out with streaming technologies. Newcomers such as Netflix and Amazon Prime gained a head start and strong market shares through moving early and the benefits of being able to design operations from scratch, leaving incumbent broadcast networks needing to make a later entry into a market where consumer habits had already been formed, the new competitors had established their brands, and content costs were starting to rise as a result of increased competition.

Which organisational structure best supports innovation?

We noted earlier in this chapter that the path from technological discovery to economic growth runs through organisations. Specifically, it runs through a relatively detailed aspect of organisations, how individual business units are located and how they interact with other parts of the organisation. A belief that 'it's hard to develop new things in big organisations' is central to Silicon Valley start-up thinking. 'Bureaucratic' hierarchies, it is held, inevitably move slowly and are innately risk averse – that is, they are inert. This thinking applies to the media, too. Many have suggested that legacy media's fixed structures block agility and limit their ability to respond to the opportunity created by digital technologies (see, for example, Filloux, 2014).

This foots to a larger debate in management theory concerning the relationship between strategy and structure. Alfred Chandler's landmark research (1962) concluded that changes in strategy result in changes in structure, implying by extension that organisations should design their structures once the strategy has been set. This view was moderated in the latter years (as is discussed in this chapter), but the underlying assumption holds – that the extent of fit between strategy and structure influences competitiveness (see, for example, Gulati and Puranam, 2009).

Central to this debate is the relationship between autonomy and innovation. Autonomy has long been positively correlated with innovation, particularly innovation arising from technological advances. Back in 1961, Burns and Stalker's investigation of innovation in the electronics industry identified two types of organisational structure – mechanistic and organic – with mechanistic structures favoured in stable environments, and organic ones in fast-changing turbulent ones. Kanter (1992) speaks of the need for firms to develop 'entrepreneurial enclaves' where innovative new businesses can develop. Lovelace (1986) found that decentralised strucures enable individuals to exercise more creative freedom (and autonomy is also a core component of organisational creativity – this point is discussed in Chapter 5).

Central to Christensen's (1997) proposals for how incumbents can master disruption is that the parent company needs to create a 'new organisational space' for the new businesses based on disruptive technologies because these will require a different business model, processes and culture, and organisations can seldom support this. The solution is to create a new organisational space. Christensen identifies three options: spin out an independent company, create a new organisational structure within the corporate boundaries, or acquire an organisation whose processes and values closely match the requirements of the new task (Christensen, 1997; Christensen and Overdorf, 2000).

Gilbert's (2002) comparative research of US newspapers' print and online operations found that newspapers that set up independent organisations for their online sites were twice as innovative as those that had integrated operations and had 60 per cent higher penetration and that conversely, integration could distract or even debilitate a new venture. He attributed this in part to the absence of 'threat rigidity' in the new venture: while the parent organisations tended to view online activities as a threat to established systems, processes and so on, the new ventures were able to view the internet as an opportunity However, should the new unit succeed, it may fall prey to 'autoimmune system rejection' (Schein, in Coutu, 2002). As their success becomes evident, the rest of the organisation can come to resent the 'upstart' and find ways to subvert it. Such situations require careful management on the part of the parent.

Decisions on whether units focused on new technologies are best housed within the parent or given independence are complex (Feldman, 2021). Is there an opportunity cost for the core business if research and development based on technologies important to the future of the industry are taking place in an independent unit? While the autonomy provided by independence from the parent can side-step inertia, what happens if that unit succeeds? Must it remain independent to maintain a distinct culture? Do the new competencies and knowledge present in the separate organisation need to permeate the parent? If this doesn't happen 'uncoordinated learning' can be the result (Schein in Coutu, 2002; Gulati and Garino, 2000). Kanter (1983) suggests that institutionalising new ventures by ensuring they become part of a legitimate and ongoing part of the business is the final challenge of entrepreneurship.

Ambidexterity: combining 'exploration' and 'exploitation'

Theories of disruptive innovation suggest that to respond to ongoing technological innovation in the strategic environment, an organisation may need to create parallel organisations that operate in tandem with, but independently, of the parent and in so doing find a way to combine adaptive strategic processes, built-in learning mechanisms, and fluid structures that operate independently of traditional functional ones found in the parent. Such considerations are central to the so-called exploration–exploitation dilemma (March, 1991), a concept that 'dominates' analyses of technological innovation, organisation design, organisational learning and competitive advantage (Gupta et al., 2006).

This concept from the adaptive school of theory concerns how organisations balance the competing demands of 'exploitation' – using existing resources and capabilities to generate short-term returns and 'exploration' – searching for new resources and capabilities to potentially bring long-term gains.

Organisations that over-engage in exploration may 'suffer the costs of experimentation without gaining many of its benefits ... too many undeveloped ideas and too little distinctive competence' (March, 1991), and 'never gain the results of its knowledge' (Levinthal and March, 1993). Those that over-index on exploitation may find themselves 'trapped in suboptimal stable equilibria' (March, 1991), where their fixed cognitive maps of sector, organisation and the potential of innovation lead them to create 'core rigidities' rather than core competencies (Leonard-Barton, 1995).

One solution is 'ambidexterity' (Tushman and O'Reilly, 1996) – the ability to combine 'explorative' and 'exploitative' units within a single structure. This allows the organisation to address current markets and technological demands, and at the same time develop new ones. The greater an organisation's ability to balance these activities, the higher the organisational performance (Tushman and O'Reilly, 1996; Gibson and Birkinshaw, 2004; He and Wong, 2004; Tushman et al., 2011). These two types of units are fundamentally different:

- The **explorative units** experiment with new technologies, products and services. They seek new customers in immature markets where there is little data on customer needs. Such units need to be small, decentralised and independent so that they can foster risk-taking, respond fast and have the kind of flexible structures and processes needed in emerging uncertain situations. These elements in turn foster entrepreneurial competencies and the knowledge to underpin more radical innovation. The 'skunkworks' set up by advertising and media firms to explore the potential of the metaverse are typical examples. They are tasked with gaining insights into how this new technology might impact clients' businesses and experiment with campaigns that extend brand presence into the immersive domain.
- The **exploitative units'** role is to maximise the performance of existing products, drive out variation, maximise efficiency and optimise revenues. They extend existing knowledge that supports incremental innovation and scale successful innovations into mature businesses that they can exploit for profit.

Burgelman (1983) proposes 'internal corporate venturing' as a means of resolving the 'fundamental paradox' between the 'chaos arising from the autonomous strategic behaviour necessary to initiate [innovative] businesses and the administrative discipline that must be imposed at some point so the parent can take advantage of the new strategic thrust' (1983: 121). Internal corporate venturing involves a firm developing an 'IVC', or entirely new entrepreneurial initiatives that originate within a corporate structure that are intended from the start to become new businesses (Kuratko et al., 2009; Govindarajan and Trimble, 2010).

This is a process by which diversified firms transform activities based on new technologies into new businesses that involve competencies not previously available to the mainstream business of the parent. Integrating the different cultures, structures, processes, management teams and human resources of these two types of units is the task of senior management. They must ensure that the strategic context, which determines corporate objective-setting and resource allocation, and the structural context (the mechanisms by which operational behaviour is kept in line with strategy) do not preclude autonomous strategic behaviour that falls outside current strategic goals. They must also show unwavering support for entrepreneurial activity, regardless of fluctuations in the parent's wider business. This in turn requires a 'flexibility and tolerance for ambiguity in … strategic vision' that allows 'experimentation and selection' (Burgelman, 1983: 1362).

Changing newsroom structures

> When you really boil it all down my job is to make sure that our journalism gets to our readers, everywhere as fast as possible, doesn't break, is on brand and has a clear strategy behind it. (Product Director, 2017 *Washington Post*)

Marc Andreessen, founder of Netscape and Silicon Valley venture capitalist, famously declared that 'software is eating the world'.[5] With this comment, he was flagging up the inexorable process by which more and more businesses and industries are run on software and delivered as digital services. Think of Uber, a taxi service, or Airbnb, an accommodation provider. In both cases, software lies at the core of the business. And in the media, too, software now underpins an increasing number of essential functions, from how content is created and presented, to the entire system by which that content is monetised and relationships with readers are established.

Four 'incursion points' have been identified where technology is entering the newsroom (Kueng, 2019):

- **Product**: Product is a new function inside media organisations. Its role is to ensure that digital content that can flourish in the digital ecosystem finds audiences, meets those audiences' needs and can be monetised. Product has long been a core function in the technology industry, where companies seek growth by producing products or services that meet customer needs and provide an exceptional user experience. For the news organisations, product is now a central function of the business (Royal,

2021; INMA 2022). It builds a bridge between the media organisation and its users, and activities encompass building the website, apps, digital story-telling formats, the content management system and many more elements. With the rise of product comes an attendant growth in UX (user experience) design.

- **Data:** The growth of data functions inside media organisations was spurred by the shift to funding models based on direct funding by those consuming the content. Once this direct relationship was established, media companies for the first time gained granular data about who was consuming their products and how. This allowed them to establish a data feedback loop, which soon became central to their activities: the more data you have, the better your product; the better your product, the more data you can collect; the more data you can collect, the more talent you attract; the more talent you attract, the better the product.
- **Social media:** Newsrooms' social media teams' role has grown from beginnings of optimising content for specific platforms to originating content tailored for those destinations. This function is important because it is the first stage in the customer acquisition funnel and allows a newsroom to prioritise audience impact and digital optimisation first.
- **Digital storytelling** is now a foundational aspect of all newsrooms. Digital storytelling formats are central to mobile consumption and digital business models. Three underlying shifts can be observed in these new approaches to journalism: the relationship between writer and reader moves towards a dialogue; the tone of this dialogue is less an 'explanation from an expert' and more an 'exchange between equals', the third is the priority placed on engaging readers, which means that digital stories can be altered after publication according to insights gained from data systems, which have created a real-time feedback loop between producer and consumer of content.

The growing centrality of digital technologies in the media, and specifically the need to produce both classic and digital news output for multiple platforms has created significant change in how newsrooms are organised (Jenkins, 2001; Deuze, 2003; Avilés and Carvajal, 2008; Doyle, 2011; García-Avilés et al., 2014). Three basic approaches (García-Avilés et al., 2008) have been observed:

- **Isolated platforms**, where a new organisational unit is established to develop content for the digital platforms, and this works independently of the main newsroom.

- **Cross-media structures**, where newsrooms are partially restructured to permit the coordination of classic and digital work routines and multiple-platform production, but where the 'traditional' structures are still discernible.
- **Full integration**, where a new centrally coordinated architecture for the multi-platform product is created.

Organisations often moved sequentially through these approaches as digital technologies also moved from the fringe of news production to the core product area. 'Isolated platforms' were an initial step, whereby they established independent units to produce digital content for digital platforms. As digital technologies became more entrenched and audiences grew, these new units were integrated into the 'parent' newsroom, often by creating cross-media structures – desks, teams and units. This shift also reflected a search for synergies and efficiency gains arising from the combination of content, staff and other resources, both of which grew in necessity as revenues from analogue products diminished. A decision to redesign fundamentally to fully integrate the newsroom often resulted from a strategic goal of becoming 'digital first'. Here, digital activities are prioritised, not only in terms of which formats are used, and when content is released, but also in terms of the strategic attention and investment they receive. Alongside these changes in digital journalism and the structures of the newsroom, a slew of new newsroom roles also emerged. These are summarised in Figure 4.7.

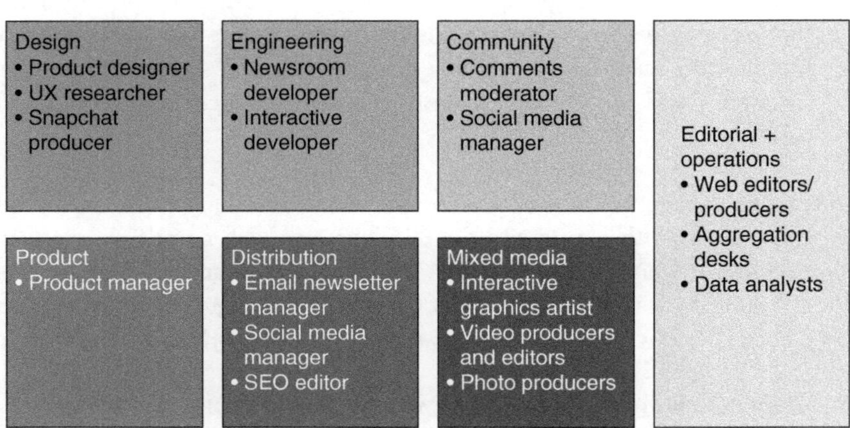

Figure 4.7 New newsroom roles arising from convergence and technology transitions (*Source*: Julia Bezier, Bloomberg, 2022)

Conclusions

This chapter has discussed how the media industry is rooted in technology and its fate is intimately connected to the path of technological innovation. Strategy is in part about how an organisation orchestrates a response to a changing environment. Technological advance is a permanent aspect of that environment. This can be a force for good – a source of new products and services, and therefore of economic growth, but at the same time it poses challenges. The appeal of established products and services declines when innovative new ones find resonance with the market. This often unseats incumbents, even leading ones, and initiates their own process of decline. And incumbents' ability to master these challenges can be undermined by the complexity arising from the interplay between innovation, social influences and organisational response.

However, not all technological advance is the same, and one of the key messages in this chapter is that media firms, like their peers in other sectors, need to be able to differentiate between different types of innovation and orchestrate their strategic responses accordingly. Their ability to respond depends not only on the 'content' of their strategic response, but also on the strategic process employed to implement that response. Specifically, as we have seen in this chapter, many relatively mundane organisational elements must be carefully conceived, tightly interlinked and well executed. Critical among these are furthering creativity and innovation, finding the correct structural option for the new venture tasked with responding to a new technology, and fostering the right culture, mindset and leadership. These topics have featured in this chapter's analysis, but are handled as stand-alone subjects in the following chapters.

Questions

1. Choose a media product. Identify its basic 'bundle of technologies'. Which new technologies could enhance or replace the current basic technology bundle?
2. The 'creator economy', 'streaming media' and 'the metaverse' are all technological advances with significant influence on the development of the media sector. Assess these against the Gartner hype cycle. Where does the technology currently stand?
3. Take a news organisation in your country and investigate how it has structured its digital activities. Does it integrate legacy and digital activities, or are these separated? How well is this structure working? If you were a consultant, would you advise any changes?

Resources

Books, articles and reports

Clayton M. Christensen's *The Innovator's Dilemma* and *The Innovator's Solution* are essential reading on the dynamics of technology transitions and their impact on organisations. In *Breaking News: Mastering the Art of Disruptive Innovation in Journalism* he applies these concepts to journalism (https://nieman.harvard.edu/articles/breaking-news/)

Clayton Christensen's application of his theories to the news sector can be read in: *Breaking News: Mastering the Art of Disruptive Innovation in Journalism.* Available at: https://nieman.harvard.edu/articles/breaking-news

The UK Audit Office's strategic assessment of the BBC's digital technologies, its resource level and future digital technology challenges can be found at: www.nao.org.uk/reports/a-digital-bbc

Geoffrey A. Moore's *Crossing the Chasm*, and *Inside the Tornado* are definitive works on the challenges established companies face when underlying technologies change fundamentally.

The Lean Startup by Eric Ries has become *the* reference for entrepreneurs seeking to set up new businesses and organisations seeking to make organisations more entrepreneurial.

Managing Media and Digital Organizations, by Eli Noam, 2018.

Marc Andreessen on how new technologies develop, disrupt and create opportunities across all sectors at: mckinsey.com/Industries/Technology-Media-and-Telecommunications/Our-Insights/Find-the-smartest-technologist-in-the-company-and-make-them-CEO

Research and industry organisations covering tech in the media

Industry associations track technology advances their specific sectors.

Broadcasting:

- International Broadcasting Convention (https://IBC.org)
- National Association of Broadcasters (www.nab.org/)
- SMPTE, the global society of media professionals, technologists and engineers (www.smpte.org/)

(*Continued*)

News publishing:

- INMA (www.inma.org/topics-main.cfm)
- WAN-IFRA (https://wan-ifra.org/)
- FIPP (www.fipp.com/) publishes an annual Innovation in Media Report
- JournalismAI is a journalism thinktank at the London School of Economics and supported by the Google News Initiative. It explores the use of AI in news journalism which offers conferences, workshops and meetings, and offers Journalism AI scholarships (www.lse.ac.uk/media-and-communications/polis/JournalismAI).

Sites, newsletters and podcasts

On technology developments affecting media and tech sectors *Benedict's Newsletter* at: www.ben-evans.com/newsletter

On film industry *The Entertainment Strategy Guy*, https://entertainment.substack.com/

On product management in news journalism:

- Lenny's Podcast: Interview with Alex Hardiman, Chief Product Officer at *The New York Times*, at: www.lennyspodcast.com/an-inside-look-at-how-the-new-york-times-builds-product-alex-hardiman-cpo-at-the-new-york-times/
- Platform Product Management at *The New York Times*, at: www.slideshare.net/productschool/platform-product-management-changing-whats-possible-by-the-new-york-times-svp-of-product

Schibsted's annual *Future Report* at: https://futurereport.schibsted.com. See also the Substack newsletter from one of its papers: *Inside Aftenposten*, at: https://aftenpo, sten.substack.com

FT Strategies' guides on subscription strategies at: www.ftstrategies.com/en-gb/insights/.

The Table Stakes project on change management for local news providers at: www.tablestakes.org

The News Product Alliance Resource Library (in Spanish as well as English) at: https://learning.newsproduct.org/?_gl=1*1e89oj1*_ga*NzY3MTM5MDgwLjE2Nzk1ODkyOTQ.*_ga_L540RW67FZ*MTY4MjA5NDg3MS4xMi4wLjE2ODIwOTQ4NzEuMC4wLjA.

Case: Strategic renewal via technological transformation at *The Washington Post*

It seemed ... that ownership by somebody who had immense knowledge of the future, of technology, of ways to deliver information to readers brought a big plus. (Former owner of *The Washington Post,* Donald Graham, on reasons for selling to Jeff Bezos)[6]

When Jeff Bezos bought *The Washington Post* in 2013, it had 'a global reputation but a local business model'.[7] Despite the fact that millions had been invested in digital initiatives, the paper had a strong international reputation (achieved in part by its track record of uncovering scandals like Watergate), but was essentially a print-focused regional publication with only a limited national readership. Financially, it was 'money-making but no longer the money-minting machine it was in the 1980s and '90s'.[8]

Bezos's goal for the paper was ambitious. He wanted to make it 'the newspaper for the world', just as he had sought to make Amazon the world's largest online store.[9] He would do this by transforming its technology, and this approach was critical in Graham's decision to sell to Bezos. Journalism was not the *Post*'s challenge; rather, it was the technology. As Don Graham put it: 'We did not have the technology skills.[10]

Bezos's strategy

[Bezos] supplied resources as ... only one of the world's wealthiest men ... could. He ... turned *The Post*'s business strategy — and, by extension, its journalistic one — upside down, stipulating that its outlook would change from local to national, even global.[11]

Bezos's game plan was to lean into the major digital shifts that had already taken place to power *Post*'s transition from print to digital, expand its global footprint and transform its finances. For Marty Baron, the paper's Pulitzer Prize-winning editor, Bezos's logic was self-evident: 'Why are we taking all the pain of the internet and not taking the gifts that [it] has to offer'.[12]

The plan had three basic steps:

- **Scale readership by moving from regional to international.** For Bezos, the distribution capabilities of the internet combined with digital formats meant that a regional paper could access global markets at minimum

(*Continued*)

cost. This had never been possible with a print product. Once the digital systems and products were up to speed, readership could be increased by moving from regional to national and then international.

- **From print to digital subscriptions**. The business model would need to shift as a result. *The Washington Post* was reliant financially on high-priced print subscriptions sold to locals in the Washington, DC region. Digital readers needed digital subscriptions and these had a lower price point than print ones. Thus, while print subscriptions would continue to be important, the strategic priority would be achieving a high volume of lower-cost digital subscriptions across the entire US and internationally.
- **Master digital journalism and digital product**. If the core product is to be digital news for international audiences, then the digital product needs to be strong enough to make that ambition a reality. This meant not simply that *The Washington Post*'s digital journalism needed to excel in meeting that broader market's needs, but the digital product experience needed to be top notch also.

Cascading innovation and technological investment throughout the organisation

Reorientating *The Washington Post* as a digital news provider was straightforward in principle: ensure the digital product meets the needs of digital consumers, that those customers are tightly connected to the product and that the number of those consumers grows. This would in turn ensure that the *Post*'s journalism has the impact it deserves. In practice, this needed widespread technological innovation (and investment). The *Post* needed to create more digital content and digital storytelling formats, build first-class systems for digital subscriptions, digital advertising and digital content management, build the pipelines and products to promote and deliver digital content to digital readers. Wide-ranging technological change was required throughout the organisation. It also needed to recruit the engineers, data scientists, product experts and UX specialists who would shape and guide this transformation.

Taken together, these initiatives spanned all variants of technological innovation listed earlier in this chapter. For example:

- **Real-time analytics in the newsroom (incremental innovation).** These give journalists permanent feedback on digital stories in real-time and allowed them to alter headings, pictures, story structure, etc. to ensure that they connected better with readers.

(*Continued*)

- **'Rich' election alerts combining text and location-specific map (architectural innovation).** The *Post*'s product innovation teams developed 'push notifications' that were sent to the lock screens of readers' mobile phones to alert them to breaking news stories and encourage them to then visit *The Washington Post*'s app or website. These are now standard for news organisations. This concept was developed further into 'rich alerts', a new feature built into the email platform that enabled iOS users to get alerts with a map giving election updates specific to their state.
- **Arc digital content management platform (discontinuous innovation).** Arc is a suite of integrated tools that replaces the combination of systems and processes required for digital news publishing. Arc allows *The Washington Post* to publish stories and videos across all digital publishing platforms and combines scheduling and workflow management, mobile app, story tools, analytics dashboard, headline testing tool, A/B testing tool and newsletter tools. Arc is also discontinuous in that it moved *The Washington Post* into a new business segment – the provision of software to other businesses. Arc is licensed to other publishers and is an additional revenue stream for the organisation.

Goal achieved, but focus on technological transformation continues

In 2017, four years after Bezos's acquisition, the *Post* had 1 million paid digital-only subscribers.[13] By 2021, this figure had risen to 3 million; 95 per cent of its digital traffic came from outside the Washington, DC area and one third of total readership was international.[14] Unsurprisingly, the number of technology staff had also increased (in 2021, the ratio of journalists to engineers was 2 to 1[15]). And Bezos's focus on technology, particularly on the performance of digital product continues, as evidenced by his bi-weekly call with product teams: 'They'll go through the flow of … a new subscription process … or a new product that will help our site load faster or be more engaging, more riveting, in the storytelling.'[16]

Case questions

1 Outline Bezos's core strategy for transforming *The Washington Post*. How did this leverage technological changes in the wider strategic environment?

(*Continued*)

2 How did the 'technology bundle' underlying *The Washington Post* alter as it moved from print to digital?

3 In terms of where technological innovation took place, did *The Washington Post* follow an exploration or an innovation approach, or did it combine the two?

4 Research recent innovations at *The Washington Post*. How would you categorise these? Are they incremental, architectural, discontinuous or disruptive?

Case: *Encyclopaedia Britannica* – unseated by technological change

Encyclopaedica Britannica is an iconic lesson in what can happen if a response to disruptive innovation fails. *Encyclopaedia Britannica* at its peak was the oldest continuously published reference work in the English language and a staple of family bookshelves. Its multi-volume sets had text contributions from leading scientists and theorists of the time, cost around $1,500–$2,000 and were sold door-to-door by salespeople who were legendary at persuading parents that the *Encyclopaedia Britannica* was essential if children were to be well educated.

In the mid-1980s, *Encyclopaedia Britannica* was confronted by the first of a series of potentially disruptive technological innovations – CD-Rom. This new format was not appealing to the publisher: why cannibalise its high-priced print version with a low-priced digital one? It maintained this view, even when Microsoft, the dominant provider of computer software for home and office, offered a joint venture to create a market leading CD-Rom version of the reference work. Microsoft went on to develop its own product, *Encarta*, which became the best-selling CD-Rom encyclopaedia in the world.

Encyclopaedia Britannica was not blind to digital technologies and had engaged in the field. In 1981, it licensed its content to Lexis-Nexis. In 1983, it launched educational software programs with Apple. In 1985, it purchased the American Learning Corporation and acquired a 75 per cent stake in *Encyclopaedia Britannica* Educational Corporation, a supplier of films and educational materials to schools. In August 1988, it partnered with Educational Systems Corp to build an electronic version of *Compton's Encyclopaedia*, a networked CD-Rom for schools. In 1993, a CD-Rom containing the entire

(*Continued*)

text of *Encyclopaedia Britannica* in searchable format was released, and a few months later this was distributed electronically to universities and some libraries over the internet. A CD-Rom for consumers was released in 1994, only a year after Microsoft's *Encarta*. In July 1995, they offered free trial access to the internet site.

Despite these moves, the publisher lost 50 per cent of revenues between 1990 and 1995, and sales had dropped by 83 per cent. A year later, *Encyclopaedia Britannica* was sold for $135 million. In the ensuing years, its new owners launched expanded and enhanced CD-Rom versions, as well as online versions that were initially subscription-based and later free. Despite these moves, the brand was unable to compete against the tremendous scale and scope of free information available on the internet. In 2012, the print version (priced at $1,395) was finally shelved in favour of a continuously updated website and educational products for schools in areas such as maths, science and the English language.

There are many lessons to be drawn from this case. *Encyclopaedia Britannica* was a global brand with unique content and with loyal readers happy to pay high prices for the product. Yet a series of advances in publishing technologies – from printed books, first to CD-Rom and then to online delivery, altered every stage of *Encyclopaedia Britannica*'s value chain – from how information was gathered, packaged and produced, to how it was distributed, marketed and consumed. *Encyclopaedia Britannica*'s existing competencies in book design, printing, binding and door-to-door marketing became irrelevant, and indeed liabilities, in that they represented high fixed costs that digital competitors did not have to contend with. In their place, an entirely new set of competencies were required. The reference publisher did not fail to respond; rather, its response was inadequate, ranging from being hesitant to undermine a high margin product with an 'inferior' new one, to mishandling played collaboration approaches from technology giants. A quarter of a century later, these issues continue to bedevil media organisations' responses to disruptive technologies.

Case questions

1 How well does the case of *Encyclopaedia Britannica* fit with Clayton Christensen's (see p. 113) theories of disruptive innovation? Why?

2 How do you explain the publisher's reluctance to enter a joint venture with Microsoft to product a CD-Rom version?

3 Is there a media product that is the natural successor to the *Encyclopaedia Britannica*? Which one and why?

Notes

1 Mathias Döpfner, 'The future of journalism', 17 May 2006. Available at: www.signandsight.com/features/756.html
2 Mike Shatzkin, *The Shatzkin Files,* 4 January 2023. Available at: https://us8.campaign-archive.com/?e=c0baa11cf3&u=c3cbf58096d38288f7327eba6&id=6184fd3a5b
3 'Netflix and video games', Matthew Ball, 24 August 2021. Available at: matthewball.vc/all/netflixgames
4 Netflix's Q4 2018 investor letter: 'We compete with (and lose to) Fortnight more than HBO.'
5 *The Metaverse,* Matthew Ball, 2022: 27.
6 Marc Andreessen, 'Why software is eating the world'. Available at: https://a16z.com/2011/08/20/why-software-is-eating-the-world
7 Francesca Giuliani-Hoffman, *CNN Business,* 16 August 2019. Available at: https://edition.cnn.com/2019/08/16/media/jeff-bezos-donald-graham/index.html
8 Steve Coll, former *Washington Post* reporter, cited in Marc Tracy, 'How Marty Baron and Jeff Bezos remade *The Washington Post*', *New York Times,* 27 February 2021. Available at: www.nytimes.com/2021/02/27/business/marty-baron-jeff-bezos-washington-post.html
9 Marc Tracy, 'How Marty Baron and Jeff Bezos remade *The Washington Post*', *New York Times,* 27 February 2021. Available at: www.nytimes.com/2021/02/27/business/marty-baron-jeff-bezos-washington-post.html
10 Beaujon, ibid.
11 Francesca Giuliani-Hoffman, ibid.
12 Mark Tracy, *New York Times,* 27 February 2021. Available at: www.nytimes.com/2021/02/27/business/marty-baron-jeff-bezos-washington-post.html
13 Andrew Beaujon, *Washingtonian,* 25 August, 2021. Available at: www.washingtonian.com/2021/08/25/inside-the-plan-to-make-jeff-bezoss-washington-post-the-everything-newspaper
14 Beaujon, ibid.
15 Beaujon, ibid.
16 Beaujon, ibid.
17 Beaujon, ibid.

FIVE

CREATIVITY AND INNOVATION

> It is my intention to restructure things in a way that honors and respects creativity as the heart and soul of who we are. (From Bob Iger's memo to Disney employees on returning to Disney as CEO, 2021.[1])

When Bob Iger returned as CEO of Disney in November 2022, his first major message to staff focused on creativity – he was going to return creativity to the heart of the organisation's activities after a three-year period where previous CEO, Bob Chapek, had rolled these areas into the distribution function. In reversing these changes, Iger was not only returning to Disney's historical roots but also underlining how creativity is essential to take advantage of new opportunities and meet the challenges in a rapidly evolving media landscape.

Creativity has always been central to the media industry and paramount for the success of organisations in it. Without creativity, the sector would not be able to produce the films, TV shows, music, games and articles that consumers enjoy. Creativity is strategic: it differentiates a media company from its competitors and makes it stand out in a crowded market (think of HBO). And, as technology evolves, the need for creativity is permeating more dimensions of media activity; it is necessary not simply to ensure a constant stream of successful products within established formats, but also to create new ways of telling stories and engaging audiences, and to create new products, work processes, ways of organising work and business models (see Bessant and Tidd, 2007).

Innovation and creativity are slippery concepts – related, but not the same thing. They are often used interchangeably, but this confuses two different streams of scientific research that have different scholarly associations, epistemological roots and areas of application. This chapter focuses particularly on creativity, partly because in recent years this element, which is foundational to the success of media organisations, has tended to be crowded out by an (understandable) focus on innovation.

Creativity refers to the process of coming up with new ideas or finding new ways to look at things. Innovation refers to the process of taking those creative ideas and turning them into something that is valuable and useful. In other words, creativity is about generating ideas, while innovation is about implementing those ideas and making them a reality. Research into creativity is based at root on psychology. It focuses on the initial inspiration – the 'bright idea' – that leads to the creation of a new product or service.

Innovation from this perspective is understood as the successful implementation of creative ideas in the shape of processes, products or services (Amabile, 1988, 1993; Woodman, in Ford and Gioia, 1995). It is the broader concept. Innovation theory concerns the processes by which products are manufactured, the organisation structures and strategies that support this process, and the relationship between innovation and corporate performance (Utterback, 1994). Thus, Janszen (2000: 8) defines innovation as 'the commercialization of something new'. Theories of innovation stem predominantly from the fields of engineering and technology management. These tend to subsume creativity under the umbrella term of innovation, viewing creativity as a subset of the broader domain of innovation, and innovation as a subset of an even broader construct of organisational change (Woodman et al., 1993). Innovation theory is closely linked to the study of entrepreneurship – thus, Drucker (1985: 26) describes it as 'the specific instrument of entrepreneurship'.

This chapter has strong links to earlier ones: creativity is the first stage of innovation, innovation is implicit in technological advance, and technological advances are a major driver of strategic change in the media. It also links to the next chapter on organisation culture – the unconscious beliefs, shared values and prevailing norms that make up culture must prioritise and promote the attitudes and activities that foster ongoing creativity and innovation (Tushman and O'Reilly, 2002; Flynn and Chatman, 2004; Dawson and Andriopoulos, 2021).

This chapter begins by reviewing theoretical understanding of creativity in organisational settings. It explores how understanding of the concept has developed over time, in the process delineating the distinction between creativity and innovation, two terms that are often frequently used interchangeably, but which in fact stem from different research streams. Socioconstructivist approaches to organisational creativity provide the foundation for the analysis. These explore the sources of creative responses in individuals, and the aspects of the work context that influence levels of creativity in organisations. This body of theory was not developed within the context of the media industry but is highly relevant to it. It addresses particular organisations with knowledge workers – professionals who are required to solve complex problems creatively – and it provides insights into the reasons behind performance differences betwen media firms.

Creativity in the media

Creativity is central to all organisations – a new idea is the uncircumventable first stage in all new organisational initiatives – whether involving products, processes or procedures (Amabile, 1988; Staw, 1990; Woodman et al., 1993), and these new products, processes and procedures are the cornerstone of an organisation's ability to adapt, grow and compete (Kanter, 1983, 1988; Porter, 1985; Van de Ven, 1986).

Creativity is arguably even more important for media firms – they don't need the odd great idea, but rather an ongoing supply (Caves, 2000; Towse, 2000; Hesmondhalgh, 2002). Performance is strongly affected by the quality of content they create, with 'create' being the operative word. The act of content generation is the sector's fundamental activity and *raison d'être*, and thus the requirement for creativity is constant.

From an economic perspective, creativity is a critical strategic resource because of the nature of cultural goods. Because they can rarely be standardised on a long-term basis and because customer demand is fickle, there is an incessant need for novelty. Viewed strategically, the higher the levels of product creativity, the higher the media firm's ability to satisfy this customer need and the greater the potential for market success and competitive advantage. This gives rise to the primacy of creativity as a strategic organisational resource, since unless employees can consistently generate ideas that can translate into commercial, saleable commodities, they cease to be able to compete.

The need for creativity – in all firms, not just media ones – is exacerbated when environments become more turbulent, an observation made decades ago by Schumpeter (1942) (DeVanna and Tichy, 1990; Bettis and Hitt, 1995; Ford and Gioia, 1995; Dutton et al., 1997; Hitt et al., 1998; Eisenhardt and Martin, 2000), especially when that turbulence involves emerging technologies (Yoffie, 1997), as is the case with the media sector. Thus, while creativity has always been critical to the media industry, technological change has both underlined the strategic centrality of creativity for the sector and expanded the scope within organisations where creativity is required. Media firms must not only be more creative with their products, but also organisationally and strategically. They must apply creativity to business models, the design of their organisations and the roles within it, and develop new products and services for entirely new categories of media platforms and audiences.

In a study of media majors' convergence strategies, Dennis et al. commented that:

> ... once associated with writers, producers and designers, creativity is now mentioned as an essential quality for managers and executives as well. Partly because some content producers are medium-centric and have little experience across platforms, business executives are increasingly asked to think creatively about integrating content, marketing strategies and audience data beyond decades old distribution channels as they seek new formats and communicative styles. Given the need for business models that exploit convergence, creativity is a critical skill set. (2006: 33)

Although strategy theorists agree on the importance of creativity to organisations, overall, surprisingly little attention has been devoted to increasing understanding of its origins and influence on performance. Indeed, this subject was long avoided, a tradition stretching back to Plato, who felt that creativity involved divine intervention and was therefore outside the scope of man's intervention. Popper concluded that research into creativity was irrelevant rather than unfeasible since creative inspiration is an irrational process and could not be accessed via scientific or systematic investigation. And for management researchers, especially those of the positivist school, the unconscious, inspirational component of creative acts made them hard to accommodate within rational management concepts.

Researching creativity

Despite these reservations, from the 1950s onwards, a steady and growing stream of researchers has investigated the nature and causes of creativity, albeit not within the context of the media industry. In the period from 1950 to the 1980s, there were two clear strands in this work: the first focused investigations on the creative individual and the second on the creative process.

Investigations into gifted individuals were premised on the assumption that creativity was determined at birth, that a few exceptional individuals are 'born creative'. This so-called 'person approach' looked at outstandingly creative individuals in the field of arts and science, often retrospectively through analysis of autobiographies, letters, journals and other first-person accounts, and sought to identify the cognitive processes and personality traits that might be predictive of creative performance (Barron and Harrington, 1981; Amabile, 1988, 1996; Deazin et al., 1999). A typical finding is Koestler's proposition that rather than being a random process, creativity results from the deliberate connection of two previously unconnected 'matrices of thought' (1964, cited in Amabile, 1996: 21). From studying gifted individuals' thought processes, research shifted to the wider personality of creative individuals – that is, to 'those patterns of traits that are characteristic of creative persons' (Guilford, 1950, cited in Amabile, 1996: 21), an approach rooted in psychometric testing.

The second major strand in creativity research concerned the process by which creative products are generated, the so-called 'process/product approach to creativity'. This concentrates on the characteristics of processes that lead to creative outcomes (Amabile, 1988, 1996; Oldham and Cummings, 1996) and has now become the dominant approach to the field (Amabile, 1983; Woodman et al., 1993).

Context was seldom an explicitly addressed variable in these studies, although the majority of these were conducted in creative or intellectual settings such as schools and cultural institutions (Ford, 1996). Over the years, the research domain has broadened to include more prosaic institutional settings (Ford and Gioia, 1995) and from group to pan-organisational environments, although investigations of small project groups have tended to dominate (Deazin et al., 1999).

An explicit focus on the influence of the work setting on creativity was absent until the 1980s when Amabile instituted a new branch of research (Staw, 1990; Ford and Gioia, 1995). This 'interactionist' or 'socio-constructivist' approach looks at how social influences and contextual factors influence creativity. Aspects previously stressed, such as cognitive skills, personality traits and process issues, are not ignored but subsumed into a larger framework. The approach is more egalitarian: creativity is not restricted to the chosen few; rather, it assumes that given the right task and circumstances most individuals are capable of creativity. To that extent it is also positivist, in that it assumes that changes in the environment can produce changes in levels of creativity. This has led to criticisms of functional-reductionism (Rousseau, 1985; Deazin et al., 1999).

This approach allows a coherent framework to be constructed concerning how strategic management can further creativity, and this provides a systematic strategy for building sustained creativity, and the backbone for the analysis and discussion in this chapter.

Factors that define creativity in an organisational context

> Content matters, that's the product that they're selling, it's entertainment. The thing that has surprised me most about Netflix is their struggles to get better at it.[2]

This chapter focuses on creativity inside media organisations, as applied to a product or service (and looks less at generating it at an individual level). Theories of organisational creativity define creativity as follows:

> A product or response will be judged as creative to the extent that (a) it is both a novel and appropriate, useful, correct or valuable response to the task at hand, and (b) the task is heuristic rather than algorithmic. (Amabile, 1996: 35)

Drawing on this, four criteria define creativity:

1 It is **novel, original** or **unique**, and solves a challenge that is open-ended, where there is no straightforward path to an acceptable outcome (in psychological terms, it delivers an heuristic rather than an algorithmic response). Originality and novelty for creative products, like those created in the media, often blend novel elements with familiar ones (Lampel et al., 2000). Synthesising these two is a highly subjective process that depends on high levels of sector expertise (the importance of expertise for sustained creativity is discussed below).

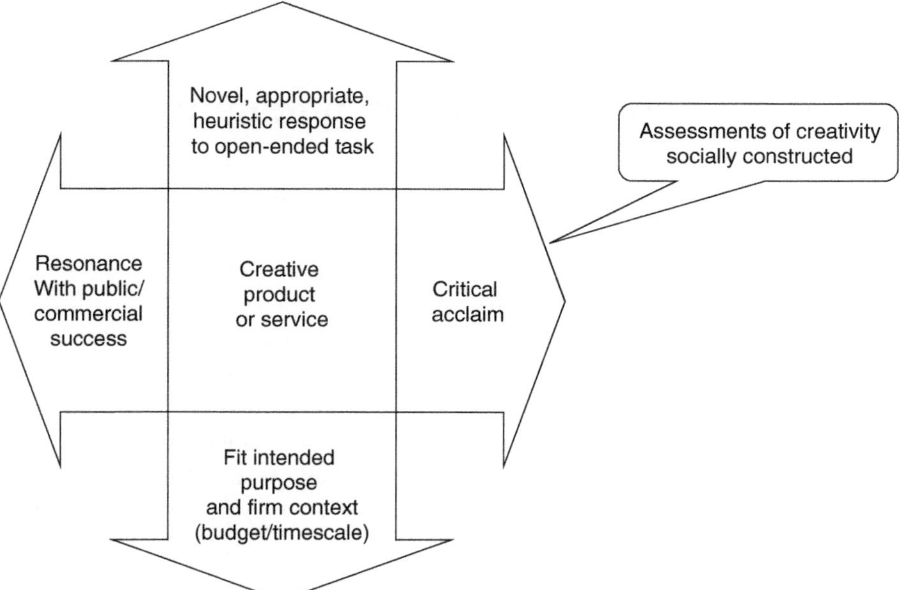

Figure 5.1 Defining criteria of creativity in organisational settings (adapted from Amabile, 1983, 1988, 1996)
© Lucy Küng

2 It **resonates with the public and/or finds commercial success**, and, by extension, it is useful, has value and/or brings benefits to others. An original product that pleases only those who created it, and perhaps a select group of industry experts, but which is not perceived by potential users or customers as valuable and novel and cannot be termed a successful creative entity according to this body of theory.

3 It **receives critical acclaim**. Assessments of creativity are socially constructed – that is, there are no absolute criteria for judging whether a product is creative or not; subjective judgement is always involved. That subjective judgement derives from the social context and development of the field. It is therefore impossible to judge the creativity of a product without some knowledge of what else exists in a domain at a given time (Amabile, 1996: 38) (which means that creativity is linked with experience and expertise of the field concerned). So, defining something as creative often includes assessments from industry experts – a function carried out in the media sector by industry awards.

4 Finally – and here the organisational perspective comes to the fore – to be creative, a product must help the organisation **meet its strategic objectives and work within available budgets and timeframes**.

Three building blocks of organisational creativity

The first stage in any new product or service depends on someone having a good idea – 'the creative spark' – and then being able to develop that idea further. Both the likelihood of having that initial idea and developing it into a concrete entity are strongly influenced by the social environment within organisations (Amabile et al., 1996). According to socioconstructivist approaches, creativity has three core components that need to be present in an organisation if creativity is to occur. These are outlined below (and discussed in detail in Amabile, 1983, 1988, 1993, 1996, 1998; Amabile et al., 1994, 1996, 2002, and the following text draws on these references unless otherwise indicated).

1. Creativity-relevant skills

The best way to have a good idea is to have lots of ideas. (Linus Pauling)

These refer to the ability to think creatively and generate different alternatives. Alternatives are necessary because individuals who have access to a variety of potentially relevant ideas are more likely to make the connections that can lead to creativity (Amabile et al., 1996). Creativity-relevant skills include:

- **Cognitive style.** This includes the ability to understand complexities, to break 'cognitive set' during problem-solving, to keep options open as long as possible, to suspend judgement, to use 'wide' categories allowing relationships to be found between apparently diverse pieces of information, to remember accurately and to break out of 'performance scripts'. Bennis and Biederman (1997) point out that members of highly creative teams tend to enjoy this kind of problem-solving activity for its own sake.
- **Creativity heuristics.** This involves ways of approaching a problem that can lead to set-breaking and novel ideas. They can be highly idiosyncratic, but they should allow the exploration of new cognitive pathways.
- **Working style.** Creativity requires a working style that has little to do with preconceptions about how 'creative individuals' go about their work. Rather, it involves a set of pragmatic abilities: to concentrate for long periods, to abandon unproductive searches or temporarily give up on stubborn problems, persistence, high energy levels, high levels of productivity, self-discipline, an ability to delay gratification, perseverance in the face of frustration, independent judgement, a tolerance for ambiguity, a willingness to take risks, and a high level of self-initiated, task-orientated striving for excellence.

2. Expertise

Known as 'domain-relevant skills', expertise represents a combination of knowledge of the existing facts and issues concerning a specific area (or domain), coupled with the experience necessary to be able to find feasible solutions to problems in that field. Expertise, unsurprisingly, arises from immersion and experience, and for that reason, newcomers to an area who lack knowledge of prior work are unlikely to be able to come up with truly path-breaking, creative solutions. Expertise in the media field tends to rest on tacit rather than codified knowledge (Lampel et al., 2000). It stems not from qualifications attained, say, in the fields of engineering or finance, but from a combination of experience derived from exposure to the field and individual judgement and intuition.

3. Intrinsic motivation

> The greatest pleasure that life has to offer is the satisfaction that flows from participating in a difficult and challenging undertaking. (Mihaly Csikszentmihalyi, 1996)

Intrinsic motivation, the final component of creativity listed here, is first among equals. It provides the cornerstone for this body of theory (which is known as the 'intrinsic motivation theory of creativity'). Intrinsic motivation will be familiar to many as 'flow'. It means being motivated to do something for its own sake, because the task is in itself pleasurable and rewarding, rather than because it is a means to meet an extrinsic goal.

Intrinsic motivation matters for creativity because it makes people curious, and encourages them to experiment and break with established ways of doing things (McGraw and Fiala, 1982; Amabile, 1988). Intrinsic motivation is linked to cognitive flexibility – the ability to change viewpoints, connect elements in new ways, and categorise issues in new ways – and it has been suggested that this is the mediating element between intrinsic motivation and individual creativity (Li et al., 1998).

In the intrinsically motivated state, or flow state, individuals are more likely to take risks, explore new solutions and experiment. Intrinsic motivation explains why many talented and highly educated individuals are keen to work in the media industry and creative arts despite relatively low salaries: the state of flow is so gratifying that people will tolerate low pay (or no pay at all in the case of industry internships), and in extreme cases physical or psychological discomfort to achieve it, something that the media industry and cultural sector wittingly or unwittingly has long exploited.

By contrast, external motivation – the motivation that results from external goals – can undermine creativity. External motivation is motivation that arises from sources outside the task – evaluation, deadlines, rewards such as bonuses, competition – a nagging parent in the case of children. It is important to note that extrinsic motivation does not preclude high-quality output. It can give rise to good work but is unlikely to lead to creative breakthroughs because it narrows the cognitive focus and precludes the path-breaking novel solutions that are the hallmark of true creativity. Indeed, external motivators such as financial rewards have been found to 'crowd out' intrinsic motivation (Frey and Jegen, 2000), as Drucker pointed out when he warned against 'bribing' knowledge workers with stock options (Drucker, 1985).

Designing a work environment to boost intrinsic motivation

> We learned that the only way for businesses to consistently succeed today is to attract smart creative employees and create an environment where they thrive at scale. (Google founder Eric Schmidt, cited in Schmidt et al., 2014)

'Organising' for creativity may sound like a contradiction in terms; theory shows that specific aspects in how work is designed have a direct impact on levels of intrinsic motivation, and therefore on creativity. Five aspects have been identified as particularly influential: encouragement, challenge, autonomy, resources, and team composition and function.[3]

1. Encouragement

If creativity is required from staff, then those in charge need explicitly to request it, and ground this request in an explanation of why it is important. Often a company will say that it prioritises creativity but takes no further steps to demonstrate that commitment. Actions that do demonstrate that creativity is a priority include how key strategic goals and key performance indicators (KPIs) are set, which projects are put at the top of the agenda, which projects or teams are given resources, and which behaviours or teams are most highly rewarded. Reactions to creative contributions are important. They need to be acknowledged and publicly celebrated if special in any way, and there needs to be thoughtful feedback. Attention must be paid to all suggestions, good or bad, and ideas that are unsuitable need to be evaluated constructively. If creative ideas are disregarded or handled clumsily, staff can feel that the interest in creativity is only cosmetic, and experimentation will be discouraged. This is dangerous since high levels of creativity need high levels of experimentation.

2. The creative challenge and how it is framed

> Creative people work for the love of a challenge. They crave the feeling of accomplishment that comes from cracking a riddle … they want to do good work. (Florida and Goodnight, 2005: 127)

Encouragement	Creativity needs explicit encouragement. Real value of project must be clear.
Challenge	Project goals should be clear, stable and feasible. Too much challenge overwhelms and demotivates.
Resources	Financial: • 'Resource slack' (over-generous funding) reduces focus and discipline. • Parsimony (too little funding) means creativity will be channelled into increasing the budgets for the project. Time: • Over-tight deadlines reduce the scope for 'combinatorial play' and bring the risk of burnout.
Autonomy	Freedom concerning means but not ends. Autonomy concerning process fosters ownership and intrinsic motivation.
Team composition	Team should comprise a diversity of perspectives, experience and backgrounds.

Figure 5.2 Contextual factors influencing levels of intrinsic motivation (adapted from Amabile, 1983, 1988, 1993, 1996, 1998; Amabile et al., 1994, 1996, 2002)

Creativity is enhanced by clearly defined overall project goals (Amabile and Gryskiewicz, 1989). A creative challenge must be clear, unambiguous and feasible – it can be complex, too. Tasks that are demanding, multifaceted and non-routine increase intrinsic motivation (Amabile, 1988; Oldham and Cummings, 1996). But the degree of stretch needs to be calibrated carefully – complex creative challenges should be mobilising but not overwhelming, and there needs to be a good match with expertise and creative-thinking skills. Kanter (2006) describes how adjusting the creative challenge increased creativity at *Time* magazine. When CEO Don Logan took over in 1992, the magazine was poor at developing new titles. He increased creativity by reframing the creative challenge: staff should experiment to find original ideas with long-term potential. With this, he reversed the previous requirement that new concepts should have immediate bestseller potential.

3. Autonomy

> We recently greenlit a particular Amazon Studios original. I was in doubt if it would be interesting enough, but the team had a completely different opinion and wanted to go ahead. I wrote back right away with, 'I disagree and commit and hope it becomes the most watched thing we've ever made.' Consider how much slower this decision cycle would have been if the team had actually had to convince me rather than simply get my commitment (Jeff Bezos[4]).

Autonomy is perhaps first among equals of the contextual factors required for high levels of intrinsic motivation. Jeff Bezos's quote clearly indicates that giving his creatives the support to make decisions as they see fit is central to his leadership approach. In this context, autonomy means that the creative team need space and scope to solve their creative challenge, which means limiting organisational constraints such as unnecessary reporting requirements or non-essential organisational tasks.

Critically, the creative team needs autonomy in terms of deciding how they will meet their goal – that is, concerning the process by which they solve their problem. This does not extend to autonomy in setting the goal itself (and the goal itself should remain clear, constant and unambiguous). This has been described as giving the team the freedom to work out how they climb the mountain, but not to decide which mountain they climb. Autonomy over process fosters creativity because it heightens the sense of ownership, and therefore intrinsic motivation, and also allows employees to approach problems in ways that make the most of their expertise.

That small group autonomy is important for creativity is an established tenet in the media. News Corp, like Bertelsmann, has long seen the creation of small, decentralised groups as critical for generating quality content within the context of a large global media conglomerate. Founder Rupert Murdoch has spoken of the need to balance encouraging independence while ensuring overall responsibility. His strategy is to give 'local' leaders the freedom to deal with problems as they arise, but he will personally intervene if necessary in crisis situations (Coleridge, 1993).

4. Resources

> If you're trying to create a company, it's like baking a cake. You have to have all the ingredients in the right proportion. (Elon Musk[5])

Money and time are the critical resources for boosting intrinsic motivation. As with autonomy, levels need to be carefully judged. They should be sufficient to allow the task to be achieved, but neither over-generous – 'resource slack' (over-generous resources) can reduce project focus and discipline (Nohria and Gulati, 1996), while miserly funding will result in creativity being channelled into the problem of finding the funds necessary to complete the task.

Deadlines for creative projects need to be carefully judged. Despite the received wisdom that deadlines focus the mind and increase creativity, if these are too demanding and unrealistic, staff will have no time to 'play' with concepts and solutions. Time to play is important since creativity results from the formation of many associations in the mind, followed by the selection of associations that are particularly interesting and useful. Time pressure will limit or remove entirely the scope for such combinatorial play, and may additionally risk burnout in the creative team.

5. Team composition

> Smart creatives ... are the product folks who combine technical knowledge, business expertise and creativity. When you put today's technology tools in their hands and give them lots of freedom they can do amazing things amazingly fast. (Google founder Eric Schmidt, Schmidt et al., 2014)

Creativity is reflexively seen as a solitary phenomenon (the lonely artist in the garret). This may be true for great cultural works generated by individuals, but creativity in organisational settings needs the coordinated contributions of a diverse team, where diversity includes perspective, expertise, background and preferred approach to problem solving.

Diversity matters because creative challenges are often epistemologically unsolvable by any one person. They require input from a range of specialist disciplines and a broad palette of expertise. Teams that are homogeneous can hinder creativity, since there will be too much similarity in experience and approach to the task, plus too much social cohesion can inhibit the exchange of ideas. Within the team, working practices need to be open to encourage the constructive challenging of ideas and shared commitment, which in time can allow the development of a strong subculture. Attention needs to be given to the team's communication skills. If these are poor, necessary expertise and insights will not be shared, particularly the tacit knowledge that emerges during the project (Kanter, 2006).

Creativity in creative organisations

A small body of work focuses on creativity in creative organisations. Lampel et al. (2000) note that because the creative quality of creative products is hard to judge since their consumption is highly subjective, defining creativity in creative contexts is difficult. They draw a distinction between commercial creative organisations and ones that are primarily engaged in cultural and artistic endeavours. Whereas in cultural organisations, creative products must 'only' satisfy artistic and cultural criteria, in commercial creative organisations they need to meet commercial objectives too, which entails their finding a market, and if they are too creative and original, this may not succeed, meaning they need to synthesise new and familiar elements (Lampel et al., 2000).

Gil and Spiller (2007: 245–6) identify several essential characteristics of creative work in creative organisations (which they describe as 'internal creative production') that cause challenges 'quite different from the standard' in organisations:

- An informational asymmetry between creatives and management because creatives have an expertise that management do not have and possibly do not understand.
- Management cannot force the creation of high-quality work; rather, they can only create conditions that are conducive to it occurring.
- The 'infinite variety' problem, which means there are an infinite number of possible solutions to any creative challenge and a manager cannot specify in advance what output is sought, nor can a creative employee specify what will be produced.
- The 'nobody knows' problem, which arises from the fact that the performance of a creative product is virtually impossible to predict, and even when a formula works once, there is little guarantee that it can be repeated in exactly that way. Thus, the average internal rate of return in the movie industry is negative (Dekom, in Squire, 2004) and the majority of new books published fail to earn back their authors' advances.
- The 'art for art's sake' problem. Creatives are intrinsically motivated and work on creative projects because of the sense of fulfilment or achievement it brings. This means high levels of commitment, engagement and ownership, but also an unwillingness to compromise on their creative solutions. This can make management interventions difficult and lead to time and cost overruns.
- Many creative products have very high development costs, which, because of the uncertainties implicit in creative markets, can spiral out of control. Even with troubled projects, problems in development do not preclude market success. This, coupled with a wish to avoid 'sunk costs', can mean that a decision is made to invest further, leading to the 'Ten-Ton Turkey Syndrome' (Caves, 2000).
- Creative expertise cannot be appropriated by organisations but resides with the owners of that talent. Particular creative talents may become identified with particular products, and future attempts to exploit that product may encounter a hold-up from that creative talent. Similarly, creative staff may not share all their creative ideas with their current

employer. Thus, creative businesses are subsidising the future career opportunities of their creative talent.

Conclusions

So far, this book has looked primarily at the strategic environment, the sectors that make up the media industries and key developments taking place in them. This chapter focuses on the impact of the strategic context on the internal organisation of the media firm. It is also unusual among the other chapters in this book in that it focuses mainly on one particular stream of theory, socio-constructivist approaches to organisational creativity, whereas previous chapters have, in the main, covered a far broader theoretical terrain. The reason for this lies primarily in this research stream's high relevance for the field. Sustained creativity is one of the prime drivers of above-average performance in the sector and the need for creativity is enlarged when environments become unstable. This body of theory provides insights into how levels of creativity may be improved.

A key message is that creativity is influenced by what can feel like relatively mundane aspects of projects – elements such as deadlines, financial resources, team composition and goal setting. Two aspects of this are interesting. The first is the sustained performance outcomes that can result when these elements are well and coherently managed, and, by extension, the scope for optimising creativity that probably exists in media organisations. The second is how some findings from this body of theory undercut received wisdom in the media industry. To take the hit model, this proposes that market success is contingent in large part on the amount invested in creative talent and processes – that higher budgets mean higher audiences. However, this framework shows that creative projects do not benefit from unlimited resources, and may perhaps even be harmed by them. This chapter also provides additional evidence of the importance of autonomy for creative teams, something that can be threatened by moves towards consolidation and cross-platform integration.

The impact of creativity in the wider organisation – in structures, processes and systems – is also explored. This underlines that not only do aspects of the creative project environment need to be carefully thought out and integrated, but they need to harmonise with wider systems, strategies, processes and business models. A more intimate understanding of these systems and their interrelationships will contribute fruitful insights into how media firms can improve both creativity and performance.

Resources

Books

Some of the best insights on creating environments that are conducive to creativity come from business leaders' biographies. For example, Robert Iger (2019) *The Ride of a Lifetime*, New York: Bantam Press, and Ed Catmull (2014) *Creativity Inc*. New York: Bantam Press.

Extensive resources are available on how to increase your own creativity. Check out Mihaly Csikszentmihalyi (2013), *Creativity: The Psychology of Discovery and Invention* (New York: Harper Perennial). To raise your children to be creative, look at Teresa M. Amabile (1989) *Growing Up Creative* (New York: Crown).

Mumford, D.D. and Todd, E.M. (eds) (2020) *Creativity and Innovation in Organizations*. New York: Routledge.

On Creativity, from the Harvard Business School Press (2022), is a compendium of the Harvard Business Reviews' top ten articles on cultivating creativity at work. Valuable for a deep but accessible dive into the subject.

A classic work in the field is *Flow* by Mihaly Csikszentmikalyi (1990), Harper & Row.

Video

If you are curious about how specific leaders prioritise or drive creativity and innovation, check out YouTube videos – for example, to learn more on Elon Musk's approach to creativity, see www.youtube.com/watch?v=Owa-tzQqVpc, and how Jeff Bezos encourages staff to be innovative, see www.youtube.com/watch?v=97h6ECZnf9o

Case: Founding CNN: creativity in systems and strategy

Creativity is increasingly required in the broader set of activities concerned with how organisations mount a response to their strategic environment. Novel ideas are needed to enable media firms to grow, adapt and compete. As we have seen, the media industry has been subject to a continuous stream of fundamental changes in the technologies used to develop and deliver products. This stream of change triggers in itself a fundamental ongoing need for renewal in terms of systems, process and strategy, irrespective of the need to develop new media products. Organisations that master these challenges can establish powerful bases of strategic advantage.

CNN, during the first 16 years of its life (from its founding in 1980 to its takeover by Time Warner in 1996), displayed creativity in terms of developing systems and strategy. Many aspects of CNN's concept have since been widely adopted by the industry – to the point that they are the norm – but they were path-breaking when they arrived. This point underlines the temporary nature of creative advantage – good creative ideas that are replicable will be replicated.

The idea behind CNN was to set up a channel that concentrated only on news and to broadcast that news around the clock. The news would be global and it would be live. CNN would aim to cover news as it happened, giving a sense of dynamism, rather than report after the fact – creating a more static output. A central new concept here was to create 'a role in the process for the viewers'. This would be achieved by avoiding the groomed, closed-set approach of the US networks in favour of open sets within newsrooms, and a presenting style that was 'on the ground', creating a sense of immediacy, authenticity, of news happening as viewers watched and allowing viewers to viscerally experience the process. Overcoming industry cynicism, this unconventional approach held real attraction for viewers and revitalised what had become a stale genre, so much so that two decades later, the CNN style had become a standard for news delivery worldwide.

The core product was pathbreaking and can be categorised as creative. Creativity was also evident in the systems and processes that supported the content proposition. The concept of CNN was designed to exploit several simultaneous technological advances and use these to reinvent the way that news is produced and delivered. These technological advances included cable television, communications satellites, suitcase-size satellite uplinks and handy cams. Resources – time and money – were limited and CNN needed to be creative in how it structured its business too. Its most famous innovation is probably the invention of the video journalist or VJ: a 'one-person television band' that is capable of covering a story without the expense of a full film crew, shooting video as well as reporting and then editing the material too.

(Continued)

Organisational creativity can be found in the network of broadcast affiliates all over the world that CNN set up. The traditional affiliate relationship to that point was one-way, from the channel or network to the affiliate, and most news organisations pride themselves on the exclusivity of their content. CNN revisited this approach by establishing a reciprocal network of 600 television stations worldwide, which both received news feeds from CNN and fed local footage back to CNN. This was initially a pragmatic solution to the need to offer global coverage without adequate resources, but it became a strategic asset in that it enabled CNN to build a global presence quickly, defray the cost of its own newsgathering and provided footage of breaking events all over the world far more quickly than its competitors could get news crews on the scene.

Case: HBO – strategic differentiation through creativity

> HBO has shaped a creative environment which almost anyone would tell you is the best place to work in town. (Peter Chernin, then President and COO News Corporation, April 2003[6])

Despite facing unrelenting industry competition and being involved in 'the two worst mergers of the century'[7] (being acquired first by AOL and then by AT&T), Home Box Office (HBO) is still widely recognised as one of the most reliable and higher performing creators of television.

HBO's origins share similarities with CNN's. It was founded by Time Inc. in New York in 1972 as a paid movie/special service cable operation. Like CNN, the early HBO was known for its frugal spending in comparison with its peers (Shamsie, 2003). It couldn't compete with ABC, CBS and NBC, so instead it counter-programmed with original entertainment content comprising one-hour stand-up comic specials and concerts, and boxing. And, like CNN, it took an early bet on emerging technologies, making an investment in RCA satellites which would allow it to cover the entire US, and, like CNN's original news services, when HBO launched into original programming, industry peers sneered.

From these inauspicious beginnings, HBO's original programming division grew into an industry leader for premium content and has over many years reliably delivered over the decades a chain of critical and commercial hits, ranging from *The Sopranos*, *Sex and the City* and *Six Feet Under*, to *Succession* and *Game of Thrones*. Its strategy is one of differentiation based on the creativity of

(Continued)

its programming. This is captured in the slogan 'It's not TV, it's HBO', which holds as good today as it did when it was first coined.

Successful – creatively and financially

> HBO remains the premier artisanal content creator — garnering nearly three times the Emmys per dollar spent than Netflix, and four times as many as newcomer Apple. (Scott Galloway[8])

HBO meets theoretical definitions of creativity to a degree unusual in an industry where the 'mud against the wall' approach to finding hits is standard (see p. 30). HBO shows are novel – an HBO's trademark is its ability to disregard the elements judged to be prerequisites of commercial successes by other broadcast networks, such as likeable characters or clear underlying premises (Shamsie, 2003). They are also **successful**. In terms of critical acclaim, in 2022, in a much more competitive field than it had grown up in, it still managed to win the most Emmy awards[9] (38), followed by Netflix, which won 26. Overall, HBO Max's SVoD service had the highest volume of award-winning content in the US,[10] a reflection of its consistent focus on premium top-end content:

> The focus on quality over quantity is key to retaining and growing a subscriber base whilst maintaining a smaller library ... Those that are victorious at well-established awards ceremonies, such as the Emmys, not only prove their quality but can help elevate a title's profile to increase engagement.[11]

HBO's creative performance has translated into **strong subscriber numbers**. Q1 2022[12] results for HBO and HBO Max showed 76.8m total global subscribers and 48.6m domestic subscribers. In Q2 2022, Warner Bros. Discovery (HBO's new owner) reported that total direct-to-consumer subscribers for HBO, HBO Max and Discovery+ were 92.1 million, but figures were not broken down by individual network.[13] Financial performance is harder to assess because HBO's conglomerate owners tend not to break out figures for its financial performance from group results, but in 2019, when HBO was owned by WarnerMedia (part of AT&T) it was reported that operating revenues for HBO were $6.75 billon.[14]

Three organisational elements drive creativity in organisations – expertise, creative thinking skills and intrinsic motivation. At HBO, its sector expertise stands out. Creative leaders combine a deep knowledge of the

(Continued)

aethestic and cultural components of entertainment content in the widest sense – script writing, plot, character, dialogue, and so on, with a deep knowledge of how the business of TV works – that is, of audience behaviour and preferences, and the nuances of a business model. Interestingly, HBO avoids over-dependence on one top creative leader. Rather, its top creative leaders are required to develop the next generation of talent to ensure that they create leaders who will 'carry the baton to the next generation.[15]

Further expertise comes from freelance creative staff. Here a virtuous circle comes into play: the critical praise received by HBO programmes attracts high-calibre writers who want to be involved in HBO programmes. Their high-calibre skills contribute to the ongoing creative quality of the channel's output, which in turn leads to commercial and critical success, continuing to attract high-quality creative freelancers.

The contextual factors that are necessary to trigger intrinsic motivation and thus creativity are also present. These are summarised in Figure 5.3. First, in terms of creative challenge, creativity is intrinsic to its strategic vision and its core mandate. Its strategic positioning is 'to be good and different' (Shamsie, 2003: 63) and its advertising strapline is 'It's not TV, it's HBO'. This means that HBO is looking for shows that are different and unique, and don't look like series that have been seen before. They 'really believe in pilots and getting the story off on the right foot. They keep things in development until it feels right'.[16] Pilots with test screening approval over 75 per cent are rejected on the basis that anything so acceptable to the 'conservative masses' is unlikely to be edgy enough for HBO, and conversely shows that may initially confuse audiences are accepted.

Explicitly demands creativity	Core mandate is 'to be good and different': 'It's not broadcasting, it's HBO'. Entire strategy is based on 'differentness'.
Sets clear creative challenge	Overall objective is crisp, concise and inspiring: to create 'series that will gain creative approval and commercial success'.
Provides adequate resources	Funding is substantial, but not over-generous. Long-term commitment to projects and writers.
Provides autonomy for creative teams	Teams have creative freedom within tightly controlled operation. Distinct HBO identity. Low bureaucracy: 'ideas aren't nibbled to death by ducks'.

Figure 5.3 HBO's factors encouraging intrinsic motivation

© Lucy Küng

(Continued)

> There is this very specific playbook they go back to: trust the artist. They are not relying on an algorithm or data to influence programming choices. Market research tells you what's in the past. It doesn't tell you what's coming next.[17]

In terms of autonomy, HBO has always sought to ensure that staff have the scope to hit stretching goals, particularly that they have the space to concentrate on the creative task. In the words of Alan Ball, screenwriter of *Six Feet Under*, 'there's less levels of bureaucracy to dig through.... To make a good show on HBO is almost easier work. You're living and dying by what you believe in, and you're not being nibbled to death by ducks' (cited in Shamsie, 2003: 64). This means that notes (comments on ideas under development) come from just one or two people, and those people are regarded as experts (in contrast, networks' notes can come from up to ten different reviewers and can be contradictory, the net result of which can be to shift the idea towards standard approaches).

Despite being successively part of large media empires, HBO, probably because of its evident success, has so far been fortunate to consistently have had high levels of independence, being physically and operationally removed from its conglomerate parent's other TV activities. Further, its policy is to give its staff scope for creativity within a tightly controlled operation – writers have high levels of artistic freedom but must seek to create series that will garner critical acclaim and approval with the viewing public. HBO's business model also contributes to creative autonomy, since cable subscription funding means that it is less reliant on fast ratings success and less burdened by regulation than the mainstream networks.

With regard to resources, HBO is adequately funded, but finances are not over-abundant. However, the fact that it is subscription-financed means that its income is relatively secure and not too sensitive to dips in the overall economy (which affect media advertising spend disproportionately). In terms of time, HBO's deadlines allow staff to play with concepts: it is unique in the industry for offering writers a five-year contract, with the explicit goal of providing creative stability and the psychological freedom to take risks.

Case questions

1 Do you agree that HBO is a creative organisation? Which other television series producers also qualify in your opinion?

2 Which factors drive HBO's high and consistent level of creativity?

3 HBO's current owner, Warner Bros. Discovery, has (at the time of writing), over $53 billion debt. It looks likely to integrate HBO into other services as a cost-saving measure. If you were CEO, would you do this too?

Case: Pixar, 'The most reliable creative force in Hollywood'[18]

Pixar Animation Studios has prioritised organisational creativity since it was founded in 1986. It came into being when Steve Jobs purchased the computer division of Lucasfilm using $5 million of his personal funds and set up a new company, of which he became Chairman and CEO (he invested a further $5 million to finance the company). At that point, the primary asset was the Pixar Imaging Computer, which had been designed for film frames but also had uses in business-to-business (B2B) fields, such as medical imaging and design prototyping.

The first decade was a struggle financially. Pixar was searching for a business model and was, as Catmull observes (2014: 52), 'mostly just haemorrhaging money'. It needed frequent cash injections from Jobs, who tried to sell Pixar three times between 1987 and 1991, but each time walked away from the deal at the last minute. The Pixar Imaging Computer had sold only a few hundred units and revenues came mainly from sales of its software. It also produced animated commercials (up to 15 a year) and, while these won awards and allowed it to hone its technical and story-telling skills, it had to lay off over a third of its employees in 1991. This period did, however, produce early indicators of Pixar's future path and future creative success in the shape of two highly acclaimed short films, *Luxo Jnr* (1986) and *Tin Toy* (1988), the first computer-animated film to win an Academy Award.

In 1991 the five-year-old Pixar signed a deal with Disney for three digital animation movies: Pixar would create these and Disney would own them and distribute them, retaining 90 per cent of the profits and the merchandising rights. Jeffrey Katzenberg, head of Disney's motion picture division, also wanted to buy Pixar's technology, to which Steve Jobs reputedly replied: 'You're giving us money to make the film, not to buy our trade secrets' (Catmull, 2014: 55).

The first movie produced under this deal, *Toy Story*, was released in 1995. It was the first full-length 3D animated feature film, the first to win an Academy Award, and broke box office records. Jobs presciently proposed this was the moment to go public: Toy Story was going to be a huge success, Disney would realise it had helped create a competitor, and when its deal with Pixar came up for renegotiation it would probably try to clip Pixar's wings, whereas Pixar should actually be seeking a 50/50 revenue split. But an equal revenue split would require Pixar to finance half the production budgets, which it currently did not have the financial resources to do. Hence the plan to go public: this would provide the necessary finance to allow Pixar to fund half of production budgets for its movies, and in return it would receive half the revenues from

(Continued)

them. Jobs had called the situation correctly. The IPO raised $140 million, and when Disney sought to renegotiate the deal, Pixar received a deal featuring an equal split of both production investments and profits (less a distribution fee of 12 per cent).

Following the success of *Finding Nemo* (2003), Pixar wanted to renegotiate again. Disney refused and relations soured, not least because Eisner had exercised Disney's right to make sequels to Pixar movies without Pixar's input. The partnership ended in January 2004, but after Eisner left in 2005 the relationship was rebuilt after reconciliation efforts by incoming CEO, Bob Iger. In 2006, Disney bought Pixar outright for $7.4 billion, Jobs joined the Disney board and Pixar's John Lasseter became Disney's Chief Creative Officer and Ed Catmull became President. Bob Iger describes how acquiring Pixar was central to the creative regeneration of Disney's own animation business:

> What I wanted to do more than anything is, I wanted to send a signal to everybody at Disney that it was a new day, that we were more open-minded about expansion, in particular about partnerships,' Iger said. 'That creativity was the most important strategy for the company. And Pixar, at that point, exemplified original storytelling and quality and creativity at its highest form.[19]

Pixar's output meets all the defining criteria for creative products outlined in this chapter. In terms of **novelty** and uniqueness, Pixar films were novel, not only in their content but because they reinvented the somewhat tired animated film genre. They abandoned hand-drawn animation in favour of digital techniques but used these to create extraordinary levels of texture and sensory detail – the matted wet rat fur in *Ratatouille*, for example.

Creativity was apparent also in a basic notion fundamental to Pixar's business model – that an animated film could be made sophisticated enough to appeal to adults as well as children, and therefore to work for both markets simultaneously.

Pixar's output succeeded at the box office, but in addition to commercial success, it also received high levels of critical acclaim, as evidenced by the many industry accolades the studio has won. In terms of fit with organisational requirements, Pixar places great emphasis on ensuring that its movies are developed on schedule and to budget (see the discussion later in this chapter on Pixar's process for resolving the inherent tension between setting stretching creative goals and the need to respect financial and time limits). Pixar has always believed in ensuring it has the best expertise on the market, as Ed Catmull explains:

> I've made a policy of trying to hire people who are smarter than I. (Catmull, 2014: 23)

(Continued)

Pixar is renowned for its technological expertise, and this has developed through a series of innovations it has made in the field of digital animation, dating back to RenderMan, a programming language that allows disparate parts of the 3D production process to connect and communicate. This was made available commercially and became an industry standard, as did a batch of associated programs covering other aspects of the computer-animation process that it developed and marketed. Its mastery of the artistic skills involved in animated filmmaking is also widely respected, as are its narrative skills in the field of storytelling, script writing, portrayal of characters and storyboarding.

Short films are a key mechanism to building new expertise. The tradition started in the early 1980s and the first wave of films functioned as a means of sharing Pixar innovations with the scientific community. Pixar stopped producing them in 1996, and then restarted, booking the costs under the R&D budget (in a similar move to digital publishers who charged early digital experiments to their training and development budget). Pixar's 'second-generation shorts' served several purposes, all central to furthering creativity. They allowed staff to develop a broader range of skills, forced technological advances (in the rendering of difficult characteristics like faces, hands or water, for example), and provided a way for the smaller teams who worked on them to form deeper relationships with colleagues, built goodwill with filmgoers, demonstrated Pixar's commitment to artistry (because the shorts have no commercial value) and provided a relatively inexpensive way to make mistakes.

Expertise is built, too, through meticulous research. Filmmakers on *Finding Nemo* visited sewage treatment plants and learned to scuba dive. Those working on *Monsters University* visited dormitories, lecture halls and research labs at MIT, Harvard, and Princeton, 'documenting everything … right down to … what the graffiti scratches looked like on the wooden desks' (Pixar Art Department Manager, cited in Catmull, 2014: 197).

The contextual factors that are necessary to trigger intrinsic motivation and thus creativity are also present. To start with **creative challenge**, at Pixar this comes from the top. Jobs's overt goal for the organisation was 'to let creativity flourish'. For Catmull, the challenge was larger than simply commercially successful creativity:

> My hope was to make this culture so vigorous that it would survive when Pixar's founding members were long gone, enabling the company to continue producing original films that made money, yes, but also contributed positively to the world. That sounds like a lofty goal, but it was there for all of us from the beginning. (Catmull, 2014: 65)

(Continued)

Part of Catmull's strategy to achieve this is to avoid a syndrome termed 'Feed the Beast'. This arises when the success of each new film enlarges the marketing infrastructure, creating a compulsion to create more products simply to fill this pipeline (Catmull, 2014). Instead, Pixar focuses on a small number of films. To keep the creative challenge manageable, creatives are encouraged to break down larger tasks into creative steps.

Pixar's resource strategy has developed through trial and error. Striving for greatness can result in very long lists of ideal features that filmmakers would like to incorporate in their projects. Deadlines are used to force both a priority-based reordering of such wish-lists, and difficult decisions about which items on the lists are not feasible and will need to be dropped. Catmull (2014: 199–200) describes how:

> We have constantly struggled with how we set useful limits and how we make them visible ... The very concept of a limit implies you can't do everything you want – you must think of smarter ways to work.

In terms of autonomy, unusually Pixar staff are authorised, whatever their position, 'to stop the assembly line, both figuratively and literally' if they feel things are going wrong. This is part of an overall approach that requires staff to solve problems when they surface, without first asking permission, which means that it is also accepted that this may result in mistakes. This philosophy extends right up to the top of the organisation, whereby Steve Jobs also encouraged Pixar to function autonomously, recognising that the organisation's considerable expertise was in a different domain to his own. As Catmull (2014: 100) describes, 'at Pixar, he didn't believe his instincts were better than the people here, so he stayed out'.

Teamwork is the basic building block of Pixar's *modus operandi*. It seeks to promote 'unfettered group invention' and stresses that its films are the product of groups, rather than of key individuals. A Pixar tool for maximising teamwork is The Braintrust, which is:

> ... the primary mechanism to push us toward excellence and to root out mediocrity … our primary delivery mechanism for straight talk … one of the important traditions at Pixar. (Catmull, 2014: 86)

This meets every few months to assess each movie as it develops. Feedback is constructive and focused on solving problems within an atmosphere of trust and mutual respect and rooted in shared beliefs. The first belief is that 'Pixar films are not good at first, and our job is to make them so' (Catmull, 2014: 90), and the second is that 'People who take on complicated creative projects

(Continued)

become lost at some point in the process' (Catmull, 2014: 91). Underlying this is an additive approach that 'starts with the understanding that each participant contributes something, even if it's only an idea that fuels the discussion or ultimately doesn't work' (Catmull, 2014: 101). Pixar's Operating Principles (Catmull, 2022: 47) seek to ensure that ideas can flow freely between team members, by explicitly stating that 'Everyone must have the freedom to communicate with anyone', and 'It must be safe for everyone to offer ideas'.

An equally important element of the teamwork process is the post-mortem. This is a meeting held shortly after a movie is completed where the team explores what worked and what didn't, and aims to consolidate key learnings. Historical data are analysed, too: Pixar tracks the rates at which things happen, and how long processes actually take versus estimates, in the goal of identifying patterns and providing inputs on where improvements can be made.

Setting the creative challenge	Overall goals are to 'let creativity flourish' (Jobs) and 'produce films that contribute positively to the world' (Catmull). Shuns the hit model – doesn't fall into the trap of 'feeding the beast'. Concentrates creative energy on a few products of the highest standard.
Resources	Financial – adequate but not over-generous. Deadlines are used as a mechanism for teams to identify real priorities and work smarter. Tries to avoid burnout.
Autonomy	'[Jobs'] talent is to identify good people and give them free rein.' Staff can 'stop the production line' if things are not working. People are encouraged to solve problems without permission, and mistakes are tolerated as the inevitable consequence.
Teamwork	Seeks to promote 'unfettered group invention'. Teams are the basic building block of output; films are produced by teams, not individuals. 'Braintrust' concept is used to push towards excellence. 'Post mortems' are used to consolidate new learning.

Figure 5.4 Factors boosting intrinsic motivation at Pixar

(Continued)

Case questions

1 Do you agree that Pixar is a creative organisation? Which other animated film produers or game studios also qualify in your opinion?

2 Which factors drive Pixar's high and consistent level of creativity?

3 Bob Iger, CEO of Disney, describes his acquisition of Pixar for $7.4 billion as his proudest decision because it led to a revitalisation of Disney's own animation studios and generated over $14 billlion in sales. Which elements of the Pixar model do you think Disney imported from Pixar to transform its own animation business? How is Pixar doing now? What could describe any change in performance?

4 Compare the description of Pixar as a creative organisation in this chapter to the Netflix case study in Chapter 6. Where are the two organisation's approaches to ensuring a strong creative pipeline similar, and where do they diverge?

Notes

1 www.cnbc.com/2022/11/21/kareem-daniel-disney-head-of-media-and-chapeks-right-hand-is-out-following-igers-return.html

2 Matthew Ball speaking of his experience of competing with Netflix while Head of Strategy at Amazon Studios, Prime in Ben Thomson, 'An Interview with the Metaverse Author Matthew Ball', *Stratetechery*, 30 June 2022.

3 These are discussed in detail in Amabile, 1983, 1988, 1993, 1996, 1998; Amabile et al., 1994, 1996, 2002, and these sources are the prime references in the following sub-sections, unless otherwise indicated.

4 'Following the leader: 30 best quotes from Jeff Bezos'. Available at: https://orbitaltoday.com/2022/07/26/following-the-leader-30-best-quotes-from-jeff-bezos/

5 John Brandon, 'Elon Musk on how to innovate'. Inc.Com. Available at: www.inc.com/john-brandon/elon-musk-on-how-to-innovate-20-quotes.html

6 President and COO Peter Chernin speaking at Booz Allen Hamilton Gotham Media Breakfast 2003, www.boozallen.com/capabilities/Industries/industries_article/659265

7 Lucas Shaw (2022), www.bloomberg.com/news/newsletters/2022-11-06/how-hbo-survived-the-two-worst-media-mergers-of-the-century?utm_medium=email&utm_source=newsletter&utm_term=221106&utm_campaign=screentime

8 Scott Galloway, 2023 Predictions, 30 December 2022. Available at: www.profgalloway.com/2023-predictions

9 https://variety.com/2022/tv/awards/emmys-2022-wins-by-show-platform-hbo-max-white-lotus-1235369416/#:~:text=HBO%20roared%20back%20to%20the,their%2019%20wins%20in%202021

10 https://advanced-television.com/2022/11/09/research-hbo-max-has-most-award-winning-content

11 Joe Hall, Ampere Analysis in https://advanced-television.com/2022/11/09/research-hbo-max-has-most-award-winning-content

12 https://techcrunch.com/2022/04/21/hbo-max-and-hbo-gained-3-million-subscribers-in-q1-as-netflix-reports-subscriber-decline

13 https://techcrunch.com/2022/08/04/hbo-hbo-max-and-discovery-report-a-combined-total-of-92-1m-subscribers-plans-for-major-restructuring/?guccounter=1&guce_referrer=aHR0cHM6Ly93d3cuZ29vZ2xlLmNvbS8&guce_referrer_sig=AQAAAE-EI8gbEh0gvC17PaQC-Mu32uE-JrUwOVsl5WWVKTeBU_wYNRcO2I0-wRqwv91DWSFjL06MfQO__zdi7pES_rih_horFM5PzKTWilhXS1FlFs4AnHe08TZwUy1kM4XNm45ltdr-Z70VbR51mdKM6i8aa90hGPIsbGJCIU3GjN7ylT

14 AT&T Inc, *2019 Annual Report*. Available at: https://sec.report/Document/0001562762-20-000064/

15 Felix Gillette and John Koblin interviewed in Lucas Shaw, 'How HBO survived the two worst media mergers of the century', *Bloomberg.com Newsletter*, 7 November 2022.

16 Ibid.

17 Ibid.

18 Kenneth Turan in the *Los Angeles Times*, cited in *Slate*, 5 June 2003.

19 Cited in Sarah Witten. Available at: www.cnbc.com/2021/12/21/disneys-bob-iger-says-pixar-was-probably-the-best-acquisition-as-ceo.html

SIX

CULTURE AND STRATEGY

> It takes deliberate work ... specific ideas about what a culture should become.... dramatic, concrete actions that seize the attention of team members and push them out of their familiar comfort zones. (Satya Nadella, CEO Microsoft[1])

'Culture eats strategy for breakfast' is almost inevitably said by someone when the impact of organisational culture is discussed. Credited to Peter Drucker (although the Drucker Society disputes that he ever said it), the saying surfaces so frequently because it rings true to painful experience: culture has an enormous impact on what can and can't be achieved in terms of strategic change. This is why Reed Hastings at Netflix and Satya Nadella at Microsoft both lead through culture (although in different ways, as this chapter explores). It's why Andy Grove, an early Silicon Valley thought leader, founder of Intel and inventor of the OKR (the goal-setting methodology based on Objectives and Key Results) put culture at the heart of his 'high output management' style. For Grove, culture is a 'user manual for quicker, more reliable decisions' (1983: 135).

Beliefs, values and emotions are part of an organisation's social architecture. They exert tremendous influence on day-to-day, minute-by-minute behaviour, let alone what strategic choices are made and whether these are implemented. These powerful but often unconscious elements inside an organisation are the subject of this chapter. We look at how researchers have conceptualised them and how managers manage them.

Interpretative school of strategy

Culture and cognition concern how individuals create shared meaning out of events and interpret what is going on. Such 'governing beliefs' and their impact is the focus of the interpretative school of strategy, which explores organisations from the perspective of those inside them. The interpretative school is complementary to the rational one. While rational approaches focus on exogenous, external changes in the environment and the content of the strategies developed to respond to these, the interpretative school focuses on the processes by which these changes are perceived and understood and the impact this has on those strategies. The challenge surrounding this school, and of working with these phenomena inside organisations, is that they are highly subjective; they operate outside conscious awareness, which means that they are hard to analyse and even harder to influence. Because of these difficulties, they can get overlooked or underemphasised in strategy work.

Culture (unconscious shared beliefs) and cognitions (conscious shared beliefs) are fundamentally different entities. This distinction (between their conscious and unconscious nature) is critical when moving from strategy to practice, when actively trying to understand and shape culture:

- **Cognitions** are beliefs and assumptions that are **known to the individual** involved, sometimes even stated, and therefore 'accessible' at surface level. This means that they are far easier to address than cultural assumptions. People know they share these beliefs or think in a certain way.
- **Cultural assumptions** are deeper, **unconscious beliefs**. They are much more influential in terms of behaviour because people don't necessarily know they think in this way or hold a particular opinion. In order to change at this level, it is necessary to first surface these unconscious ways of thinking. This is a complex process that needs skill.

This distinction is critical for researchers and for managers. If the goal is to understand and change culture, then methods surveys or questionnaires will not succeed, because you are seeking to access beliefs that people may not know they hold. Surveys and questionnaires can certainly help understand climate and sentiment inside an organisation, but to understand culture ethnographic and anthropological approaches are needed.

Not all theorists uphold this distinction and bundle the cognitive and the cultural together. For example, Johnson (1987) defines strategy as the product of the ideologies (cognitive maps) held by individuals or groups in an organisation that are preserved in the symbols, rituals and myths of the organisation (culture). DiMaggio and Powell (1983) refer to an organisation's cognitive 'pillar', which includes the taken-for-granted unconscious cultural beliefs and values. This is correct to the extent that both phenomena belong to a single social architecture, but for those trying to change or manage culture, the distinction is critical not least in terms of designing the change process.

This chapter explores both culture – the set of collective unconscious beliefs that influence behaviour and outcomes – and cognitions – the explicit and sometimes stated beliefs and assumptions held by individuals in an organisation. For each, it explains the core concept and its origin, explores its role in the strategy process, and discusses with the help of case studies how this plays out in the media industries.

Culture

> ... external change almost inevitably leads to new strategies ... more mergers and acquisitions, more digital transformation, and more new methodologies ... the right culture can make work happen much faster and better, and the wrong culture can stall or kill the effort ... as the speed of change increases, culture becomes even more relevant. (John Kotter in Heskett, 2022)[2]

The impact of culture on strategic outcomes is now widely acknowledged – culture is an oft-cited culprit when organisations experience difficulties implementing strategies. But while the existence of organisational culture is widely accepted, the concept itself remains vague; and while cognition is often viewed as a strategic issue, culture falls into a no-man's land between organisation and strategy.

Culture turned 'mainstream' in the 1980s when several researchers proposed that if an 'appropriate' culture (a combination of values, norms and behaviours) is compatible with the strategy of an organisation, performance improvements will result (see, for example, Pascale and Athos, 1981; Peters and Waterman, 1982). The assumed relationship between culture and corporate success in these texts at least was straightforward: good performance resulted when culture and strategy were in harmony, and management's task was to ensure that culture was brought into line with strategic initiatives.

As the 1990s progressed, the intricacies and challenges involved in reconciling culture and strategy started to be acknowledged. Culture, it emerged, was far more than an organisational variable that could simply be manipulated and harnessed as needed; indeed, when culture and strategy were in opposition, it appeared that culture normally won out (thus the well-known adage, 'culture eats strategy for breakfast'). The term 'culture' started to morph into a metaphor that 'encodes an enormous variety of meanings and messages into economical and emotionally powerful forms' (Bolman and Deal, 1991: 250) that should be the starting place for strategy (Hampden-Turner, 1990).

What is culture?

> It is far more common for leaders seeking to build high-performance organizations to be confounded by culture ... Many either let it go unmanaged or relegate it to the HR function ... They may lay out detailed, thoughtful plans for strategy and execution, but because they don't understand culture's power and dynamics, their plans go off the rails. (Groysberg et al., 2018)[3]

The essence of an organisation's culture is 'contained' in an underlying paradigm of unconscious assumptions shared by members of the organisation. The assumptions are a quintessential and usually unacknowledged driver of strategic actions: they direct how people perceive the environment and the challenges or opportunities it presents, and how they react to the strategies designed in response.

All other things being equal, provided the cultural assumptions and the strategies are appropriate to the environment, the organisation is likely to experience success. That success will reinforce the 'rightness' of cultural assumptions. But a strong culture forged through success can also become a liability in that it creates a rigidity that impedes the ability to adapt. The mechanism is as follows. Cultural assumptions about the correct responses to the problems of internal integration and external adaptation are formed through organisational success. Continued success validates these further and they are passed on to new members as the 'correct' way to feel and act. In this way, an organisation's culture is perpetuated. Yet should the competitive environment change markedly, members of the organisation must change their core assumptions substantially. But such changes are hard to make (Schein, 1992). Revising basic assumptions means altering some of our deepest cognitive structures. This destabilises our cognitive world, releasing large quantities of anxiety (Schein, cited in Coutu, 2002). Many employees would rather hold on to existing cultural beliefs than experience such anxiety.

One of the most precise and widely used definitions of culture comes from Edgar Schein (Schein, 1992). His definition of culture is foundational to work in this field:

> Culture is a pattern of basic assumptions shared by a group of organisation members that were learned as it solved problems of external adaptation and internal integration and that are taught to new members of that group as the correct way to respond to such problems.

Culture is therefore a group construct; it concerns the accumulated learning shared by the members of a group that has been acquired as the group works together and deals with its external environment and internal growth. This process gives rise to a set of tacit assumptions about how things do and should function (what works, what doesn't, what matters, what doesn't, how to approach problems, and so on), which determine perceptions, thoughts and feelings, and function as short-cuts to decision-making.

If you want to understand an organisation's culture now, look to its founding circumstances. These, particularly the nature of the individual who founded a culture and the circumstances where this took place, play a disproportionate role in shaping the subsequent development of unconscious, shared assumptions (Bolman and Deal, 1991; Kotter and Heskett, 1992; Schein, 1992). Indeed, building and shaping an organisation's culture is 'the unique and essential function of leadership' (Schein, 1992: 212) – as we can see on the emphasis that leaders like Satya Nadella and Reed Hastings place on it.

Leaders employ several 'culture-embedding mechanisms' to create the culture they want. These can be subtle, including, for example, what they pay attention to, measure and control, how they react to critical incidents and crises, the criteria by which they allocate resources, rewards and status, and the criteria by which they select, promote and 'ex-communicate' members (Schein, 1992: 231). These factors are discussed in detail in transformational leadership (see p. 206).

Layers of culture

For Schein (1992), culture has three distinct but interconnected layers.

- The top layer comprises '**artefacts**' – behaviour, dress style, rituals, publications, stories – phenomena that are highly visible. These are easy to access but hard to interpret without prior understanding of the deeper levels of culture.
- The second level comprises '**espoused values**' – officially expressed strategies, goals and philosophies. Elements at this level may ostensibly show the underlying beliefs in the culture (and often claim to), but in reality they reveal more about how that group feels that it should present itself publicly or would like to be seen. Espoused values can be used to check hypotheses about underlying assumptions, but are not an accurate representation of them.
- '**Basic assumptions**' are the third and deepest level of culture, and these contain the essence of an organisation's culture. They are the unconscious, taken-for-granted beliefs, perceptions and feelings about the organisation and its environment shared by members of the group or company, which act as

> the ultimate source of values and drivers of actions. Such basic assumptions contain the key to a culture and are the tools by which the two higher levels – espoused values and artefacts – can be interpreted or encoded.

These basic assumptions at the heart of a culture take the form of an interrelated belief system or paradigm. According to Schein (1992), it is because they are not an assortment of beliefs, but an interconnected system that they have so much power. This deepest level of culture concerns the underlying belief structures that give purpose to the working life – 'the … expressive social tissue around us that gives … tasks meaning' (Pettigrew, 1979: 574). Uncovering and deciphering an organisation's culture is not easy because the underlying assumptions at the heart of a culture operate outside conscious awareness. Critically, they are not accessible at the surface attitudinal level, meaning that they can't be accessed using surveys (Schein, 1992). This makes researching culture complicated. It requires deep access to the organisation.

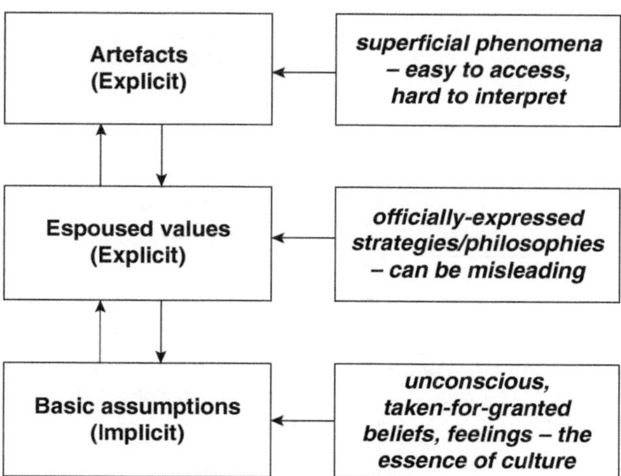

Figure 6.1 Layers of organisational culture (Schein, 1992)

The BBC's culture

The unconscious assumptions at the heart of the BBC's culture around the turn of the millennium are shown in Figure 6.2 (Küng-Shankleman, 2000). These were:

1 **'Public funding makes us different'**: This shared belief created a sense of higher purpose, a conviction that the BBC makes an important contribution to the nation and exists in the public good and in the service of that

public. This was a powerful intrinsic motivator, but also, by placing the BBC apart from its commercial rivals, also served to estrange it from the commercial world.

2 **'The best in the business'**: This assumption is related to the ethos of professionalism, a concern to offer broadcasting of the highest possible quality. Allied to this belief was a sense that its programme-making excellence was intrinsically linked to licence-fee funding: guaranteed funding enabled creativity and professionalism to flourish and a critical creative mass to develop, which enabled the BBC to raise public service broadcasting to the highest standards possible. However, its belief in its creative and professional prowess also created a risk of complacency and insularity, and gave rise to an anti-commercial, anti-managerial bent, a sense that BBC staff should prioritise creative- over business-related goals.

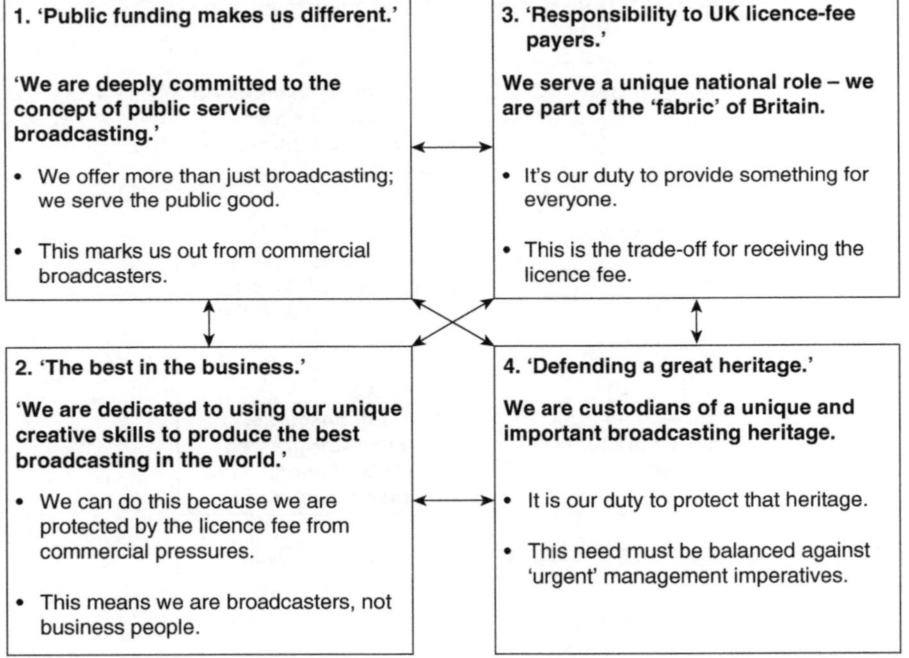

Figure 6.2 The BBC's paradigm of cultural beliefs (Küng-Shankleman, 2000)
© Lucy Küng

3 **'Responsibility to UK licence-fee payers'**: Licence-fee funding created a conviction that the BBC had a responsibility to provide something for everyone who paid it. This in turn created a deep respect for audiences and a strong priority on serving its licence-fee payers.

4 **'Defending a great heritage'**: For BBC staff, the organisation's long tradition, national role and international reputation was a source of great pride. The motivation stemming from this counteracted a frustration that was felt by some about the increasing focus on management and the bureaucratic nature of some internal processes. However, the BBC's commitment to its heritage also engendered resistance to management initiatives that threatened to damage that heritage.

Dimensions of culture

Although we assume that an organisation's culture is monolithic and speak of it as a singular entity, in any given organisational setting, a range of subcultures will also be present, and these will also affect how issues are viewed and decisions made. Members of an organisation will share the values particular to that organisation, culture, but will also share assumptions with individuals in other cultural groupings – professional cultures (say, journalists or product managers), industry cultures – for example, in the tech industry – and national cultures, who have similar professional or personal circumstances or experiences. These cultural pluralities mean that an organisation's culture is multifaceted and there will be a diverse set of cultural norms at play. For example, members of staff at a movie studio will share assumptions common to the film industry, assumptions common to their particular studio, but also assumptions common to their profession within the movie industry and to their national culture. These subcultural distinctions can give rise to conflict – for example, between the 'technical creatives' – the photographers, lighting engineers and cameramen who are involved with the 'nuts-and-bolts' aspects of content creation – and the 'talent' – the actors, directors and writers (Wolff, 1998: 127). Some of the most common subcultural groupings are shown in Figure 6.3.

Subcultures

These are composed of individuals inside an organisation who share some degree of commonality. Networks of underrepresented groups, war correspondents, cohorts of trainees who join the organisation at the same time or individuals working closely together on a new project for an extended period all fall into this category. These cultures can be very strong, depending on the depth of the experiences they share.

Figure 6.3 Dimensions of organisational culture

Professional cultures

Professional cultures are shared by individuals with a common profession or industrial background. In recent years, professionals working in the field of product have become a prominent subculture in the media sector (the resources section of this chapter provides details of associations and their extensive publications). Much research into culture in the media industry has concentrated on the culture of journalism. The American Society of Newspaper Editors (cited in Picard, 2004) identified a number of fundamental cultural values shared by newspaper journalists, including fairness and balance, editorial judgement, integrity, diversity, and community leadership and involvement. Georgiou (1998) describes how journalists' culture interacts with strategic change initiatives (note there are similarities in his findings to the shared cultural assumptions at the BBC discussed earlier in this chapter):

> ... commitment to the organisation is both an emotional and a calculative one. In the case of journalists ... the emotional attachment ('I believe in what we do') can be very strong. This high level of commitment means that anything that is perceived as diminishing a journalist's ability to 'do the job' is likely to face fierce resistance. Conversely, anything that demonstrably makes the job 'easier' is likely to be adopted quickly. (Georgiou, 1998)

Industry cultures

An industry culture is a value orientation common to those working in a certain industry. The success of Silicon Valley has been ascribed to the unique combination of shared culture values that have both given rise to and are the product of how organisations are structured and operate. The speed of technological development in the environment mandates high levels of adaptability, achieved in part through high levels of collaboration and outsourcing, giving rise to loose network structures (Saxenian, 1994), and clusters of highly entrepreneurial organisations that are flatter and more egalitarian than is the norm for US industry, and where there is cross-functional interaction at all levels. Structure and culture together have created a micro economy that can adapt fast: as existing companies die, new ones emerge, allowing capital, ideas and people to be reallocated, a phenomenon termed 'flexible recycling' (Bahrami and Evans, 1995). Many other parts of the world have sought to replicate this combination – for example, Manhattan's Silicon Alley, LA's Silicon Beach, Lagos's Silicon Lagoon and the Dubai Silicon Oasis.

The media industry's shared culture is described in very different terms. Frequently cited are its anti-commercial overtones, reflecting a shared belief that media businesses are 'different' (this cultural strain was present in the BBC's culture, discussed earlier in this chapter):

> ... the people who work in and own and manage businesses, newspapers, broadcasting stations, etc., are terribly in love with those businesses and have a devotion to reinvestment and to expanding that often doesn't defy economics but has little to do with economics. (Savill and Studley, 1999: 28)

This assumption derives in part from the creative imperative of content creation. But it also reflects a deeply rooted belief that content should not simply entertain, but also fulfil important societal and political functions, ranging from enriching the life of consumers to promoting democracy and furthering social cohesion. This has two strategic implications: first, it creates a sense of 'higher purpose', which can be an important motivator, and second, it can create an antipathy towards strategic change, which can hinder adaptation to a changed strategic environment.

National cultures

The underlying foundational assumptions shared by members of an organisation can differ significantly from one part of the world to another. Work-related values differ substantially in different international contexts, as shown by Hofstede (1980). These differences persist, despite the use of common technologies, networking platforms and increasing international competition (Heskett, 2022).

Cognition

> Your beliefs are cause maps that you impose on the world, after which you 'see' what you have already imposed. (Karl Weick, 1995)

The cognitive school of strategy draws on cognitive psychology. Culture and cognition are closely linked, as we see in Karl Weick's quote that opens this section: culture concerns the 'beliefs' or 'cause maps' that direct what we 'see' – that is, our cognitions. Morgan (1986) uses the metaphor 'organisations as brains' as a collective term for the field.

Like cultural approaches, cognitive approaches to organisations are premised on the assumption that individual behaviour is guided by sets of governing beliefs. These develop through a range of sense-making processes and affect how we perceive and interpret information about our environment. Cognitive approaches are therefore constructivist in that they assume, as Kant and Hume put it, that what exists is a product of what is thought: there is no objective measurable reality; rather, we each construct our own realities based on our individual interactions, experiences, perceptions, needs, and so on. Organisations, by extension, are open social systems that interpret their environment according to the cognitive frameworks of individuals in the organisation (Fiske and Taylor, 1984; Abelson, 1995).

Weick's (1995) notion of 'sensemaking' is central to cognitive organisational theory. Sensemaking is the process by which ambiguous and complex information is absorbed from the environment, processed and meaning constructed to guide decision-making. Processing activities involve many elements common to strategic analysis: defining, prioritising, constructing frameworks and highlighting significant factors. The mental models that emerge are 'abstract representations' of knowledge that are created in a path-dependent way and retrospective (Weick, 1995): 'the past shapes the template for understanding the future' (Bogner and Barr, 2000).

Simon's (1955) concept of bounded rationality is key to cognition theory (Gavetti and Levinthal, 2000). This observes that human thought processes are rational but have limitations (Simon, 1955; March and Simon, 1958). Human information-processing capabilities are limited: we can never fully grasp every facet of ambiguous and complex issues or comprehend the world in its entirety. To manage the situation, to reduce uncertainty and complexity, we apply 'inferential heuristics' – that is, rules of thumb we develop based on our previous experience. These heuristics simplify decision-making by providing short-cuts, but they also impoverish it by limiting the amount of information we process and the number of options we consider.

Different types of knowledge structures

Reality is an illusion, albeit a very persistent one. (Albert Einstein)

The structures of governing beliefs have been conceptualised in a variety of ways. Some of the best-known 'knowledge structures' are listed below, but note that collectively, the terminology here is imprecise.

- **Cognitive maps:** A mental structure by which equivocal information in the environment is organised so that organisation members can make sense of it (Weick, 1995).
- **Schemas or schemata:** As first defined by Bartlett (1932) and Piaget (1952), these are knowledge systems comprising ideas, conclusions and presumptions, etc., which have emerged over time on the basis of experience. They allow information connected to a specific subject to be organised in hierarchical levels, and therefore speed up assessments of events, likely consequences and appropriate responses. They allow disparate information to be organised and ambiguous data to be assessed quickly. However, information that cannot be accommodated into the schema can be ignored, meaning that they can be inaccurate representations of the world.
- **Mental models (or causal maps):** Understood as deeply ingrained assumptions, overt and covert, that capture the relationship between different factors, and which develop through interacting with a complex environment. They influence how the world is understood and what action is taken.
- **Paradigms:** An over-arching set of beliefs, or 'conventional wisdom' about the nature of the world, usually in the context of an industry. A classic use is Kuhn's (1970) theory that 'shared beliefs' and 'conventional wisdom' constitute a dominant paradigm that governs any particular science at any particular point in time by serving as a means of defining and managing the world and providing a basis for action.
- **Frames:** Understood as 'underlying structures of belief, perception and appreciation through which subsequent interpretation is filtered' (Schön and Rein, 1994: 23).

Changing culture

> We've been to hell and back with cultural change at *The New York Times*. (Mark Thompson, CEO of *The New York Times*, 2020)[4]

'It's easier to change a strategy than change a culture', observed management theorist John Heskett (2022: 17). That is because strategic change almost by definition requires an organisation to alter its cultural assumptions, and, as we have seen in this chapter, those shared beliefs are largely unarticulated. As environmental turbulence has grown, organisations have needed to change strategy more frequently. This change has often proved painful and slow, and attention has come to rest on the relationship between unconscious shared assumptions and their impact on the ability of an organisation to change strategically.

In their research into 'architectural innovations' (apparently minor improvements in technological products that do not concern the components of a product but rather its 'architecture' – that is, the knowledge embedded in the structure and information-processing procedures, Henderson and Clark describe how 'old [mental] frameworks' hinder such innovations because:

> ... incumbents may not realise that an innovation is architectural because the information is screened out by the information channels and communication channels that embody old architectural knowledge ... the effect is analogous to the tendency of individuals to continue to rely on beliefs about the world that a rational evaluation of new information should lead them to discard ... organizations facing threats may continue to rely on their old frameworks. (Henderson and Clark, 1990: 17)

For Christensen and Overdorf (2000), the failure of many incumbents to seize the potential of disruptive innovation stems in large part from shared cognitions:

> The larger and more complex a company becomes, the more important it is for senior managers to train employees throughout the organization to make independent decisions about priorities that are consistent with the strategic direction and the business model of the company. A key metric of good management, in fact, is whether such clear, consistent values have permeated the organization. But consistent, broadly understood values also define what an organization cannot do. (Cited in Day and Schoemaker, 2000: 69)

Shared values build identity, create cohesion, speed decision-making, but also create rigidity. A central tenet of the interpretative school of strategy is that changing strategy means changing culture and mindset. Because interpretative elements change slowly, strategic change will be slow too, happening via a process of 'logical incrementalism' (Quinn, 1980).

In the 1940s, Kurt Lewin developed a model to structure the culture and mindset changes that accompany strategic shifts. Like many classic management theory concepts, many decades after its development, it is still influential and widely used, often in tandem with Kotter's 8-Stage Transformational Change (see p. 209).

Lewin's model identifies three stages in the process of cultural change: **unfreezing**, **changing**, or moving to a new model, and **refreezing**.

Stage	What is involved?	Steps in the Kotter model
Unfreezing	Open minds. Build understanding that change is needed. Explain the rationale for change. Determine what needs to be different. Encourage new ideas and behaviours. Ensure strong support from management. Create concern about not changing. Tackle doubts and concerns, and build a sense of psychological safety about change.	1. Create a sense of urgency. 2. Form a guiding coalition. 3. Create a vision for change. 4. Communicate the vision.
Changing (= move to a new level)	Decide on the changes needed. Implement them. Keep the organisation informed as the change programme is implemented. Build an understanding of new elements and new 'ways of doing business'.	5. Remove obstacles. 6. Create short-term wins. 7. Build on change.
Refreezing	'Lock in' by integrating them into the 'normal' way of doing things. Adapt processes and systems to ensure they reinforce the changes. Ensure the changes will be sustained.	8. Anchor the change in the organisation culture.

Accessing deep cultural assumptions – the 'culture web'

Because the deepest cultural assumptions are usually unconscious, members of a group can seldom articulate them (without specific intervention), meaning that they are difficult to access, let alone change. Johnson (1992) holds that these assumptions are enmeshed in everyday aspects of the wider organisational context that together make up a cultural web. Spot and decode these, and the underlying cultural values will become clear.

Johnson's (1992: 32) cultural web identifies six key elements rooted in the paradigm of cultural assumptions.

- **Stories and myths.** These reinforce or encapsulate cultural values. They are shared between members of the group, with outsiders and with newcomers as part of their socialisation into the organisation.
- **Symbols.** These can be tangible – buildings, cars, office spaces, and so on, or intangible – behaviour, habits, modes of address, which industry awards are most respected, etc. Symbols can convey enormous amounts of information about a culture, especially about what confers status and what behavioural expectations are at play. For example, in the early days of Amazon, Jeff Bezos wanted to build a culture of frugality. To symbolise this, desks were made of cheap doors from a hardware store with legs bolted on. This was to emphasise that Amazon looked for every opportunity to save money so it could deliver the best products for the lowest cost.
- **Power structures.** These concern how power is distributed inside the organisation. It can be explored by looking at which individuals, groups or roles have the most official power, or carry the most influence or have the most say when key decisions are being made.
- **Formal structures.** These are the elements that concern how formal decisions are made, and who has the power to influence them, but also informal power structures. Netflix, as we can read in the case in this chapter, has deliberately sought to simplify the overt structure of the organisation, relying instead on smart people using their best judgement. For this to work, they seek to hire specific types of individuals.

- **Control systems**. These determine what is measured, monitored, rewarded or controlled, and show what the organisation considers important. In the cases on *The Guardian* and the BBC's 50:50 initiative in this chapter, using data to monitor specific aspects of daily work was used to shift cultural assumptions in order to achieve specific strategic changes.
- **Rules, routines and rituals.** The work processes and activities that determine the nature of daily work in the organisation. When Ben Horowitz and Marc Andreessen started their venture capital fund, they wanted to build a culture of respect for the founders and entrepreneurs they were working with. To ensure that this attitude was understood by all staff, they implemented a $100 fine for any staff member who turned up even a few minutes late for a meeting with an entrepreneur.

Conclusions

This chapter focuses on issues central to the adaptive school of strategy, cognition and culture. Both concern the influence of shared assumptions on organisational outcomes, and both have common roots in psychology and an acknowledged impact on strategic issues. But interpretative approaches to strategy represent a relatively recent wing of strategic theory – one that has expanded rapidly in recent years, but which still lacks the cohesion and clarity of, say, the rationalist field. This chapter has tried to build an understanding of interpretative approaches by discussing the underlying theories and analysing the role of interpretative phenomena in the media industry. A central argument of this book is that this body of theory is highly relevant to the media industry, as evidenced by the very many cases of leading industry actors ascribing their current strategic challenges to cultural and cognitive inflexibility. Understanding of interpretative phenomena inside media organisations can both complement the insights gained through the application of positivist models of strategy, but contribute to the successful implementation of adaptive strategic initiatives.

Resources

Books and articles

Organisation Culture and Leadership, Ed Schein. Jossey Bass (2010).

Win from Within, John Heskett. Columbia Business School Press (2022).

No Rules Rules, Netflix and the Culture of Reinvention, Reed Hastings and Erin Meyer. Virgin Books, (2020). Netflix Culture as described by the organisation: https://jobs.netflix.com/culture

'How Netflix Reinvented HR', Patty McCord. *Harvard Business Review*. (1 January 2014).

Hit Refresh, Satya Nadella. Harper Books (2017).

To understand start-up culture and how to build one, *The Hard Thing about Hard Things*. Ben Horowitz (2014).

Videos

To explore how a leader can create a high-performance creative context, see 'Lead like the great conductors', a TED talk by Itay Talgam.

Case: *The Guardian* – changing culture with data

> I thought I could go into the newsroom and talk to people I've worked with for 10 years and just say, 'Let's stop doing that' ... But nobody did ... Nobody wants to change ... they had 200 years of habit to support carrying on doing exactly what they had always done.

The UK's *The Guardian* newspaper has an august heritage. First published in 1821 by a group of businessmen seeking to champion civil liberties and free trade, a century later it has transformed itself into a leading global digital news brand that has won a Pulitzer Prize for its coverage of leaked US NSA documents. In 2022, two thirds of its readers were digital and from outside the UK, it had 160 million monthly unique views globally, and profitable digital editions in North America, Australia and New Zealand.[5] Financially, things were tougher: in 2020 reported revenues were £223.5 million with a cashflow loss of £29 million, and more losses were forecast, a situation described by

(Continued)

the parent GMG as 'unsustainable'.[6] Unlike many of its 'broadsheet' competitors, *The Guardian* has stuck to a free online model: digital readers are invited repeatedly to subscribe voluntarily or donate, but neither is mandatory. This has resulted in an unusual business model, 'a mix of free, fan and subscriber'.[7]

Like most news publishers, *The Guardian* began running digital operations alongside its print ones. But as its digital offering grew, so too did the need to implement subtle but fundamental changes in how it did its journalism. To achieve these, journalists would need to alter long-held assumptions about how to approach their work. This task fell to Chris Moran, now Director of Editorial Innovation, and evolved from modest beginnings (changing headlines for digital) to addressing more fundamental issues, such as accommodating digital attention spans and focusing journalistic investment on mission-critical output. Underlying all this work was a need to shift deeply held cultural assumptions that had arisen in the print era and were limiting success in a digital one.

Digital headlines are different

Early on, data flagged up that print headlines did not work well for the digital product. This was the start of the project:

> ... a good print headline alludes to something as opposed to explaining what the article is about. In digital the job is different ... the context is removed, which means that all you're doing with print headlines like that is harming the journalism.

Chris assumed that once he explained the problem and what was needed, journalists would adjust. But they didn't. His message conflicted with wrong-held assumptions about what made a 'good headline', which journalists did not want to challenge. He addressed this in several stages.

- **Step 1: 'this worked well, this didn't'.** Chris started by sending out a simple morning email to a few newsroom leaders who might be most open to change. He included samples of headlines from the previous day, showing which worked and which didn't:

> It was written for people like me who didn't understand these numbers ... I showed that pieces of journalism that everybody cared about were doing well because their headlines worked ... and gently suggested that a few pieces that hadn't done so well maybe would have done if the headline had been different

- **Step 2: A five-minute slot in the daily editorial conference.** The email had increased awareness, but the headlines weren't changing. As a next

(Continued)

step, Chris and his colleagues were given a slot in the morning meeting. They kept the same communication approach: simple and constructive, giving clear examples of what had worked and why, and explaining how this could help serve *Guardian* journalism:

If there was an article, which we felt we hadn't got across to readers as we had wanted we talked about it … but very carefully, giving a general top line, say whether it's good or bad, and then digging into what could be different.

- **Step 3: Headline by headline, one-on-one intervention.** While understanding was growing, there were still too many headlines that didn't work. Granular explanation and support were needed:

I asked every single sub-editor to send me every single headline via chat … 50% of the time I said, 'That's great. Just carry on.' But when I did intervene, I made it a conversation … I tried to educate people, and show them that I wasn't squeezing traffic mindlessly … But even then, there were still sub-editors who would simply refuse.

- **Step 4: Ophan, an automated data dashboard.** This approach worked but it wasn't scalable. A hack day was held, bringing engineers and journalists together to collaborate on an automated tool that would give journalists the data they needed for their digital journalism to succeed:

We created a real-time SEO dashboard ... Real-time is fundamental. If you don't have data coming straight into the newsroom, as quickly as possible, then it's very likely you won't succeed.

- **Step 5: Introduce Ophan slowly**. Given the concerns about clickbait, the dashboard needed to be introduced carefully. To start, only a small group had access. As these users became converts, their colleagues started to request access too. Use and acceptance spread organically:

The more we showed it to people, the more they said, 'Oh, that looks useful ... Can it tell me where readers are coming from? Can it help me understand how what I'm publishing about Iran is being read?' Then you're in a virtuous cycle … you've got a momentum going.

- **Step 6: Focus on attention, as well as page views**. Journalists now knew how many readers 'came' to a story, but *The Guardian's* goal is not to maximise reader numbers but to maximise the impact of its journalism. Chris started to explore how the dashboard could drive digital impact. This meant capturing how long readers spent on stories:

(Continued)

We want to grow our audience responsibly, so seeing how long people spent on an article helped ensure that. Having attention time alongside pageviews means we can assess not only whether journalism is reaching readers, but also if that reach was engaging them.

- **Step 7: Adjusting article length**

Digital data flagged up a *fundamental* aspect of digital reading: online attention spans are short. Readers move on quickly if interest wanes. Online readers favour precision, brevity and clarity. Journalists, however, often assumed that the longer an article, the more value they were creating for their readers. Chris didn't want to prescribe what length was correct, but simply get journalists to reflect in advance on what would be best for what they were writing. A 'nudge' was needed, and a new field was built into Ophan:

We simply added a field, to be filled by journalists, that said, 'This article should be this long' ... And we changed internal arrangements so that if sub-editors received an article that was significantly longer than the commissioned length, they could simply hand it back.

- **Step 8: Tackling overpublishing**

Long-held assumptions – about what makes a good headline, about article length – were changing. But the longer the newsroom worked with data, the more a deeper challenge became apparent. Too many articles were being published that readers weren't reading in sufficient numbers. Analysis showed that 30 per cent of articles made up just 2 per cent of digital readership. That 2 per cent represented a wasted investment of intellectual capital and journalistic skill. And at this point *The Guardian* was loss-making. It needed to invest its resources wisely. This didn't mean that articles that were not highly read were without merit, but journalists did need to reflect before writing on whether this new article matched *The Guardian*'s mission and audience needs. To prompt reflection, a further change was made:

We introduced a screen that shows the bottom-ranked items … incredibly powerful, the thing that's driven most change ... Data tools traditionally show the top, the best of what's going on. We didn't just unleash it, and say, 'Hey, there's loads of crap going on here.' We did this hand-in-hand with cultural messaging, which was, 'surely when we are this resource-strapped, we don't want to be spending any of that resource on stuff that isn't being read?

(Continued)

***The Guardian's* culture change through data, in review:**

> ... the reason Ophan changed culture ... is that it absolutely chimed with what we were trying to do with our journalism.

At *The Guardian*, the precision with which data insights were introduced into journalists' daily work, coupled with a communications strategy designed to build acceptance of those changes, meant it could revise often unconscious shared assumptions about high-quality journalism. These changes are summarised in the table below:

Print assumption	Digital revisioning
'The more readers, the more impact we have, and the more successful we will be.'	'High online readership is very important but doesn't translate automatically into more impact or higher revenues. Counterintuitively, less is often more.'
'Once we have a reader "on site" they will stay for a while and read several articles.'	'Digital attention spans are short and competition for attention is fierce. We need to fight to get reader attention and work hard to keep it.'
'In print we are constrained by the physical product. With digital we have more space, we can have more articles, and they can be longer.'	'Our resources are limited, and we need to focus on the articles that are most important to our journalistic mission and goals and think carefully before publish. We need to focus investment where it matters most.'
	"We can't promote all articles equally online, and reading times are shorter. Articles of marginal interest, or that are too long make no sense when resources are stretched."

The data dashboard, Ophan, was central to the cultural change. It worked in part because its design was rooted in underlying cultural values:

> ... it was built on the common good for our journalism. It chimed with what we were trying to do, open journalism. If your argument is 'We are going to stay outside of a paywall, because we believe the journalism we create is a positive and everyone should have access to it' then you need to amplify your positive journalism as far as you possibly can. If that involves changing words and headlines, then the trade-off is obvious.

A deep understanding of underlying cultural values, combined with clarity on the journalistic mission together afforded a change process based on data that reshaped *The Guardian*'s journalism for the digital ecosystem and worked with rather than against the culture of the newsroom:

(Continued)

> Start with something specific that you're trying to change. If you're able to change it using the data, then that leads you into interesting places and probably ensures that things go well ... I think that's why some people who have tried to copy us fail; they think what they're doing is about data, introducing data in the newsroom ... What they're missing is the aim needs to be, 'We want to improve a specific aspect of our digital journalism, and the data will help us do that'.

Case questions

1. Using Lewin's model, analyse how Chris Moran 'unfroze' attitudes in the newsroom. What tools did he use? How did he frame his messages?
2. Using Johnson's cultural web, on which elements did Chris Moran focus as he sought to change cultural assumptions?
3. How would you describe *The Guardian's* culture? How did this affect the choices Chris made and the design of the data dashboard?
4. What techniques were used to 'refreeze' the newsrooms around new practices?

Case: SVT News and Sport – unfreezing and refreezing culture to achieve audience goals

> ... wow ... we should have done this a long, long time ago. (Interview Christina Johannesson and Lucy Küng, 2022)

The 2015 terrorist attacks in Paris were a watershed for Sweden's public service broadcaster, Sveriges Television (SVT). Not only did audiences criticise its slow response, but it also raised fundamental questions: if SVT could not provide the news audiences needed when they needed it, why should the public pay for it?

This audience reaction and the public debate that followed it were to trigger a revolution at SVT, but one that would ultimately transform SVT News and Sport. Five years later, it emerged as a stronger news provider with a deeper relationship to a larger audience. Resources had been shifted from broadcast to online, processes for creating news had been streamlined, there was more content of higher quality, and the local news coverage had grown to span 48 stations. It was the preferred digital news source for the coveted 20 – 39-year-old

(Continued)

age group, digital visitors had increased fivefold, and its digital journalism was winning prizes. Staff engagement levels had risen sharply too.

New leader, new goals and new structure

Anne Lagercrantz was appointed Head of SVT News and Sport in October 2015. This division had around 850 employees providing content for Sweden's 10 million inhabitants, and while the department was organised around broadcasting, an increasing number were consuming digital news on mobile phones. A major transformation was needed and changing culture would be central to this: digital needed to be the centre of activities and they needed to get much closer to their audiences. Christina Johannesson was tasked with the cultural transformation, and with colleague Kristian Lindquist spearheaded transformation initiatives in the news output. They started their work by delving into the audience challenge and found two core interlinked issues: while SVT's national position was strong, its connection with younger generations was poor and getting weaker (the average age of broadcast news viewers was 65+), and SVT was not performing well on digital (partly the cause for its weak connection to younger viewers).

A restructuring came next. All SVT newsrooms, departments and teams were gathered around a single shared news service. At the same time, broadcast and digital were separated in the national newsroom. Resources were redistributed from broadcast to digital and niche units – for example, science and investigative – were moved into the central digital function. A single website was introduced, svt.se, and all digital news was consolidated on this site, rather than distributed over many. A video desk, Live Desk and Morning Studio, was established. Multitasking – where the same content is used on both television and online without major processing – was abandoned in favour of focused digital roles. Scheduling was tightened also; both the tempo and volume of work increased. The newsroom had to produce better and more digital content, and keep broadcast output at the same level as before, and all without any substantial increase in funding. Setting up a breaking news desk ready to go live within minutes around the clock demanded tougher schedules for late nights and weekends.

Very few roles remained the same. SVT needed to clarify the nature of the roles it needed going forward – a significant task. Once the new requirements were clear, all staff were required to apply for the jobs they wanted. As a result, 70 per cent of managers and leaders changed roles with 25 per cent of reporters shifting from broadcast to digital roles.

Unfreezing with FIKA

> ... we were in deep mud ... we were making progress in digital in a big way ... but the culture in the newsroom ... made the transition slow ... managers were exhausted.

(Continued)

A lot had been achieved, but SVT was not moving as fast as it needed. Cultural values were slowing change. Journalists are trained to be sceptical, to question, and these traits naturally extend to their organisations. Internal change initiatives are subject to the same questioning as those from politicians or business people. Christina was convinced that the journalists needed to understand at an individual level why change was necessary and created the 'FIKA' project in response.

FIKA was designed as 'learning not marketing': over 350 news and sport staff went on the road to have a coffee, meet and chat with the people they were creating news for. This was a huge and complex project to set up, but it had a powerful impact; staff realised how far their working assumptions about audiences had drifted from those audiences' needs. As a result of their FIKA experiences, they acquired a visceral sense of who audiences were and what they needed. Other initiatives were introduced to bolster the mindset shift. 'Personae' were created to help newsmakers understand different target groups, 100+ newsroom leaders were trained in audience analytics, and seminars were held to introduce new ideas on leadership, society and developments in the media.

'We don't feel like leaders. People tell us in great detail what to do.'

FIKA was a success. Increased audience knowledge was boosting audiences especially on digital. But it still felt like the culture of the newsroom was holding back change. A new project was started in 2018 to change the leadership culture in the newsroom.

The first step was defining the problem. Insights from individual interviews, workshops attended by a hundred editorial leaders and survey data were analysed to reveal phenomena inside SVT News and Sport that were blocking change. Fundamental was a lack of clarity. The new structure was complex, there were many platforms and new roles. It was not always clear where roles began or ended, or who had the authority to take decisions. A lack of clarity on goals left people disempowered and decisions that junior people should have been able to make were getting deferred upwards unnecessarily:

> People felt they needed to ask senior people for direction all the time in great detail, and this ended up with the 'mother bird' syndrome – leaders have baby birds asking them for direction all the time that they have to feed with answers ... managers ... were under enormous pressure to have answers to everything and ... people were frustrated because they were waiting for answers, instead of making decisions by themselves ... This was not sustainable ... It didn't allow change at the speed we needed.

(Continued)

A new leadership programme

> When you transform an organisation with 1,000 people, it's not one transformation, it's 1,000 transformations. It's about people, and each individual needs guidance when the whole organisation is supposed to move in a certain direction, and that's why we needed to emphasise the feedback and coaching leadership for everyone.

It was clear to Christina that deep cultural transformation is not possible without granular work at an individual level. A new leadership programme was created, grounded in three principles:

1 Set clear expectations – clarify roles, goals and mandates.

2 Instil a leadership style that empowers and does not micromanage – train leaders to coach and unleash the talent in their teams.

3 Build a feedback culture where everyone gets regular scheduled coaching and feedback.

This involved a range of initiatives. Short programmes were run for nearly 200 leaders throughout the division. Over 600 staff were trained in how to give and receive feedback, and a simple template was created for every employee that clarified that individual's role, responsibility and whom they should give feedback to or receive it from.

The result: culture shift

SVT News and Sport succeeded in changing its shared cultural values. It now sees itself as a digital media company that is focused on serving its audiences, that understands that excellent content needs great teamwork. The two tables below summarise how cultural values shifted.

Old cultural values	Revised cultural values
'We know what the audience needs.'	'Listen to the audience before you turn to gut feeling.'
'We are a TV company.'	'We are a media company.'
'Individual performance is what matters.'	'We perform as a team.'
'Strategy is not our concern.'	'We understand our strategic goals, and how we can individually contribute to achieving them.'

(Continued)

This shift was achieved via a series of initiatives.

Initiative	Outcome
Audience analysis.	Clarity on audience needs and core audience challenges.
Set strategy. Give each unit: • Key success factors. • Strategic key performance indicators (KPI).	Provide staff with information on what they need to achieve.
Introduce new structure.	Shift resources to digital and quality of digital output.
Re-evaluate all roles.	Shift resource to digital.
Shift more into digital.	Ensure SVT News and Sport has digital expertise it needs.
Create new digital specialist roles.	
FIKA	Tighten connection between organisation and audience.
Audience personae	Tighten connection between organisation and audience.
Audience analytic training	Tighten connection between organisation and audience.
Seminar series	Provide continued impetus to change.
Clarify individual roles, including performance targets and decision-making sphere.	Make expectations from each role clear and ensure that individuals have what is needed to perform well.
	Increase speed, professionalism and creativity.
	Build foundation for performance management.
Train leaders in coaching.	Build skills needed to shift behaviour and support teams in reaching targets, create psychological safety around change.
Train everyone in feedback.	Create feedback culture and improve performance management.

Case questions

1 Why did SVT News and Sport need to change some of its underlying cultural values? What changes in the environment was it responding to, and how did its status as a publicly funded news organisation impact on this situation?

(Continued)

2 What were the cultural shifts SVT needed to achieve? What other changes needed to be made in the organisation to achieve the culture change?
3 What techniques did Christina use to unfreeze attitudes in the newsroom?
4 What tools were used to refreeze the newsroom and reinforce the new values?

Case: How Netflix drives performance through culture

> The Netflix Culture Deck struck me as hypermasculine, excessively confrontational, and downright aggressive. (Erin Meyer, 2020, xvii)

Netflix is one of the most successful of new players in the streaming economy. Growth has been aggressive – achieved on the back of a series of pivots:

- from DVDs to streamed distribution;
- from offering content licensed from other studios to building studios and creating its own content;
- from being a US player to being a global player;
- from focusing on subscription numbers to sales and operating profit;
- from subscription funded to advertising and subscription funded, and charging for password sharing.

As CEO, Reed Hastings sought to proactively design a culture that fuelled growth and created strategic agility. Rooted in the importance he placed on simplicity and focus, he incorporated specific and explicit policies for how decisions are made and people interact, all with the goal of building an organisation that instinctively does the right thing, that needs less managing and leading. Hastings' underlying belief was that if you create the right context, the right norms, and the right guide rails, you can give more freedom to employees, help them build their individual decision-making abilities, meaning that their decisions will get better and better over time. This approach is enshrined in the

(Continued)

Netflix slide deck, now downloaded millions of times, written by CEO Reed Hastings and his then Chief of Talent, Patty McCord[8, 9], and in the book *No Rules, Rules* by Reed Hastings and Erin Meyer (2020). (All references are from these sources unless otherwise stated).

A number of factors are essential to this approach, as discussed below.

High talent density

Having the best talent is at the core of Netflix's system. It pays 'rock-star' salaries to exceptional individuals on the basis that a single stellar performer is worth ten adequate ones. Overall, this also allows a leaner workforce and makes leadership simpler – each manager leads fewer people and can do it better.

Staff who don't classify as 'A list' players don't stay. If a co-worker's performance moves from stellar to 'adequate', then it's time for that individual to move on (but they will receive a generous severance payment). This approach means investments in performance improvement programmes, and the opportunity costs of weak performance, are avoided.

Frequent feedback

> It is tantamount to being disloyal ... if you fail to speak up when you disagree ... or have feedback that could be helpful. (Redd Hastings and Erin Meyer, 2020, p. 18)

Giving and receiving feedback – always with positive intent – is expected to be part of daily work: the more people share and learn, the more teams accomplish, effectiveness and motivation increase, and the need for control structures and systems is reduced. The emphasis on feedback means that should a staff member be asked to leave, this should not come as a surprise – the performance issues will already be known already to both sides. To ensure this is the case, staff are also encouraged to ask their managers at least yearly, 'If I were thinking of leaving, how hard would you work to change my mind?'

Highly aligned, loosely coupled, with few internal controls

> I had the great fortune of doing a mediocre job at my first company. We got more bureaucratic as we grew. (Reed Hastings, Netflix CEO[10])

Having high-calibre talent allows you to focus on innovation and reduce the need for control processes that undermine people's ability to decide for themselves. Reduce these and people will have more scope to use their own judgement. It's easier to hold people accountable, problem-solving is dispersed and fast, and motivation goes up (it's Vacation Policy and Expense Approvals operate under the policy of 'act in Netflix's best interests') and the company becomes more responsive.

(Continued)

Specific meetings ensure that people are aligned with Netflix's strategic North Star. Executive Staff and Quarterly Business Review Meetings are held for all leaders; these last a couple of days. One-to-one meetings are held for the next five layers down in the organisation chart, and these serve also to align people around strategy and ensure that the company context is understood.

Be transparent, even with sensitive stuff

Hastings believes that if you employ smart individuals, and treat them as adults who can handle complex information, then commitment and buy-in will be higher, strategy and the financial objectives will be widely understood, meaning more individuals are able to make educated decisions without involving those higher up. Potentially sensitive financial data is shared widely, but with some conditions – if transparency affects an individual's dignity or privacy, information will not be disclosed, and staff understand there are serious consequences if sensitive data is circulated outside of Netflix. Only one document (for the CEO and his six direct reports) is not widely shared. To further create a climate of openness and trust, leaders do not have individual offices or assistants, and are expected to go to meet others, rather than have staff come to them.

Accelerate innovation

The speed of industry development means that Netflix has to prioritise innovation. Netflix needs people throughout the organisation to be able to think freely and implement bold ideas, so it has established a learning process to accelerate innovation:

1 Farm for dissent: actively seek out different perspectives. For big initiatives, create memo explaining idea and inviting input, allow everyone to see any comments made. If relevant, distribute a shared spreadsheet asking people to rate ideas from -10 to +10 with comments. For smaller ideas, socialise them first – set up meetings outlining the idea and stress-test the thinking.

2 Test it out.

3 Place your bet.

4 If it wins, celebrate it. If it fails, sunset it; capture the learnings and don't make a big deal of it.

5 A couple of times a year, review innovation bets on a simple form divided into things that went well, things that didn't and ones that are still open. Discuss each set and what was learned.

(Continued)

Case questions

1 What are the shared cultural assumptions at the heart of Netflix's culture?

2 What are the strategic benefits of its unusual and rigorous approach to people and culture?

3 Would you like to work at Netflix? Why?

Case: 50:50 at the BBC – changing gender representation

> 78% [of teams] reached 50% women contributors, indicating that cultural change is taking hold and that it is sustainable.[11]

Men have long traditionally been more represented in the media than women, and these portrayals often reflect sexist stereotypes. This was an issue for the BBC, as it was for other news providers worldwide, and while many were aware of this problem, there was a dearth of solutions. For the BBC, as for its peers, this gender imbalance stemmed from a combination of hard-to-tackle inertial factors ranging from long-established routines – for example, lists of which external experts could speak well on particular news topics – to historic hiring practices, and, of course, unquestioned unconscious beliefs played a role too.

Ros Atkins, a BBC news journalist and presenter (and a white male with no HR or diversity expertise) decided to tackle the persistent imbalance in the gender representation of BBC News output. He came up with 50:50, a very simple tool that was also very successful: four years after its launch, 61 per cent of teams working with the programme had featured at least 50 per cent women contributors – an increase of 26 per cent since teams started monitoring this. The programme was later expanded to include representation of ethnicity and disability, and for teams that had been monitoring this for at least 18 months, 53 per cent had achieved their targets for disability representation (an increase of 35 per cent) and 65 per cent achieved their targets for ethnicity representation (an increase of 7 per cent). 50:50 has since spread worldwide and outside the media sector: it is now used in over 140 organisations in 30 countries in industries ranging from fashion to finance,[12, 13] and it is also the subject of a Harvard Business School case study.

(Continued)

What is 50:50?

50:50 is an extremely simple process. It invites participating teams (who elect to join on a voluntary basis) to measure the gender of contributors in their content and track this regularly. This analysis shows their performance, and it is then up to them to decide how to respond and improve their representation. It was built on equally straightforward premises: BBC News teams influence who contributes to their programmes; if they can be made aware of gender imbalances in the range of contributors who are selected, then they are in a position to select different contributors, and thus the imbalance will be redressed. Atkins's logic proved correct. Uptake spread organically within the BBC, progress was monitored across the organisation and published annually. By 2022, 750 teams across the organisation had adopted it, and 250 of those teams had expanded their monitoring to include the representation of disability and ethnicity contributors.

Data at the heart of the change process

As with *The Guardian* case in this chapter, data played a central role in changing cultural assumptions and work practices. It created an ongoing reminder of the need to change and an objective focus for argumentation, as Ros Atkins explains:[14]

> Having data available and being collected systematically removed the, 'well I think we're doing quite well,' or 'I think we're not doing quite well'. It has provided the foundation for discussions.

As with *The Guardian's* case, for data to work as a change lever, it needs to be as recent as possible, as Atkins points out:

> The potency of data to drive cultural change decreases with every minute that passes from the time that something was created … the data is at its most potent in the immediate aftermath of creating something … so, the whole thing is geared around measures you produce and share immediately after you create something.

But unlike *The Guardian* (where data was generated automatically and delivered via a dashboard), the BBC's 50:50 data was generated by the teams themselves. Ros sees this as central to the initiative's success:

> I'd seen lots of diversity monitoring, but I couldn't see it making that much difference … so, the big idea was, get the people making the content do the measuring … you make them look the numbers in the eye at the moment that they're producing content … it forces engagement.

(Continued)

Why did 50:50 work?

The 50:50 case is multidimensional. It is a successful diversity initiative, a culture change initiative, and can also be categorised as a creative response to an organizational problem.

In terms of **culture change**, the project worked in many ways to change underlying assumptions and work practices as a result. Lewin's model (p. 175) provides an overview of how this worked:

Stage in model	How did it play out in 50:50?
Unfreezing	The self-monitoring process 'unfroze' minds by creating persistent awareness of the issue and clarity on specifically what needed to change in BBC News' output.
Changing – moving to a new level	The data generated from the process showed what needed to change and provided constant feedback on the impact of the changes that were being made. As this continued, this approach became habitual, part of standard practice.
Refreezing	As more and more teams in the BBC voluntarily signed up to 50:50, as pan-BBC progress was publicly published and reported on with some fanfare by the Director General, and as more and more companies worldwide adopted the programme, 50:50 not only became an acknowledged success, but also gradually anchored in everyday routines and rituals, and in this way part of the BBC's cultural web (see p. 176).

Central to the success of each stage in the Lewin model is that the 50:50 programme is more 'middle-out' than a 'top-down'. Ros was convinced that harnessing peer groups would maximise the change of cultural acceptance. This dynamic played a role in all of the Lewin model stages:

> … rather than use management edicts to drive sign-up, we targeted individual teams within departments … I targeted the team that I thought would make the biggest success of it, not the team that was the highest profile … I was convinced that if you had a success story within a department of one team, and you made a fuss of them, and you made a fuss of them with their boss, and you just generally celebrated their success … the other teams in the department might well look at that and think, well maybe we could do this too. And it's just worked again, and again, and again, and again. And once you have that peer group dynamic up and running, it helps recruitment. It helps the performance because different teams within sections want to outdo each other. (Interview Ros Atkins and Lucy Küng, 2022)

In terms of boosting organisational creativity, 50:50 also conforms with the best practices discussed in the previous chapter. The project process encouraged intrinsic motivation and buy-in, which is essential to generate a creative response to an organisational problem, as outlined in the following Table:

(Continued)

Factor increasing intrinsic motivation	Presence in the 50:50 programme
A creative response is explicitly demanded	The 50:50 programme did not prescribe what changes teams should make to address the imbalance in their output. Rather, they were expected to design and implement their own solutions.
Challenge is clear, deliverable and inspiring	The goal was extremely clear (50:50 in terms of representation), deliverable, because teams had significant influence on the content they created, and inspiring because it tapped into widespread unease about unequal representation and provided a simple path to correct this.
Provides autonomy for teams	As we saw in Chapter 5, autonomy is first among equals in terms of generating intrinsic motivation. The 50:50 approach gave teams autonomy: they could decide whether to participate or not, and they also had agency over how to address any issues they found.

Autonomy and agency were central to the success of 50:50 in Ros's opinion, as was the fact that it had been conceived not by managers or consultants, but by a journalist. He knew that for this to land, it needed to be seen as coming from 'one of us':

> Newsrooms, and content production environments, are deeply cynical places, rightly so … if you're going to ask them to do something new, on top of their busy day, you need to make sure you're seriously credible. Now, if you come from them, you are instantly more credible. So quite often, diversity champions, or leaders within big corporates, can come from outside of the content production environment … and I'm not being disparaging about the work they do … they do very important work at a corporate level. But, if you want to persuade a group of cynical, sometimes even grumpy journalists or content producers that they should take on something new, it's quite disarming if you're standing in front of them going, 'I do the same thing as you'. You can immediately have a different conversation.

Case questions

1. Look at the analysis of the BBC's organisational culture on p. 168. Did the 50:50 initiative resonate with any of these underlying values in particular? If yes, which ones and why?
2. The 50:50 approach was initially introduced in the newsroom to be implemented by a specific subculture in the BBC – journalists. How well do you think this approach would be received by professional subcultures? Would there be a difference, and if yes, why?

Notes

1 Satya Nadella, *Hit Refresh, 2017*. HarperCollins, p.100.
2 Foreword to *Win from Within*, James Heskett, 2022.
3 Boris Groysberg, Jeremiah Lee, Jesse Price and J. Yo-Jud Cheng, 'The leader's guide to corporate culture', *Harvard Business Review*, January–February 2018.
4 Mark Thompson, 'New York Times CEO shares his guide to thriving in the next decade'. Imna.org.blogs, 19 January 2020.
5 Interview with author, 2017.
6 'The Guardian to end print?', *Flashes and Flames*, 31 July 2020.
7 'The Guardian to end print?', Flashes and Flames, 31 July, 2020.
8 Peter Martin, Head of Audience Development, cited in Peter Bale, 'How Newsrooms Succeed in Google Search', INMA, December 2022
9 https://jobs.netflix.com/culture
10 Reed Hastings and Erin Meyer, *No Rules Rules: Netflix and the Culture of Reinvention*. W.H. Allen, 2020.
11 Cited in Lucas Shaw, 'What Netflix will look like in 2023, *Bloomberg Newsletter*, 17 October 2022.
12 www.bbc.co.uk/5050/impact2020
13 www.niemanlab.org/2019/05/the-bbcs-5050-project-shows-equal-gender-representation-in-news-coverage-is-achievable-even-in-traditionally-male-areas
14 https://hbr.org/2019/06/tackling-the-underrepresentation-of-women-in-media
15 Interview with author, 2019.

SEVEN

LEADERSHIP

> Leaders' strengths and weaknesses will determine the strengths and weaknesses of the organization ... the personality of the leader … creates the environment for how the organization grows or shifts. (Maria Ressa, Rappler Founder and Nobel Prize Winner, 2021)[1]

The leaders of media organisations have always commanded intense scrutiny from regulators, policymakers and the media itself. This reflects in part the power the media exerts – to influence public opinion, build a personal profile, gain access to politicians and, by extension, influence regulation and trade terms. And the media (and increasingly the adjacent tech sector) has a long tradition of flamboyant leaders who figure large in the public eye from the press barons of the early twentieth century like William Randolph Hearst, through media moguls such as Rupert Murdoch, to today's digital empire-builders such as Mark Zuckerberg.

Great attention is paid to these larger-than-life individuals, but analysis of leadership in the media industry – the tools, techniques, and practices they use – has received far less attention. It has been suggested that leadership is 'arguably the single most neglected area of research and theory development in the field of media management' (Mierzjewska and Hollifield, in Albarran et al., 2006).

This chapter explores leadership in the media industry and its influence on strategy. It reviews theoretical approaches to the subject and explores the strands within this body of research most frequently applied to the sector. Cases contextualise the theory and provide insights into how these approaches play out in practice.

What is leadership?

The study of leadership can be traced back to the ancient Greeks. Research from a management, rather than an historical, perspective began in earnest in the 1920s and in the ensuing years, leadership has been investigated from many different theoretical standpoints using an enormous variety of different methodological approaches.

As research has progressed, perspectives have shifted dramatically. Universal recipes that assume there is 'one best way' to lead have been buttressed by contingent approaches that stress the context-dependent nature of the leadership task. A tight instrumental focus on traits, skills and styles has been broadened to involve the interactive processes between leaders and those led. A narrow leader-centric focus on the leader's abilities and attributes has evolved into integrated conceptual frameworks encompassing a leader's relationships with those led, and the strategic context. Objectivist approaches that see leadership as an absolute and measurable entity have been challenged by subjectivist ones that view leadership as something constructed through social interaction. But it is worth noting that today all these approaches co-exist. The job profiles used by executive search experts reflect a skills approach. Leaders seeking to accelerate digital transformation turn to theories of transformational leadership. To repair or renew the cultural fabric of organisations, especially at mid levels, often needs collaborative leadership or servant leadership methods.

As this chapter shows, there is an extensive body of theory on leadership, but it lacks commonly accepted definitions and is riven by methodological divisions. Debate persists concerning fundamental issues, such as what leadership is (Bass, 1990; Yukl, 2002; Northouse, 2004, 2022). For example, does leadership reside in a set of qualities or characteristics belonging to those acting as leaders (Jago, 1982), or in a social influence process that seeks to get a group of individuals to move towards a specific objective (Jago, 1982; Kotter, 1988; Northouse, 2022)? Consensus is also lacking on where leadership is to be found. Some researchers view the terms of manager and leader as interchangeable (Conger, 1999), the assumption being that authority inevitably involves a degree of leadership. Others, for example transformational theorists, assume that leaders are senior figures involved in strategic decision-taking. Trait theories classify anyone with responsibility for achieving a given task that involves a group of individuals as a leader, especially if that individual has the specific competencies required or an influence over the situation.

Trait approaches: born to be a leader

Known as 'great person approaches', trait theories are the result of some of the earliest systematic research into leadership. In vogue from the early 1900s to the 1940s, these view leadership as residing in a set of definable, measurable inborn traits that are found in 'natural leaders' (Jago, 1982), which range from physical characteristics such as height, to aspects of personality and temperament, motivation, needs and values. Researchers sought to identify the traits that were linked positively with successful leaders and often turned to historical figures such as Napoleon or Gandhi for their data. The assumption was that once the 'right' traits had been identified, potential leaders could be identified by screening for these (Jago, 1982).

Trait approaches held great intuitive appeal but, despite extensive research, a consistent, definitive list of leadership traits that applied across all contexts and which could predict leadership ability never emerged (Stogdill, 1948; Jago, 1982). Subsequent work in the field, as discussed in this chapter, highlighted the contextual nature of leadership: there can never be a universal recipe – the traits needed in any given organisation depend on the situation in hand. It was also acknowledged that leadership is a relational, not an individual construct. Leadership rests on two parties – the leader and those led.

Recently, research interest has returned to trait theories, but with a focus on different types of traits and the assumption that traits are inborn is also increasingly absent: newer research recognises that leadership traits can be acquired. While earlier researchers explored characteristics such as intelligence, masculinity, dominance, and extraversion, newer research highlights traits connected to leaders' social intelligence, their ability to understand their own and others' feelings and behaviours and shape actions around that. This perspective is fundamental to the charismatic and authentic approaches to leadership discussed later in this chapter.

'Newer' leadership traits identified by more recent researchers include:

Intelligence	Leaders tend to have higher intelligence than non-leaders. However, too high intelligence can be counterproductive as leaders with very high intelligence levels may have difficulties communicating with followers, become impatient and their ideas may be too advanced for followers to accept.
Self-confidence	The ability to be certain about one's competencies and skills, including a sense of self-esteem and the belief that one can make a difference. This is important to be able to influence others.
Determination	The desire to get things done, to be proactive, to be assertive and to persevere to achieve goals.
Integrity	Honesty, trustworthiness, having a strong set of principles and taking responsibility for their actions. Leaders exhibiting this trait inspire confidence because they can be trusted.
Sociability	Social leaders have good interpersonal skills and create good relationships. They are friendly, outgoing, tactful, and diplomatic.

Source: Northhouse, 2022: 32–5

Risk-taking: essential trait for the ambitious leaders?

> The biggest risk is not taking any risk. In a world that is changing really quickly, the only strategy that is guaranteed to fail is not taking risks. (Mark Zuckerberg)[2]

> Speed matters in business. Many decisions and actions are reversible and do not need extensive study. We value calculated risk taking. (Amazon Leadership Principles)[3]

Audacious bets in any industry are guaranteed to generate press coverage. This was as true in previous eras with media moguls such as Joseph Pulitzer, as it is today of tech titans such as Jeff Bezos or Elon Musk. These gambles are often reflexively framed as intrinsic to the nature of the entrepreneurial leader.

Viewed through the lens of leadership theory, a pronounced entrepreneurial orientation leader is a trait, and its components include being closely abreast of environmental change, employing a visceral mixture of intuition and experience to interpret events, and a strategic orientation to hunt out opportunities in the environment and make bold resource commitments in response to that change (Mintzberg et al., 1998).

This pronounced penchant for risk is central to understanding of the 'media mogul', as anyone who has watched the HBO series 'Succession' will know. Logan Roy, the lead character is an archetypical risk-taking larger-than-life media mogul (reputedly modelled on Rupert Murdoch). Indeed, the media mogul is defined as someone who:

> ... owns and operates major media companies, who takes entrepreneurial risks ... who largely built up his own media empire: ... [the] entrepreneurial element can include the launching of new media enterprises ... but often consists of largely buying up, and taking over, existing media companies. (Tunstall and Palmer, 1998: 105)

A valuable nuance regarding the leadership trait of risk-taking was introduced by McClelland (1961) in the sixties and is still relevant today. He distinguished between 'gambling' and 'calculating', suggesting that successful entrepreneurial leaders do not in fact take risks but highly calculated gambles, and this trait was honed by years of experimentation. Rupert Murdoch (founder of News Corporation) and Ted Turner (founder of CNN) have both been credited with a pronounced facility for risk, and both reportedly gambled since childhood

(Bibb, 1993; Shawcross, 1994; Auletta, 2004) and continued with risk-taking strategies as they built their empires. It has been said that 'no one else bets the farm quite like Murdoch' (Gibson, 2007), who is 'the most gifted opportunist in the media' (Pooley, 2007).

The start-up world also links the concepts of risk-taking, entrepreneurialism and leadership, which are tightly linked. In his influential book, *The Lean Start-Up*, Eric Ries defines start-up leadership as 'creating conditions that enable employees to do the kinds of experimentation that entrepreneurship requires' (2011: 35). Michael Moritz of Sequoia Capital, and investor in Instagram, Reddit, Tumblr, WhatsApp and YouTube, suggests that 'the ability to resist [doing what others expect of them] is the difference between being a manager and a leader'.

Skills approaches: leadership can be learned

Trait approaches are absolute: they assume that there is one best way to lead and that depends on a set of immutable predispositions, inborn leanings or abilities that individuals either have or don't have. Skills approaches are more egalitarian. They see leadership as residing in a combination of skills that can be acquired through training programmes, growing experience, mentoring, and so on (Northouse, 2004). Thus, leadership is within the gift of many, rather than a few.

Research in this field seeks to hunt out the learnable skills, knowledge and behaviours that make for effective leadership (Jago, 1982; Mumford et al., 2000; Northouse, 2004, 2022). Katz initiated this stream of research (Katz, 1955) when he identified three core categories of leadership skills (Northouse, 2004):

- **Technical skills**. The ability 'to work with things', including analytical skills, as well as expertise in domain-appropriate tools and techniques.
- **Human skills.** The ability to work effectively with people colleagues at all levels, being sensitive to their perspectives, needs and motivations, and being able to create a climate of trust.
- **Conceptual skills.** The ability to work with abstract ideas and hypothetical notions.

The concept of a 'skill' was expanded in the 1990s into 'capabilities', which were defined as the 'knowledge and skills that make effective leadership possible' (Mumford et al., 2000: 12). As research progressed, the cognitive skills of solving problems and constructing solutions became a focus. These require a facility with abstract and hypothetical ideas that allows a leader to identify complex relationships and predict future events from current trends (Yukl, 2002), and find solutions to new, unusual and ill-defined problems (Mumford et al., 2000; Northouse, 2004, 2022).

Amazon has a clearly defined set of Leadership Principles[4] that its managers are expected to follow:

> We use our Leadership Principles every day, whether we're discussing ideas for new projects or deciding on the best approach to solving a problem. It is just one of the things that makes Amazon peculiar.

These focus particularly on the skills of leadership, for example:

Learn, dive deep into the detail	'Leaders are never done learning and always seek to improve themselves.' 'Stay connected to the details, audit frequently.'
Moving fast	'Speed matters ... Many decisions and actions are reversible and do not need extensive study.'
Pay attention to others	'Leaders listen attentively, speak candidlyand treat others respectfully.'
Disagree and commit	'Leaders are obligated to respectfully challenge decisions when they disagree, even when doing so is uncomfortable or exhausting.'

A digital environment places specific challenges on leaders. In the final section of this chapter, David L. Rogers provides an overview of the jobs of a leader in a digital era.

Shared or distributed leadership

> At Netflix ... we have a loosely coupled system. Decision making is highly dispersed, and we have few centralized control processes, rules, or policies. This provides a high degree of freedom to individuals, gives each department greater flexibility, and speeds up decision making throughout the company. (Reed Hastings and Erin Meyer, 2020, 216–2107)

Distributed leadership is seen as a potentially valuable response to the challenges posed by VUCA environment and other contexts requiring high levels of innovation. It is seen as permitting faster responses to complex issues (Morgeson et al., 2010), which in turn can increase competitive advantage (Porter and Beyerlein, 2000). Teams with shared leadership have been found to have higher levels of trust and cohesion, and less conflict (Bergman et al., 2012).

This concept emerged in the field of educational institutions. Because it is popularly understood to bring benefits such as bringing decision making closer to the customer and the market, creating space for creativity and collaboration, and therefore increasing innovation and trust, ownership and engagement, it has also found traction in sectors affected by fast, complex change. It has theoretical roots in theories of distributed cognition and activity theory (which views human behaviour as contextualised in a situation).

In shared leadership contexts, leadership authority rests not with specified individuals, but is shared among members of a group. Members of that group come forward to provide leadership as needed, and then step back to allow others to lead (Kogler Hill in Northouse, 2022). Decision making is dispersed and autonomy and authority are devolved to those best placed to make decisions. Shared leadership is therefore collective leadership. In the best case, it means that the leadership skills available for any initiative encompasses the entire repertoire of the entire team (Day et al., 2004). By extension:

- Anyone who engages in leadership activities is a leader – leadership is conferred by task, not position.
- Anyone who is influenced by leadership activities is a follower.
- A person can lead in one situation and follow in another – the roles of leader and follower are dynamic.
- Influence flows two ways – followers may influence leaders, as well as leaders influencing followers.

Models of shared leadership see leaders at the top as supported by a network of leadership practices distributed across an organisation: leadership is not projected downward from the top, but involves tasks and responsibilities that are carried out at all levels and by a range of indivual (Fletcher and Käufer, 2003). Thus, the approach links leadership with group processes and teamwork, and increased interest in distributed leadership reflects the increasing use of team structures in organisations. This in turn stems from several factors: the increased complexity of products and services requiring more interfunction collaboration, globalisation meaning that organisations are internationally dispersed, and flatter organisational structures (Kogler Hill in Northouse, 2022). As team structures become more common, interest grows in how teams are best led. Effective leadership processes have been identified as the most critical factor in team success (Zaccaro et al., 2001).

Learning as leadership skill

> Digital leadership requires the ability to reimagine and reinvent that business itself. What business are you in? How do you create value for customers? (Rogers, 2016: 239)

Finding appropriate solutions to such problems becomes more difficult as environments become turbulent. Extremely turbulent environments are described as 'VUCA' – that is, characterised by volatility, uncertainty, complexity and ambiguity. The risk of cognitive rigidity and erroneous conclusions increases in step with environmental instability: leaders must not only become more structured and vigilant in environmental scanning and problem-solving (Ancona, 1990), but also capable of challenging and updating their operating assumptions of unlearning.

Schein (1992) terms this learning leadership, which is based on double loop learning – a central concept from the field of education. It concerns the process by which people become aware of the assumptions and beliefs that underlie the knowledge that generally supports their decision making (Argyris, 1977). It is based on the premise that there are two types of learning:

- **First-order, or single-loop, learning.** This arises through repeated exposure to similar types of problem. The type of knowledge that arises is advantageous in stable contexts, especially if other players are new to an issue and do not possess it, but it can be a liability in turbulent ones since it reduces the likelihood of recognising a need for change (Weick, 1979).
- **Second-order, or double-loop, learning.** This is important in unstable contexts. This involves questioning the governing norms, unlearning prior assumptions, and developing new heuristics (Tushman and Anderson, 1986) and is central to improving the organisation's ability to adapt (Virany et al., 1992).

The skills approach is pragmatic and inclusive. It explores the skills that make up effective leadership and maps out a route by which individuals can become leaders by acquiring those skills, and assumes that anyone who can learn the necessary skills has the potential for leadership (Northouse, 2022). Not surprisingly, it often acts as the conceptual basis for recruitment activity, leadership development programmes, the design of business education programmes and industry development initiatives.

Leadership skills in the media

There is a slim body of research into leadership skills required in the media sector. Sanchez-Tabernero (in Küng, 2006) identifies the ability to 'build great teams', which requires a long-term orientation, an ability to motivate, strong beliefs and an understanding of consumer tastes. While not addressing the media industry specifically, Burns and Stalkers' (1961/1994: 102) research into environments that further innovation identifies two leadership skills: to grasp the changing dynamics of the strategic environment, particularly technological ones, and recalibrate the internal organisation in step; and to 'define the work situation, displaying … the commitments, effort, and self-involvement … the individual … should attempt to meet'.

The ability to see business opportunities in turbulent environments surfaces frequently in analyses of successful media leaders. In her research into the pay television platform Sky, Spar (2001) highlights Murdoch's skill at designing business models that exploit multiple uncertainties – in that case, advances in satellite and encryption technologies, a regulatory vacuum arising from the confluence of domestic and EU broadcasting regulation, and the UK government's desire to increase competition in UK broadcasting:

> Again and again, the same pattern unfolded: Sky would recognise how some emerging technology could enable the firm either to leap through a regulatory barrier or consolidate a competitive foothold. Then Sky's managers would move to grasp this technology, develop it, create whatever standard might be necessary, and thus control its usage by any other parties. This was how Murdoch had first used satellite technologies to circumvent the otherwise solid net of British regulation: this was how Sky operated throughout the next decade. (Spar, 2001: 156)

Digital skills, including digital leadership skills, are highly sought as multiple sectors confront the challenges of digitalisation (see p. 7). The hard skill dimension of this concerns leaders' understanding of how IT, digital technologies and data can make organisations responsive to customer needs and changing markets.

From a softer skills perspective, digital leadership focuses on the capabilities necessary to innovate and to drive digital transformation. This includes skills such as how a leader works with teams, including their ability to build teams, build culture, empower interaction, devolve decision making, collaboration, capture learning from failed projects, motivate and influence within a team context.

Style approaches

> Instead of simply continuing … Jobs' autocratic leadership style, Cook has played to his strengths and placed emphasis on advancing cooperation among Apple's arsenal of talent. This is extremely indicative of the democratic style of management, which encourages consensus building, particularly among high-level employees prior to mutally consented decision making. (Investopedia, 2021)[5]

From the late 1940s onwards, researchers started to focus on leadership style – on leaders' behaviour and the impact of this on others (Stogdill, 1974; Jago, 1982; Yukl, 2002). These 'Style' approaches therefore expand the concept of leadership to include leaders' relationship with followers – and this expanded view became intrinsic to much subsequent leadership theory.

Like the Skills approach described above, Style, or behavioural, approaches also see leadership as something that can be learned rather than something that is inborn. That learning in how to lead is the result of experiences, knowledge and opportunities that generate responses that contribute to development as a leader.

Research by the University of Michigan identified two critical dimensions of leadership style. The first is employee-centred and focuses on a leader's concern for people. The second is job-centred, and centres on a leader's concern for what is produced, or output (Stogdill, 1974). These classifications derived from early work in the field, the Ohio State Studies, which involved followers answering a questionnaire on the behaviours of their leaders (in this work, the relationship behaviours were termed 'consideration' and task behaviour was termed 'initiating structure', which encompassed tasks that organised work and defined the roles around it.

These two fundamental dimensions – leadership activities focused on people and those focused on the job or task – remain at the core of style approaches:

- **Relationship behaviours** focus on the well-being of followers, approaches that help followers feel comfortable with themselves, with each other and with the situation, and include consideration, the degree of two-way communication and consultation, mutual trust, respect and warmth a leader exhibits towards his followers.

- **Task behaviours** are focused on achieving goals, they seek to help followers achieve their objectives by structuring it, setting out roles, establishing policies and procedures, facilitating relationships between group members and establishing channels of communication.

Each dimension will always require some element of the other, so leaders need to combine them to influence followers to achieve their goals, what is critical is the leader's ability to judge how much of each is required, according to the situation (Northouse, 2022). For example, the quote at the start of this section suggests that Tim Cook's leadership style while Apple CEO prioritises on relationship behaviours, while that of his predecessor, Steve Jobs, focused primarily on task behaviours, on achieving goals.

Cook's leadership style preferences is supported by the limited research that existis into leadership styles in the media. This suggests that consensus-based approaches are more appropriate than hierarchical authoritarian ones because creative employees resent being told what to do (Davis and Scase, 2000), will not accept unquestioningly directions from above (Lavine and Wackman, 1988), and when working as news journalists, need editorial freedom and protection from managerial or owner influence (Curran and Seaton, 1981). Aris and Bughin (2005) propose two leadership styles for media organisations, which broadly match the two core dimensions in style approaches to leadership: an inspirational, charismatic, hands-on style (which focused on relationship behaviours; and a performance-orientated, structured style, involving systematic setting of strategic corporate and individual goals.

Transformational leadership

A major recent concept in leadership theory is 'transformational leadership'. This is a broad approach that has spawned subtheories, including charismatic and authentic leadership, and together this school has gained much traction inside the media industry. The origins of this approach are credited to political sociologist Burns (1978), who identified a leader who changes organisations elementally – transforms them – by evoking followers' intrinsic motivation and harnessing this to realise performance outcomes that exceed expectations. The focus on intrinsic motivation distinguishes transformational from 'transactional' leadership, where followers act in a certain way in return for specified extrinsic rewards (Conger, 1989).

The transformational leader 'pulls' levers in the social architecture of the organisation to achieve wide-scale change (Conger, 1989; Senge, 1990; Bass and Avolio, 1994; Bass and Steidlmeier, 1999). The leader's vision for how the organisation should look post-transformation is the starting point – this vision needs to be compelling enough to encourage individuals to question assumptions that might hold back the change process, find new solutions to existing problems and select new courses of action (Senge, 1990). The leader's charisma, termed idealised influence in this body of theory, stems in part, from strong internal ideals (Kunert, 1994) and builds emotional commitment to the vision by engaging followers' higher order needs and encouraging them to transcend self-interest in order to reach new goals (Bass, 1985; Kotter, 1996; Hitt et al., 1998). The transformational leader also changes the cultural assumptions (Morgan, 1986; Sackmann, 1991; Schein, 1992), employing a set of mechanisms to embed new ones.

At the heart of transformational leadership is the interplay between leader and follower. Central to how she or he guides the organisation to a fundamentally different place is that the emphasis is placed on followers' needs, values and performance, and developing them to their fullest potential. This involves coaching, mentoring and providing growth opportunities. The entire spectrum of a leader's actions can act as signs and symbols to the organisation, underlining priorities and emphasising desired behaviours – for example, which issues a leader pays attention to, decisions about who is promoted or who 'gets sent to Siberia' (Schein, 1992), reactions to critical events and how resources are allocated. Mintzberg and Westley (1992) note that transformational leaders often have a strong facility for language, particularly symbolism and metaphor. This process of changing a group's shared cultural assumptions also means changing that group's social identity, since leadership and identity are interdependent.

The basic steps by which a transformational leader moves the organisation are (Northouse, 2022):

- Makes followers aware of the importance and value of specific goals that lead to an 'ideal' future state for the organisation.
- Gets followers to place these goals, which relate to their team or organisation, ahead of their personal goals.
- Persuades followers to address higher-level needs.

Transformational leadership occupies a central place in leadership research (Northouse, 2022). It has relevance for the media sector as it confronts digital disruption – first in its emphasis on intrinsic motivation, and second because it focuses on how leaders can bring about fundamental change and harness followers to pull off major transformation. In his exploration of how incumbent businesses threatened by digitalisation should adapt their organisations, Waldman (2010) proposes a leadership approach that echoes many tenets of transformational leadership. He views the ability to 'bring people with you in challenging times' (2010: 130–1) as the essence of the leadership task. This requires clarity ('people need to know what is happening: why, how and when'), consistency ('don't just present a plan once; present it time and time again ... you are leading people on a journey, not a set of random dance moves'), and collaboration ('getting people working with people from different parts of the business, tackling business problems collectively, is energising and constructive. It makes people feel they are part of something bigger').

Transformational leadership has four components: admiration, attention, aspiration and adaptation:

Admiration (idealised influence)	Leaders are strong role models. Followers admire them, absorb their vision, respect them, trust them and emulate their behaviour. Leaders' behaviour is rooted in high moral and ethical standards.
Attention (indvidualised attention)	The leader 'knows' the people in the organisation as individuals, listens to them, including views that oppose their own, shows concern for followers, and seeks to empower them by investing in their development so they can become fully actualised.
Aspiration (inspirational motivation)	The leader works with emotions, articulates a clear set of values, inspires followers to share these and commit to their vision, and understand how their work contributes to the purpose of the organisation, and leads with optimism and courage.
Adaptation (intellectual stimulation)	The leader encourages followers to develop innovative solutions to challenges, to question assumptions and established 'ways of doing business' and creates a climate that encourages experimentation and learning, encourages inclusive decision-making, rewards innovation and creativity.

While transformational leadership has great intuitive appeal and is now widely applied across a range of contexts, it has its critics. No causal link between transformational leaders and changes in followers or organisations has been established (Antonakis, 2012, cited in Northouse, 2022). Transformational leadership theories have also been criticised as a representing return to trait theories, where exceptional individuals generate exceptional responses from individuals by drawing on inborn personality traits, rather than a set of behaviours that can be acquired (Bryman, 1992).

Kotter's eight-stage process for transformational change

Kotter's approach starts by drawing a central distinction between the role of the leader and that of the manager: leadership is about change, while management is about maintenance. Thus, the leader's job is to 'do the right things', which means set the vision and design strategies to achieve it, empower others to make vision happen, and motivate and inspire people to move out of their comfort zone. The manager's role is to 'do things right'. This means turn strategies into action steps, plans and budgets, ensure the organisation can realise the vision, and check progress and trouble shoot.

Kotter believes that the leader must not only recognise when fundamental change is needed, but also ensure that this happens. Change efforts mostly fail, not because the strategy or vision is wrong, but because culture, bureaucracy, politics, lack of trust, lack of teamwork, arrogance, fear of the unknown, block the change efforts. Kotter's prescription for change seeks to eliminate these barriers.

It has eight steps, which need to be followed sequentially, with no skipping ahead. These are:

1. Establish a sense of urgency.	This means alarming people enough to get them to let go of the status quo. Pay special attention to ensure that key people who may end up much worse off are on board and understand what needs to be done and why, otherwise they may become 'change critics'. Work hard on this stage – building urgency will pay off later.
2. Create a guiding coalition.	A change project needs a strong change team behind it. Check that all the 'true leaders' are on board and visibly committed, and make sure it's diverse. All departments, all levels invest in team building so that it really works together.
3. Create a vision.	The new vision must provide a compelling reason why people should abandon self-interests and buy into uncomfortable changes. Craft the language – the entire change team needs to be able to describe the vision in five minutes or less. Everyone required to give it should practice the 'vision speech' often.

(Continued)

4. Communicate the vision.	The new vision will have to compete with hundreds of other messages, new and old, so double down on ensuring that this message cuts through and is heard. Communicate it directly as much as you can, but also ensure that all other actions and communications underline its message – for example, in terms of what issues a leader pays attention to, who is promoted and rewarded (and who is side-lined).
5. Empower others to act on the vision.	Get rid of barriers to change fast, including people who are resisting change. Anything that undermines the vision – job descriptions, bonus criteria, internal rules – must go. Ensure that those who take risks, break with tradition and make change happen are rewarded.
6. Create short-term wins.	Ensure that there are some visible successes early on. Transformation takes time and quick wins ensure that the urgency doesn't fade. Look for potential wins that are fast, feasible and failsafe, avoiding anything expensive or involving 'change critics'. Analyse the pros and cons of short-term wins you are thinking about before embarking on the project as failure with an early goal can hurt the entire initiative.
7. Build on change.	Be careful not to declare victory too soon. Reinvigorate the change process with new projects and change agents. After each success, analyse what went right and what could be done better. Keep checking systems and policies to see if they fit the vision. Hire and promote people who get the vision and will take it further.
8. Anchor new approaches in the culture.	The final stage is to ensure that changes are consolidated and the organisation doesn't slip back. Show that the changes are bringing success, so take every opportunity to demonstrate their benefits until they become an accepted part of 'the way we do things around here'.

Authentic leadership

> The traditional leadership narrative is all about you: your talents, charisma, and moments of courage and instinct ... real leadership is about your people and creating the conditions for them to fully realize their own capacity and power. To do this, you have to develop stores of trust. (Francis Frei and Anne Morriss, 2020)

'Authentic' leadership is a recent approach that combines elements of leadership, positive psychology, organisational behaviour and ethics theory (Northouse, 2022). It is defined as:

> ... a pattern of leader behavior that draws upon and promotes both positive psychological capacities and a positive ethical climate, to foster greater self-awareness, an internalized moral perspective, balanced processing of information, and relational transparency on the part of leaders working with followers, fostering positive self-development. (Walumbwa et al., 2008: 94)

Authentic leaders share an intertwined set of behaviours that are rooted in positive psychology and a personal sense of ethics (Walumbwa et al., 2008). These make the leaders appear trustworthy and credible (Northouse, 2022) and in turn generate a range of positive outcomes for the wider organisation (Prakash et al., 2021), which arise from changes in the psychological state of followers. They include increasing commitment and team effectiveness (Leroy et al., 2015), fostering creativity (Semedo et al., 2016), optimism and engagement (Stander et al., 2015), and willingness to invest in work and solve problems proactively (Hu et al., 2017).

Researchers have indentified four central behaviours that are a mix of 'intrapersonal' processes that occur 'inside the leader', and 'interpersonal' processes that take place between leaders and followers (Avolio et al., 2009; Gardner and Carlson, 2015; Miao et al., 2018):

Self-awareness	The leader has a deep understanding of self. This includes an awareness of personal values, emotions, motivation, strengths and weaknesses, how these influence his or her decisions and actions, and how these elements impact followers.
Balanced processing	The leader is able to use all available information to make decisions and can be objective in analysing situations. This includes understanding others' views, especially those who disagree.

(Continued)

Internalised moral perspective	The leader has a strong internal moral compass and high ethical standards, and these guide behaviour. The leader's actions are consistent with these standards. Taken together, this helps generate a positive ethical climate inside the organisation.
Relational transparency	The leader communicates honestly and openly and presents her or his true self in interactions. This generates honest relationships and encourages self-development throughout the organisation.

Charismatic leadership

> His remarkable charisma … drew people to him even when they knew he might attack at any moment. (A colleague describing Steve Jobs, in Young and Simon, 2005: 201)

Charismatic leadership is a close cousin of transformational leadership (Hunt and Conger, 1999). It happens when a leader employs personal magnetism to evoke followers' trust and to influence them to act in certain ways in the pursuit of specific goals (Bass, 1985; Conger, 1989, 1999; Conger and Kanungo, 1998; Yukl, 2002). Like transformational approaches, charismatic leadership is understood as collective, processual and attributional – that is, it exists in the perceptions of others. It can improve employee satisfaction, motivation and performance (Yukl, 1999).

Vision is a central tool of charismatic leadership. Steve Jobs's vision was to build 'insanely great' machines that will 'make a dent in the world' swept away rational objections, and an Apple employee describes the impact this had on followers: 'We really believed in what we were doing. The key thing is that we weren't in it for the money. We were out to change the world' (Trip Hawkins, cited in Young and Simon, 2005: 62).

A vision should appeal to followers' higher-order needs and link with their own values and ideals. This engenders emotional commitment and encourages group members to cooperate to achieve their collective task (House, 1977; Conger, 1999; Yukl, 2002). A charismatic leader's vision may represent a marked departure from what has gone before, but not be so dramatic that followers might reject it, and it should resonate with follower disenchantment with current conditions. To embed their vision, the charismatic leader models the behaviours, norms and values followers should adopt. He or she may also act unconventionally – making self-sacrifices or taking personal risks, for example – to underline the importance of the changes that need to be made.

The distinction between transformational and charismatic leadership is not easy to establish. The fields certainly overlap. Conger (1999) sees charismatic leadership as an offshoot of transformational leadership, now of almost equal stature. Certainly, charisma is central to transformational leadership. However, Bass (in Yukl, 1999) argues that a leader can be charismatic without being transformational. It is suggested that the emotional component on the part of leaders and followers distinguishes charismatic leadership as particularly concerning the compelling nature of the vision and the way it is communicated (Conger and Kanungo, 1998). Further, while transformational leadership is normally understood as a positive concept, charismatic leadership has a shadow side – as can be inferred from the quote about Steve Jobs above.

Howell (in Conger, 1999) sees leadership as running a spectrum from leaders who empower and develop their followers, to authoritarian and narcissistic ones who use their power for personal gains. Conger (1999) argues that a charismatic leader may well possess elements of both poles. The success of charismatic leadership is affected by context (Bryman et al., 1996). While charismatic leaders improve employee satisfaction, motivation, and performance, they can also underestimate threats in the organisational environment, screen out negative information, be overly self-confident and have an inflated sense of their own importance (Yukl, 1999). A charismatic leader's strategy may fail if implemented either too early or too late in a strategic initiative (Conger and Kanungo, 1998).

Leading for creativity

An important aspect of strategic leadership in the media relates to the connection between leadership and creativity. This is another under-explored issue, although general suggestions have been made for organisations that need creativity – for example, that hierarchical, paternalistic management styles limit creativity, and inclusive ones that distribute creative decision-making throughout the organisation promote sustained creativity (Mauzy and Harriman, 2003).

For insights into how leadership intersects with levels of creativity inside organisations, we can refer back to theories of organisational creativity. These identify three obvious links. The first is intrinsic motivation. This is central to transformational and charismatic leadership theories, and to creativity theories, although it confers different advantages: in creativity theory, intrinsic motivation catalyses expertise and creative-thinking skills in the pursuit of novel solutions; in leadership theories, intrinsic motivation promotes followers' receptivity to higher-order goals and suppresses self-interest.

The second link is vision. A leader's vision drives strategic action, especially when seeking to achieve transformational change. Vision is central to creativity also, since no new product or service can be created without a clear vision that is simple, achievable, but also stretching and inspiring. The 'right' vision will resonate with pre-existing intrinsic motivation and lay the seed for ultimate success by sparking both a creative response to the core concept and a deeper-lying sense of commitment to its fundamental goals.

The third link involves establishing an environmental context conducive to creativity. This is addressed, albeit tangentially, in the 'initiating structure' dimension of leadership discussed in style approaches, where the leader is viewed as the architect of the work environment, dictating the nature of creative challenges, how resources are allocated, and establishing wider contextual elements such as structure, coordination mechanisms, culture, business processes and management. The provision of autonomy for teams required to be creative also features. At Pixar, Ed Catmull's leadership approach explicitly sought to build an environment where creativity flourishes, and many components of this correlate closely with theories of organisational creativity. A fascinating dimension of this concerns his focus on failure and extracting learning from this. For example, he tried to ensure that teams feel safe to fail: 'Part of our job is to protect the new from people who don't understand that in order for greatness to emerge, there must be phases of not-so-greatness' (Catmull, 2014: 132). Indeed, failure itself is not a problem, although, as creative director Andrew Stanton puts it, 'People need to be wrong as fast as they can' (cited in Catmull, 2014: 97). There are not only post-mortems after movies are complete, but mid-mortems halfway through the process. During these sessions, participants are asked to list the top five things they would do again, and the top five they wouldn't. Performance data is used to stimulate discussion and challenge assumptions based on subjective impressions. This focus on and reframing of failure as an opportunity for growth and creativity has an emotional dimension in that he requires leaders to be honest about their mistakes to make it safe for others to do the same, reflecting the belief that 'being open about problems is the first step toward learning from them' (Catmull, 2014: 111).

Indeed, a fourth point of connection concerns emotions. Emotional commitment by the leader and emotional engagement on the part of followers are fundamental to transformational and charismatic leadership. Emotions – desire, enjoyment, interest – are also present in the intrinsically motivated state, which is central to organisational creativity. The role of emotions in leadership has been acknowledged – Burns (1978), for example, argued that the genius of Mao Tse Tung was his understanding of others' emotions.

Conclusions

Leadership in the media is an under-researched field. Leadership theory is extensive but, because it is disjointed, it is hard to apply systematically to the sector. This chapter therefore needs to be viewed in the spirit of seeking to capture the current state of knowledge and giving impulses for further research.

It does, however, underline the close link that inevitably exists between leadership and strategy, and the relevance of this interrelationship for the media industry. It suggests that the media leadership role encompasses three different spheres: the outer, strategic environment that provides a starting point for strategy; the inner environment, the organisational eco-system comprising the many different organisational phenomena – particularly the interpretative ones – which must be brought into alignment if a strategy is to be implemented; and the internal relationship with the self – the ability to reflect and learn and to connect with others. It also highlights the range of 'sub-roles' contained in the media leadership task (or the number of leadership hats that must be worn at once) and the strategies that can be employed to pull off this extremely challenging requirement.

The chapter also shows that the task of leadership in the media sector contains many inherent paradoxes: the span of competencies and talents required is best served by multi-leader structures, yet these clearly complicate the decision-making process; the intricacies of the environment mandates that leaders develop heuristics to reduce complexity, but these can also limit strategic options when that environment changes too dramatically; the power, influence and responsibility make huge requirements in terms of self-knowledge and emotional maturity, yet individuals possessing such characteristics are unlikely to be able to stomach the temperamental, ego-driven, hard-nosed, power-hungry individuals that populate the sector. Paradoxes such as these are one of the subjects covered in the next chapter, which seeks to identify common themes and issues from the ideas presented in the book so far for researchers, students and practitioners.

Resources

Books and articles

Peter G. Northouse, *Leadership Theory and Practice* (Sage, 2022).

Lucy Kueng, *Hearts and Minds: Harnessing Leadership, Culture and Talent to Really Go Digital* (Reuters Institute for the Study of Journalism, 2020).

Brad Stone, *Amazon Unbound* (Simon & Schuster, 2021).

Satya Nadella, *Hit Refresh* (William Collins, 2017).

Robert Iger, *The Ride of a Lifetime* (Bantam, 2019).

Begin with Trust (Frances Frei and Anne Morris, *Harvard Business Review*, May–June 2000).

Amy Edmondson, *What Psychological Safety Looks like in a Hybrid Workplace*. Available at: https://hbr.org/2021/04/what-psychological-safety-looks-like-in-a-hybrid-workplace.

Scott D. Anthony, Clark Gilbert and Mark W. Johnson, *Dual Transformation: How to Reposition Today's Business While Creating the Future* (Harvard Business Review Press, 2017).

Ringtone: Exploring the Rise and Fall of Nokia in Mobile Phones. Yves Doz and Keeley Wilson (Oxford University Press, 2016).

Videos

Frances Frei, *How to Build (and Rebuild) Trust* (April, 2018). Available at: www.ted.com/talks/frances_frei_how_to_build_and_rebuild_trust?language=en

Satya Nadella interviewed at Code 2021. Available at: www.youtube.com/watch?v=-Osca2Zax4Y

Amy Edmondson, *Fearless – Creating Psychological Safety for Learning, Innovation, and Growth*. Available at: www.youtube.com/watch?v=_1Ub1.xfSQ1s

Clark Gilbert discusses *Dual Transformation at the Deseret News*. Available at: www.youtube.com/watch?v=M8AcNbtIo8Y

Clark Gilbert on *The Three Crises of Leadership*. Available at: www.youtube.com/watch?v=PzquYWxHRV4

Case: Greg Dyke's transformational leadership at the BBC

> When I went to the Harvard Business School back in 1989, I luckily came across a brilliant professor called John Kotter, who was the first person whom I had come across who talked about the difference between management and leadership.

Kotter's eight-stage process for leading strategic change (Kotter, 1996) is one of the most widely applied leadership concepts in the media. One of the most well-documented applications is when Greg Dyke, Director General of the BBC, followed this methodology to 'transform' the organisation. This process was turned into a teaching case study for business schools and key steps in this are outlined in this chapter (Pg. 209–210).

Dyke named his initiative, 'Making it Happen'. It was designed to make the BBC more creative and to repair the damage done to the social fabric of the organisation by a previous radical restructuring product, 'Producer Choice'. While the latter was hailed as visionary, it was extremely complex and resented internally as the brainchild of consultants (Spindler and van den Brul, 2006–7).

Dyke believed that greater creativity and better service to audiences would ensure the BBC's survival as a publicly funded broadcaster in a multi-channel environment. 'Making it Happen' was Dykes's answer. Rather than driven by consultants, it should be a 'do-it-yourself' intervention designed to harness the energy, commitment and ideas of the BBC's thousands of staff (Spindler and van den Brul, 2006–7).

Dyke employed several strategies to build commitment. First were the 'Just Imagine' brainstorming workshops where 10,000 staff contributed over 25,000 ideas about the BBC's challenges and how these might be overcome. A handful of the best ideas were implemented very publicly within weeks to demonstrate that staff involvement was valued. Dyke also abandoned the formal communication style of his predecessor. All staff were on first-name terms, meeting documentation was reduced to a minimum and yellow cards stating 'Cut the Crap, Make it Happen' were distributed for staff to use if they saw good ideas being rejected or bureaucracy surfacing.

Next, Dyke published a new set of BBC values, which he stressed should become the bedrock of the new culture. Staff teams were asked to propose how the BBC could realise its new goals, and from these emerged a BBC-wide change plan with five main sections: Providing Great Leadership; Making the BBC a Great Place to Work; Getting Closer to our Audiences; Inspiring Creativity Everywhere; and Working as One BBC (in total over 40 separate

(Continued)

initiatives). These were presented to staff through televised, interactive BBC-wide 'conversations' involving 17,000 staff at over 400 meetings.

Research two years in showed that 62 per cent felt 'Making it Happen' was making a real difference, 22 per cent were actively championing change, 58 per cent felt valued, and 50 per cent felt management behaviour was consistent with BBC values.

This project conforms to transformational leadership theory (Kanter, 2004). Dyke harnessed staff members' intrinsic motivation and altered the BBC's social fabric to achieve fundamental change. He encouraged staff to rethink their assumptions, find new solutions to the BBC's problems and change day-to-day behaviour. He succeeded in shifting the culture, making it more creative and open to change, and through his personal style – approachability, informality, directness, communicativeness – modelled the behaviours he wanted staff to emulate.

Despite this success, Dyke was ousted a couple of years into his term as a result of a crisis that arose when in 2003 a BBC radio reporter claimed that the UK Government had made a false claim in an intelligence dossier and escalated when a weapons expert who had briefed the BBC committed suicide. In 2004 the Hutton Inquiry was tasked with investigating these events and found fault with the BBC's management and editorial systems – and by implication its top leadership. Both Dyke and the BBC Chairman resigned. Dyke's resignation brought thousands of employees into the street in protest and a full-page newspaper advert was taken in his support – evidence of the emotional bond his leadership approach had forged with BBC staff.

Case: Leadership clarity secures *Daily Maverick's* future

Ben Whitelaw and Styli Charalambous

> The 'Securing our Future' program aimed to create more relevant journalism that would create deeper relationships with our audiences and drive audience growth and revenue opportunities. (Styli Charalambous, CEO)

Daily Maverick is one of the largest independent news publishers in South Africa, and one of the most feared and respected in the media landscape. It was founded in 2009 by Branko Brkic (Editor in Chief) and Styli Charalambous

(Continued)

(CEO) to take on legacy news offerings and against a backdrop of political hostility to independent journalism with the stated mission to 'defend truth'.

As a start-up, it launched with just five staff. By 2022, the team numbered 120 (during which time the number of journalists in South Africa had shrunk by more than half). With over 10 million monthly unique visitors, the company has a crucial voice in a challenging political environment and where general unemployment hovers around 35 per cent.

'Securing our Future' – A strategic blueprint

Daily Maverick has never been scared to go against the grain. In 2018, it launched 'Maverick Insider', the first news membership program on the African continent, seeking to generate membership fees to supplement advertising revenue and finance newsroom growth. While maintaining a free-for-all model, voluntary membership totalled 24,000 by May 2023. Another contrarian move saw them launch a weekly print publication in the middle of pandemic lockdown in 2020.

Having grown into a medium-sized organisation, *Daily Maverick* still had the structure and processes of a smaller newsroom. It needed to mature, and Charalambous had seen how industry titans like the *New York Times* had transformed by becoming data-driven and audience-centric. Could the same approach help ensure that the *Daily Maverick* would thrive as an independent sustainable media organisation for many decades to come?

Charalambous enrolled in the Craig Newmark CUNY Media Innovation and Leadership Executive Program in 2020 and devoted his time to reimagine how the organisation works. He developed a 56-page 'Strategic Blueprint', and from this created 'Securing Our Future', a two-year change program using Kotter's transformational leadership model.

Stages in the program

The program had three core goals that would both guide the organisation towards a strong future and keep it anchored in its core journalistic mission.

- Be more strategic.
- Understand audiences better.
- Do data right.

These goals would contribute to building a more effective culture of innovation across the organisation.

An eight-stage process was designed, based on Kotter's approach.

(Continued)

Step 1: Creating urgency

Daily Maverick was performing well, but if staff wanted to 'secure our future' it needed to put audience needs at the heart of operations. A shared sense of urgency had to be created, starting with the founder, Branko Brkic, by stressing the importance of undertaking the project while both were intimately involved in the organisation.

A benchmark survey to understand current awareness (or lack thereof) of the company's vision and strategy, understanding of their audience and extent of data use. Online feedback sessions to gauge interest in the project built on the survey. These were optional, but two-thirds of staff attended where they learned what the program would mean in practical terms.

These interventions built a shared urgency around the need to change and stressed this was a collaborative process over which the staff had agency. Valuable learnings also emerged that were fed back to the leadership team. For example, the recent growth spurt had put the organisation under strain, and adding new teams with inadequate planning and less than ideal onboarding.

Step 2: Building a coalition

Change programs need a guiding coalition, and Charalambous built a working group that met bi-weekly to convert 'Securing our Future' into a project plan and steer the project.

Because 70 per cent of staff in the organisation worked in editorial roles, senior journalists and editors were represented in the group to ensure credibility with the wider organisation. An outside coach supported the process and a media expert supported company-wide communication and training.

A tracker was built to structure the project and a Slack channel created to share links and updates between meetings. This coalition of changemakers was supplemented by several key hires and internal moves, including the recruitment of an audience development manager to drive the organisation's acquisition and engagement efforts.

Step 3: Create a vision to direct the change effort

The strategic goals were clear, but Charalambous wanted to ensure that these were anchored in a strong shared vision about the purpose of *Daily Maverick*. To develop the vision, he held a session on 'What is journalism for?' with pre-readings from *The Elements of Journalism* by Kovach and Rosenstiel and *Constitution of South Africa*.

(Continued)

Their interpretation landed on the constitution's ask of the press to help protect South Africa's fledgling democracy and that journalism should help people navigate life. What also emerged was the congruence of the *Daily Maverick's* vision that people should 'know more and know better' having spent time with its journalism.

Step 4: Communicate the vision

A Town Hall was held to share the vision of the project. Charalambous was aware there were still concerns that data-driven methods would result in click-baiting tactics and responded by focusing on how they would create more relevant journalism, allowing the work of journalists to achieve greater impact.

Building on this message, a monthly internal newsletter, 'Future Proof', was created to report on the project's progress, and on innovations in the journalism industry. Regular Q&As were held with staff, and care was taken at these to stress the collaborative and inclusive nature of the project.

Step 5: Empower others to act on the vision

It was critical that everyone bought into the program and understood its goals. In 2021 staff were surveyed again, and responses highlighted that there was work to do. People were not confident in applying data or audience thinking to their work and needed help to connect their work to the wider goals of the organisation. There were still concerns about restrictions on editors' decision-making power and how the use of data would play out in daily decision-making.

Senior staff tackled these issues themselves (rather than bring in a consultant). Online meetings that mixed editorial and commercial colleagues in small groups were held where people participated in hands-on projects that encouraged the use of data and audience insights.

Throughout, leaders addressed staff concerns honestly and directly, and stressed that everyone was driving towards the same shared vision. A key slide highlighted 'The future of Daily Maverick is down to all of us', a reminder that everyone had a part to play, and that this project needed collective effort and buy-in.

Step 6: Plan for and create short-term wins

There were times when progress on transformation felt slow and 'stuck in the mud'. Highlighting small yet important wins kept morale high and momentum edging forward. These included:

- showcasing newsroom articles commissioned after data analysis;
- creating new roles with a strong data element;

(Continued)

- pursuing new innovation projects; and
- showcasing industry awards won by the organisation.

These were positive affirmations and reminders of the strategy and direction of the project.

Step 7: Consolidate improvements and produce more change

Larger moves were made to consolidate progress. Jillian Green, a trusted voice in the newsroom and part of the guiding coalition, was promoted to deputy editor-in-chief, demonstrating the importance of the program in the context of the newsroom's long-term vision. Training sessions continued and a new effort to identify 'key editorial themes' for the next year was conducted.

Staff were randomly allocated into small groups (with colleagues from different locations they may not have met in person before) to research the most pressing needs of the country and identify key themes that *Daily Maverick* should dedicate resources to.

It not only generated excellent ideas, but also doubled as a team-building exercise. This was followed by the newly appointed audience development manager providing company-wide training on interpreting analytics and how to action insights.

Step 8: Institutionalise change

At this final stage, a set of foundational elements were created to ensure the strategy was understood and that data analytics were anchored in everyday work to ensure the organisation stays close to audiences:

- A leadership steering group (exco) to coordinate the business unit leaders.
- Personalised coaching for managers from the CEO and program consultant.
- Training sessions and regular staff communications, as well as updated onboarding to ensure the company's vision, mission, and strategic goals are always understood.
- Audience analytics and surveys on a daily, weekly and monthly basis so that journalists can incorporate insights into commissioning and resourcing decisions.
- Daily editorial reports providing a narrative explanation of how user needs are being met.
- Engaged journalism using online tools to solicit feedback and questions from readers to create journalism that has higher engagement.

(Continued)

'Securing our Future' results

The *Daily Maverick's* mission is to 'defend the truth'. For the truth to have impact, it also needs to have reach, and 'Securing the Future' has delivered on this. Since embarking on the change plan, not only is the *Daily Maverick*'s journalism more relevant, its relationship with audiences deeper and its revenues higher, but monthly unique visitors to the website grew 235 per cent from 3.4 million in August 2021 to an all-time high of 11.4 million in March 2023.

Case questions

1 What were CEO Charalambous' biggest strategic concerns concerning the future of the Daily Maverick?

2 How did the guiding coalition seek to ensure all staff felt involved and consulted in the program? What measures did they use to communicate with staff?

3 Look at the analysis of 'Industry culture' on p. 171. Why could the shared values of journalists potentially conflict with a strategy focused on data analysis?

4 Look at the 'Three jobs of a digital leader' on p. 227. Did Charalambous lead in this way? Which leadership skills were particularly important for him and his colleagues in their transformation program?

Case: What kind of leader does Disney need?

Robert A. Brookey and Lucy Kueng

> Be genuine. Be honest. Don't fake anything. Truth and authenticity breed respect and trust. (Bob Iger, 2019)

On 31 December 2021, Bob Iger retired from The Walt Disney Company, a move that had been postponed when COVID-19 lockdowns began across the globe. Iger's preferred replacement as CEO, Bob Chapek, had been appointed on 25 February 2020, but Iger's tenure was extended by the Disney board to navigate the unprecedented challenges of the global pandemic, where Disney

(Continued)

faced greater risks than many media and entertainment organisations because of its global network of theme parks, cruise ships and live theatre productions. (It was forced to close its parks for a while and suspend its cruise holidays).

Iger's career at Disney was notable for several reasons, but primarily for his ability to acquire companies and content, and significantly grow the company. Iger oversaw the acquisitions of Pixar, Marvel, Lucasfilm and 20th Century Fox, and by some accounts more than quadrupled Disney's net income during his time at Disney. He is also responsible for developing and deploying the Disney+ service, a platform on which all the brands from his various acquisitions reside.

Iger's 'true leadership principles'

Prior to his (first) retirement from Disney, Iger published his biography, *The Ride of a Lifetime: Lessons Learned from 15 Years as CEO of the Walt Disney Company*. The biography traces his career in media and explains his leadership philosophy. In his prologue, he identifies ten principles of 'true leadership'. Authenticity features large, he writes: 'Be genuine. Be honest. Don't fake anything. Truth and authenticity breed respect and trust.' Iger's account of his leadership style mirrors the four behaviours central to authentic leadership. The table below illustrates how these behaviours are manifest in Iger's own career success.

Self-awareness	While a new employee at the ABC network, a news producer exposed his genitals to Iger in a gesture of 'complete disdain'. Iger notes: 'Forty years later, I still get angry when I recall that scene. We've become much more aware of the need for fair, equal, non-abusive treatment in the workplace, but it has taken too long.' Iger would draw on this experience when he confronted John Lasseter, CCO for both Pixar and Disney, on charges of sexual misconduct.
Balanced processing	Roy Disney and Stanley Gold sued the Disney board to challenge Iger's appointment as CEO. Once in position, Iger assembled a team of Disney executives including CFO Tom Staggs, general counsel Alan Braveman and communications chief Zenia Mucha, and sought their input regarding the ruptured relationships with Roy Disney and Stanley Gold. His analysis of Roy Disney's motives reveals Iger's capacity for balanced processing: '[Roy Disney] was just … looking for respect and getting it had never been especially easy for him.' Iger offered Roy Disney an emeritus appointment to the Disney board, an office on the Disney lot and a consulting fee; these concessions appeased Roy and he dropped the lawsuit. Similar skills were evident in his handling of activist investor Nelson Peltz, to the extent that he was able to assuage Peltz's concerns without conceding a board seat (something that had not been possible at three other companies Peltz had taken positions in – Heinz, Du Pont and P&G).

(Continued)

Internalised moral perspective	A young boy was killed by an alligator at Disney World. When he spoke with the child's father, Iger promised him that he would do whatever he could to prevent another attack. Iger observes, 'I gave him my promise. I knew from a lawyer's perspective that I should be careful about what I was saying, that I should consider whether that was somehow an admission of negligence ... but I didn't care about any of that in this moment.'
Relational transparency	Iger carefully honed his vision for Disney as incoming CEO: 'A company's culture is shaped by a lot of things, but this is one of the most important – you have to convey your priorities clearly and repeatedly. In my experience, it's what separates great managers from the rest. If the leaders don't articulate their priorities clearly, then the people around them don't know what their own priorities should be ... You can do a lot of the morale of the people around you (and therefore the people around them) just by taking the guesswork out of their day-to-day life.'

'I can't think of a better person to succeed me in this role'[6]

During his tenure as Disney CEO, Iger's prescient strategy and deal making grew the company's market value to over $350 billion. In one key task he failed – selecting his own successor. Iger's choice, Bob Chapek, had been with Disney for nearly 20 years, and had held leadership roles in home video, distribution, consumer products and resorts and parks. Yet even before Iger finally departed Disney at the end of 2021, questions were surfacing about Chapek's leadership style, and these continued into his CEO-ship. During 2021, Chapek became embroiled in a lawsuit with Scarlett Johansson regarding her compensation for *Black Widow* and had to issue a public statement reasserting Disney's commitment and respect for talent. In 2022, he baulked at challenging Florida's 'Don't Say Gay' legislation, and then changed his position in response to employee pressure and issued a challenge to the legislation, evoking the ire of Florida governor Rob DeSantis, who then sought to eliminate the special legal privileges enjoyed by Disney World. Later, in a speech, Chapek referred to Disney World as 'the happiest place on earth', whereas 'the happiest place on earth' is actually Disneyland (Disney World is the 'most magical place on earth'). This mistake was revealing: these phrases are central to the brands of the two parks, and as CEO of Disney, and ex-leader of theme parks, Chapek should have known the difference.

Back to Iger, 'coporate jedi'[7]

In 2023, Iger was summoned back from retirement to replace the successor he had personally chosen. In addition to the missteps outlined above, under

(Continued)

Chapek's stewardship, the Disney stock price had fallen, and Disney+'s growth had stalled. Trian Partners, an investment fund had acquired a 0.5 per cent stake, and Nelson Pelz, its founder was demanding the board take decisive action to address governance and strategic failures to improve financial performance, and a seat on the board. Even though it had only five months previously extended Chapek's contract by three years, in November 2023 the board fired Chapek and rehired Iger for a period of two years.

On his return, Iger had a complex set of challenges. The legacy businesses, broadcast and cable television, which delivered the lion's share of profits, were in structural decline. The new streaming business, Disney+ had by some measures more subscribers than Netflix but acquiring this market share had brought heavy losses – $1.5 billion in the last quarter of Chapek's stewardship. Morale inside the organisation was low.

He moved fast to address the concerns of the organisation and its shareholders and dismantle many of the changes Chapek had made. He reorganised Disney with the goal of putting creativity at the centre of the organisation. He rolled film, TV and streaming together into a unified entertainment unit. ESPN was turned into a stand-alone business.

Iger also made several tough business decisions to address the concerns of the board and shareholders, and Nelson Pelz's criticisms. Noting that 'nothing was off the table' in terms of returning Disney to financial health and growth, he promised to make streaming profitable by 2024 and to return to paying dividends by the end of 2023. He increased subscription prices for Disney+, and, like Netflix, launched a lower-cost advertising-supported tier. He also declared he was open to the idea of licensing Disney content to competitors, thus opening up a new revenue stream. In early 2023, he announced 7,000 redundancies and $5.5 billion in cost savings, including $3 billion in content reductions (making fewer shows and movies, and aiming to reduce 'undifferentiated content'). These changes placated Nelson Pelz, who dropped his demand for a seat on the Disney board.

The release of *Avatar: The Way of Water* early in 2023 was a good omen and seemed to suggest that the tide was turning. It became the fourth highest-grossing movie of all time (at the time of writing) and the biggest box office hit of 2022. Yet Iger had one big challenge ahead in his second stint as Disney CEO – one he failed to master the first time around: to find his successor.

Case questions

Chapek and Iger are very different leaders. Compare and contrast their leadership styles, and reflect on the respective strengths and weaknesses of each, by answering the following questions:

(Continued)

1 Consider Iger's ability to acquire and incorporate established media brands, particularly Marvel, Lucasfilm and 20th Century Fox. How might an authentic leadership style facilitate the productive deployment of the content from these different brands?

2 Consider Chapek's handling of the lawsuit with Johansson and the political conflict in Florida. Does Chapek reflect the behaviours of an authentic leader? How might Iger have handled things differently given his leadership style?

3 The pandemic disrupted distribution and exhibition markets, so Chapek would seem well placed to handle this disruption. Iger's career was in programming and the development of content. Do these different areas of the media industry (distribution and exhibition/programming and content) require different leadership styles? What styles might be best suited for these areas, and why?

4 Put yourself in the position of the Disney board looking for Iger's successor. What skills, competencies and leadership styles are critical, and how would you prioritise them? Use these insights to write a job profile for the CEO role at Disney.

The three jobs of a leader in the digital era

***David L. Rogers*[8]**

In the digital era, the accelerating pace of change means that every organisation must transform itself not once, but continually. To meet this demand for flexibility and speed, we see organisations switching dramatically away from a traditional top-down style of management. In its place, we see a new model of the 'bottom-up' organisation, where leaders push decision-making down, where market insights flow bottom-up, and where strategy and transformation happen at every level. Digital native businesses like Amazon, Netflix and Alibaba have all embraced this new model, achieving speed at scale by pushing decision-making down to the lowest level. One of the bedrock principles of agile software methods is the use of 'self-organising teams', which once given clearly defined goals, are allowed to figure out on their own how to best achieve them. Meta embraces a bottom-up model where leadership sets high-level strategy, but it is up to individual teams to set the mission, vision and strategy for individual products.[9] Amazon's Jeff Bezos saw that 'distribution of invention throughout the company–not limited to the company's senior leaders–is the only way to get robust, high-throughput innovation'.[10]

Rethinking leadership from the bottom up

If the digital era requires a shift from top-down hierarchies to more bottom-up organisations, our old model of leadership must change as well. In the past, the leader was 'decider-in-chief'. But in the digital era, the goal of leader should be to make as few decisions as possible. Inevitably, every leader will have to make some decisions, but these should be only the toughest and most important ones, when they truly have to. But what does that leave for the leader themselves to do? Leaders in a digital era have three essential jobs.

Table 7.1 The three jobs and three roles of leaders in the digital era

Job of leader	Role of leader
Define a vision of where we are going and why.	Leader as **author**
Communicate that vision in words, stories, symbols and actions.	Leader as **teacher**
Enable others to bring that vision to life.	Leader as **servant**

Define

The first job of a leader is to define a vision of where the organisation is going and why. This could be a statement of purpose or impact the business seeks to have; it could be a statement of strategy with key opportunities or problems to be solved; it could be a statement of the culture that the organisation is striving for.

A well-defined vision is not a description of what your organisation does, but a clarification of what you seek to achieve. The aim is to provide a guiding direction to the efforts of others, and to inspire employees with a clear sense of purpose to their work.

A great leader will articulate where you are going and why, but not how you should get there. They seek to set the context for others to act, not to craft their operating plans. They will vigorously debate questions of strategy, but trust others to execute and choose the right tactics. In defining the organisation's vision, the leader takes on a role much like an author. They start by studying and learning from many inputs, inside and outside the organisation. This requires getting in the trenches and listening to the perspectives of customers, partners and employees at every level. As a leader, Steve Jobs was famous for reading and answering his own public email address so that he could learn from customers. Many of Jeff Bezos's most important business insights came from memos drafted by very junior employees at Amazon. The leader must then work to synthesise all of these perspectives and insights. And then they must simplify them – looking for common themes and a central thread – to define a future vision that will be able to guide the actions of others.

Communicate

The second job of a leader is to communicate their vision – to every stakeholder inside and outside the organisation. Effective leaders communicate both what their vision is and why it matters. Or as Lucy Kueng summarises it, 'This is our problem, where we are going, and why it is necessary.'[11]

Leaders communicate these ideas in carefully chosen words, stories and symbols, to make sure the ideas are unmissable and unforgettable. In his very first letter to shareholders in 1997, Bezos introduced the phrase 'Day 1', which became a rallying cry within Amazon for long-term thinking and a perpetual mindset that the business is always just on the inception of its journey. As Bezos wrote two decades later, 'Day 2 is stasis. Followed by irrelevance. Followed by excruciating, painful decline. Followed by death. And that is why it is always Day 1'.[12] In talking about Microsoft's vision, CEO Satya Nadella tells the story of the first product built by the company's founders: a BASIC interpreter for the Altair, for use by hobbyist computer programmers. Nadella uses this story to defines his company as a 'toolmaker' and to explain his vision for the firm: 'Our mission of empowering every person and every organization on the planet to achieve more is really a look back to the very creation of Microsoft.'[13]

Leaders not only communicate; they over-communicate. They don't just tell their story to employees on the biggest stage at their largest annual meeting. Leaders communicate through every tool and means possible – in public forums and private conversations. They repeat the same ideas and themes over, and over, and over. They are relentless. As Kueng says, 'As a leader, you are never not communicating. If you say something only once, people will assume you didn't really mean it.'[14] At Acuity Insurance, CEO Ben Salzmann is in a perpetual state of communication to his employees and partners alike – from social media posts, to company meetings in a theatre built in-the-round in their headquarters, to his weekly 'gossip' audio messages sent out by voicemail to every employee.

Lastly, great communicators don't just speak; they ask questions and they listen. Rather than declare 'we need to do X!', leaders ask 'How might we achieve Y?'. They are approachable and regularly get out and take in the perspective of customers, partners and employees at every level. Salzmann says, 'There isn't any employee here who would feel uncomfortable talking to me.' (And I've seen him walk the halls enough to know it's true.) By listening, they find out if they are heard – and if not, why not? What barriers remain? Leaders remember the adage: 'The single biggest problem in communication is the illusion that it has taken place.'[15]

Through it all, leaders recognise that every interaction they have – with an employee, a customer or a shareholder – is a chance to teach what they believe about their organisation. As social entrepreneur Wendy Kopp says, 'Leadership is teaching.'[16] Or in the words of Antoine de Saint-Exupéry: 'If you want to build a ship, don't drum up the people to gather wood, divide the work, and give orders. Instead, teach them to yearn for the vast and endless sea.'[17]

Enable

The third job of a leader is to enable others to bring their vision to life. Again, this is a reversal of the traditional view of leaders in a command-and-control structure. Leaders lead less by taking action themselves, and more by enabling the actions of others.

The first way that leaders enable others is by removing obstacles or road-blocks to their work. This often means aligning processes in the organisation to help, rather than hinder, the efforts of those working to pursue your vision. It is a leader's job to align every process they approve – from compensation to organisational structure, to metrics and KPIs – with their guiding vision. Processes carelessly chosen or inherited unthinkingly can undermine culture, strategy and the most purposeful efforts of your employees.

Leaders enable the work of others through their choices of who to hire, who to promote and who to remove from key positions. Leaders give those people the autonomy to act and provide them with the tools and technologies that will make a difference in their work. Leaders help their people to grow in their own abilities, developing the talents they need to realise the goals that they set for themselves. And leaders advocate internally for those who need support to make change happen.

Crucially, leaders empower others by getting them the resources they need. This starts with the allocation of financial capital in support of their stated priorities. Leaders put their money where their mouth is. But just as important is the allocation of human capital. The most vital resource that any new initiative needs is the right people. Who will decide that a talented and sought-after executive will be pulled out of your core business in order to work on a new venture that has yet to turn a profit? In Silicon Valley, there is a saying that 'leaders vote with headcount'. As a veteran of Facebook explained to me, companies like Meta and Alphabet have plenty of money to throw at new ideas. Their scarcest resource for new projects is good engineers. They are what really matters in resourcing a team.

The last resource that a leader must allocate is their own limited attention and mental bandwidth. Any leader can only give their sustained focus and counsel to a limited number of priorities at one time. As *The New York*

Times finally began to commit in earnest to a digital-first future, one of the key changes made was to change the responsibilities of top leaders. The paper's print edition, long cherished as the historic version, would continue to be produced (because its subscribers were among the most loyal, and its advertising business was profitable, though declining). But the company was reorganised so that news would be developed in a digital-first approach, with a separate team pulling from that digital content to assemble each day's print edition. A few experienced managers were charged with overseeing this declining, but still vital, print operation. This allowed the rest of the *Times*' leadership to focus all their attention on future growth areas such as audio, video, paid apps and the all-important digital news subscriptions. For any leader, one of the most important choices to be made is where you will put your daily attention.

By enabling others – through resources, attention and mentorship, and the removal of obstacles – leaders take on a role in service of others. The third job of leaders matches closely to the concept of 'servant leadership' formulated by Robert K. Greanleaf, which defines leadership as service to the needs and growth of their followers.[18]

Notes

1 Harvard Kennedy School PolicyCast, 9 December 2021. Available at: www.hks.harvard.edu/more/policycast/nobel-peace-prize-winner-maria-ressa-how-social-media-pushing-journalism-and.
2 Facebook CEO Mark Zuckerberg talking at Y Combinator's Startup School, cited in Steve Tobak, 31 October 2011. Available at: www.cbsnews.com/news/facebooks-mark-zuckerberg-insights-for-entrepreneurs
3 www.amazon.jobs/en/principles
4 www.amazon.jobs/en/principles
5 The Investopedia Team, 'What is Tim Cook's Managerial Style?', Investopedia, 2 August 2021. Available at: www.investopedia.com/ask/answers/032515/what-tim-cooks-managerial-style.asp.
6 Bob Iger speaking at Disney's annual shareholder meeting, 11 March 2020, www.cnbc.com/2022/03/20/disney-ceo-chapek-iger-falling-out.html
7 'Thrills and spills', *The Economist*, 21 January 2023.
8 Adapted from 'The Digital Transformation Roadmap' © 2023.
9 Talk on 'Product Management at Facebook' by Abhimanyu (Abhishek) Muchhal, 2 April 2020.
10 2013 letter to shareholders. Available at: https://ir.aboutamazon.com/files/doc_financials/annual/2013-Letter-to-Shareholders.pdf

11 Lucy Kueng speech at INMA Conference in Washington, DC, 4 June 2018.
12 Jeff Bezos' Letter to Shareholders in Amazon's 1997 Annual Report https://www.aboutamazon.com/news/company-news/amazons-original-1997-letter-to-shareholders
13 Quotes from www.businessinsider.com/satya-nadella-microsoft-ceo-qa-2017-4. He called the same story their 'creation myth'. Available at: www.linkedin.com/pulse/conversation-satya-nadella-his-new-book-hit-refresh-tim-o-reilly
14 Lucy Kueng speech at INMA Conference in Washington, DC, 4 June 2018.
15 This quote is popularly attributed to George Bernard Shaw, but with no evidence. Earliest source was in business writing. Available at: https://quoteinvestigator.com/2014/08/31/illusion
16 'Walk the Walk' by Alan Deutschman, p. 158 – he may be paraphrasing Wendy Kopp.
17 https://jobs.netflix.com/culture (accessed 17 June 2022). This quote's origin is not completely clear and may be a paraphrase. See: https://quoteinvestigator.com/2015/08/25/sea
18 First formulated in his 1970 essay 'The Servant as Leader', which credits inspiration to Herman Hesse's 1932 novel *Journey to the East*. Greenleaf expanded his thinking in his book *Servant Leadership* in 1977.

EIGHT

CONCLUSIONS: GENERATIVE AI AND THE DISRUPTION OF DIGITAL

Over the past quarter of a century, the media industry has undergone a significant transformation, driven by technological advancements, specifically digital transformation. The first wave of digital transformation was marked by the introduction of online news and the digitisation of print media. This brought widescale change, from the creation of new revenue streams, such as online advertising and subscription-based services, to the creation of new functions such as product, data and social media management. But it also left many organisations struggling to adapt to the pace and scope of change. The second wave of digital transformation was marked by the introduction of social media, mobile devices and streaming services. This broadened the scope of digital transformation, with the audio visual and gaming sectors particularly affected, and bringing powerful new competitors into the media ecosystem, ranging from Meta and Amazon to ByteDance, Epic and Netflix.

That is a much-simplified account of two decades of change, one that omits many important developments. But the net result of these changes is that digital processes, digital products and digital thinking are now central to how most media organisations now operate. Digital has moved from the periphery of the organisation into the heart of strategy, workflows, processes and roles. Companies that fail to adapt to digitalisation or started too late are struggling, and those that have done so have not only a competitive advantage now, but a greater likelihood of a long-term sustainable future.

However, ongoing technological innovation, particularly the development of generative AI, threatens to disrupt that digital transformation. This technology has the potential to automate central activities, bring new competitors into the sector, and disrupt established business models. Yet again, media companies must adapt. Those that are successful in leveraging generative AI – both to create new value and to prevent value destruction – are likely to have a competitive advantage; those that adapt too slowly may see their business, audiences and revenues recede.

Generative AI and its impact

Generative AI is a subset of artificial intelligence that uses machine learning and algorithms to generate content of all types. While the technology had been in development for many years, it landed like a tornado in 2023 with the launch of a set of easily accessible free tools, including ChatGPT, DALL-E and Midjourney.

This development has far-reaching implications for the media industry. Generative AI tools, trained on extensive amounts of existing data (much of which has been produced by humans in media organisations), can algorithmically manipulate that data to generate synthetic media of virtually every type, including journalistic articles, books, song lyrics, scripts, story ideas, code, images and video, among others. The output of these tools is often indistinguishable from human content and can be produced quickly and at scale.

Tools based on generative AI are penetrating deep into every aspect of media work: they can summarise, transcribe, translate, produce headlines, 'write' in a specific style and create photographs or illustrations of any scene that can be described in text. Their output can be redrafted, rethought and revised easily. The table below shows a sample of potential applications in the media, from supporting news and book publishing to enhancing the creative processes of broadcasting, film, gaming and music production, and book publishing. It points to the far-reaching impact of this technology and the scope of its potential application.

Sector	Applications
News publishing	Article writing, fact-checking, summarising, comment moderation, document analysis, translation, transcription, image optimisation, engagement optimisation, gender balance detection.
Broadcasting, TV and film	Idea generation, scriptwriting, character and dialogue development, storyboard and animatic creation, special effects and virtual actor creation, audience preference analysis, filming schedule and location optimisation, post-production colour grading and special effects, personalised content generation based on individual viewer habits and preferences.
Gaming	Realistic game environment creation, game level design, non-playable character generation, game narrative and character library management.
Music	Song and lyric writing, vocal rendering, new composition and personalised music generation.
Book publishing	Editing support, including changes to sentence structure and vocabulary, book summary and blurb generation.

Exploring generative AI's strategic impact

Generative AI technology is having a profound impact on the media industry and media work. Developments are at an early stage, but to explore its strategic impact, we can apply the concepts and models explored in this book.

Gartner hype cycle

This model captures the path that a new technology typically takes from launch to maturity. When applied to the development of generative AI, contradictory conclusions can be reached. It can be argued that the technology has effectively bypassed or leapfrogged the curve, moving from launch to widespread use in a matter of months. Alternatively, its development can be interpreted as having a prolonged phase of high-level hype, which is atypically combined with high levels of broad-based experimentation. Either way, the application of this lens underlines the exceptional speed with which this technology is moving. Chat GPT reached 100 million monthly users (MAU) in two months (in contrast, TikTok took nine months to reach 100 million MAUs, and Google Translate needed 78 months[1]).

The swift adoption of generative AI can be partially explained by considering the bundle of underlying technologies required for widescale adoption. Unlike the metaverse, generative AI was able to build upon existing tools and services that were already widely adopted in everyday life and businesses. For instance, Bard, a generative AI tool, is available to any individual with a Google account, while Bing, which is integrated with generative AI functionality, can be accessed by anyone with a Microsoft account. By building generative AI into pre-existing tools and services, its integration becomes more seamless and widespread.

Value chain

This model provides a framework for analysing a firm's activities and identifying areas where value can be increased at each stage, ultimately impacting the overall value created by the firm. As with the advent of the internet, this is the tool many are turning to first to grasp how generative AI will impact firms and identify risks and opportunities.

Generative AI presents a significant opportunity for organisations to enhance their value creation by automating core activities, improving efficiency, reducing costs and providing additional value to customers. There are few stages in the value chain where generative AI will not bring substantial changes (see Figure 8.1, which shows its impact on the value chain of news publishing).

Generative AI has the potential to automate and augment primary activities, such as content creation, production, distribution and marketing, within media organisations. Additionally, support activities can be similarly transformed by integrating generative AI into company-wide processes, ranging from communication, such as email and press releases, to finance and controlling functions, including tracking, analysing and projecting financial outcomes.

Plan	Source	Produce	Edit	Publish	Engage	Archive
Automate planning	Find more stories in data. Find more data in stories	More efficient automated production of content	Optimise use of images & video	Better personalised distribution of content	Make content moderation manageable	Leverage archive content with enhanced image/ video search
	Fake news/deep fakes recognition	Better automated transcription and translation	Identify bias in writing		Deeper sentiment analysis	
					Optimise for engagement and subscriptions	

Figure 8.1 Application of generative AI to news publishing value chain (Source: Ezra Eeman)

Core competencies

Realising these changes to the value chain means not only rethinking tasks, processes and workflows, but also changing the competence profile.

New competencies are required. For example, an understanding of AI and its capabilities, including the ability to evaluate and select appropriate AI tools and platforms. This in turn requires sub-competencies in natural language processing, machine learning and deep learning algorithms. Data capabilities will need to expand, too, particularly the ability to recognise and label, predict, uncover patterns, cluster and generate.

According to theories of organisational creativity, the integration of generative AI into media requires a new set of domain-relevant skills. These skills can be acquired through immersion and experience, with individual judgement and intuition eventually playing a role.

Generative AI raises a host of ethical concerns in issues such as bias, privacy, misinformation and disinformation. Organisations need an understanding of these issues and develop principles and policies to ensure this technology is used ethically and responsibly.

Generative AI is also competence-destroying. As the application of the Porter Five Force model below shows, generative AI demolishes many entry barriers connected with the ability to create, produce and curate content. These were once the province of media professionals and creative workers. Now they are accessible to many. By extension, unique capabilities that organisations have invested in building, and which are central to their competitive differentiation and the margin they command, risk being eroded.

Porter's Five Forces model

Here too, the impact is wide-ranging and disruptive:

- AI lowers entry barriers (anyone can produce professional-like content), increasing the threat of new entrants to compete with established companies.
- It reduces the bargaining power of suppliers like journalists and other creators (because professional content becomes easier to produce).
- It increases the threat of substitutes (all those new content providers).
- Taken together, these factors fuel competitive rivalry, especially because the sector has many locked-in players with a high emotional commitment to the field who are fighting for the same customer group.

However, as value chain analysis shows, the use of generative AI technologies can confer competitive advantage, by automating and enhancing core activities, increasing efficiency, reducing costs and increasing the value of products. AI intelligence allows media organisations to tailor content more closely to user needs, leading to increased viewership and engagement.

In the eye of the storm, still

These continue to be interesting times for the media industry, and interesting times in which to be writing a book on strategic management in the sector. Industry boundaries are blurring. The pace of change becomes ever faster as the industry is harnessed ever more tightly to the technology sector. The fruits of two decades of painful disruption are being themselves disrupted. Yet again, the industry is at a point of fundamental transition.

This is a context that presents both enormous challenges and fascinating opportunities, for researchers, students and strategic actors in media organisations. The developments, strategic concepts and cases included in this book have been selected with this context in mind, and I hope they provide enlightenment to anyone involved with strategic management in the media, whether from a theoretical or a practical standpoint.

As I worked on this third edition of *Strategic Management in the Media,* I was struck anew by the unique nature of this industry and the profound disruption the sector has experienced since the first edition of this book was written. I was equally impressed by the remarkable commitment demonstrated by those working in a field facing a staggering degree of challenge. The industry has not only acknowledged the need for change, but has actively embraced it, a feat that is never easy for individuals or organisations. Adapting David Bowie, this is a sector that knows how to 'turn to face the change' and will continue to do so. Other sectors have much to learn from it.

Resources

The development of the media industry, particularly the impact of generative AI is exhaustively covered in a plethora of media formats. Academic publications are fewer – a function of the newness of the field and the length of time required to research and publish scholarly articles. This field is developing exceptionally fast and new resources are constantly emerging. The elements below represent just a sample of what can be found and a jumping off point from which to delve deeper.

Articles and books

Caswell, D. (2022) Producing news in the age of Artificial Intelligence. *Medienwirtschaft*, 3, 2022.

Fountaine, S., McCarthy, B. and Saleh, T. (2019) Building AI-powered organizations. *McKinsey Quarterly*, 1–11.

Newletters, podcasts, videos and research initiatives

Hard Fork Technology Podcast. Discusses technology issues often with a media focus, https://podcasts.apple.com/us/podcast/hard-fork/id1528594034

People vs Algorithms. Explores developments in the digital economy, with a focus on the impact of tech innovations on revenue and business models, https://www.peoplevsalgorithms.com/

The AI Podcast by Nvidia, https://blogs.nvidia.com/ai-podcast/

Inside My Head newsletter by Linus Ekenstam on Substack.

MIT AI ML Club channel on YouTube has lectures on how AI can be used to produce various types of content.

JournalismAI is a global initiative that empowers news organisations to use artificial intelligence responsibly, backed by the London School of Economics and the Google News Initiative. https://www.lse.ac.uk/media-and-communications/polis/JournalismAI

Note

1 Eyerys, cited in exponential view. co, 4 May 2023.

REFERENCES

Abelson, R.P. (1995) 'Attitude extremity', in R.E. Petty and J. Krosnick (eds), *Attitude Strength: Antecedents and Consequences*. Mahwah, NJ: Lawrence Erlbaum. pp. 25–42.

Abernathy, W.J. and Utterback, J.M. (1978) 'Patterns of innovation in technology', *Technology Review*, 80(7): 40–7.

Argyris, C. and Schön, D.A. (1995) *Organizational Learning II: Theory, Method, and Practice*. Addison-Wesley.

Aitkenhead, D. (2010) 'Clay Shirky: Paywall will underperform – the numbers don't add up', *The Guardian*, 5 July. Available at: www.theguardian.com/technology/2010/jul/05/clay-shirky-internet-television-newspapers

Albarran, A.B. and Moellinger, T. (2002) 'The top six communication industry firms: structure, performance and strategy', in R.G. Picard (ed.), *Media Firms: Structures, Operations, and Performance*. Mahwah, NJ: Lawrence Erlbaum. pp. 103–22.

Albarran, A.B., Chan-Olmsted, S.M. and Wirth, M.O. (2006) *Handbook of Media Management and Economics*. Mahwah, NJ: Lawrence Erlbaum.

Amabile, T.M. (1983) *The Social Psychology of Creativity*. New York: Springer.

Amabile, T.M. (1988) 'A model of creativity and innovation in organizations', in B.M. Shaw and L.L. Cummings (eds), *Research in Organizational Behaviour*. Greenwich, CT: JAI Press. Chapter 10, pp. 123–67.

Amabile, T.M. (1993) 'Motivational synergy: toward new conceptualizations of intrinsic and extrinsic motivation in the workplace', *Human Resource Management Review*, 3(3): 185–201.

Amabile, T.M. (1996) *Creativity in Context*. Boulder, CO: Westview Press.

Amabile, T.M. (1998) 'How to kill creativity', *Harvard Business Review*, September: 77–87.

Amabile, T.M. and Gryskiewicz, N.D. (1989) 'The creative environment scales: the work environment inventory', *Creativity Research Journal*, 2: 231–54.

Amabile, T.M., Hadley, C.N. and Kramer, S.J. (2002) 'Creativity under the gun', *Harvard Business Review*, August: 52–61.

Amabile, T.M., Hill, K.G., Hennessey, B.A. and Tighe, E. (1994) 'The work preference inventory: assessing intrinsic and extrinsic motivational orientations', *Journal of Personality and Social Psychology*, 66: 950–67.

Amabile, T.M., Conti, R., Coon, H., Lazenby, J. and Herron, M. (1996) 'Assessing the work environment for creativity', *Academy of Management Journal*, 39(5): 1154–84.

American Press Institute (2006) 'Newspaper next: blueprint for transformation. American Press Institute'. Available at: www.Americanpressinstitute.org

Ancona, D. (1990) 'Top management teams: preparing for the revolution', in J. Carroll (ed.), *Applied Social Psychology and Organizational Settings*. New York: Lawrence Erlbaum. p. 99.

Ancona, D., Malone, T., Orlikowski, W.J. and Senge, P. (2007) 'In praise of the incomplete leader', *Harvard Business Review*, February: 92–100.

Anderson, C.W. (2013) 'How journalists' self-concepts hindered their adaptation to a digital world', *Nieman Lab*, 17 January. Available at: www.niemanlab.org/2013/01/c-w-anderson-how-journalists-self-concepts-hindered-their-adaptation-to-a-digital-world

Ansoff, H.I. (1957) 'Strategies for Diversification'. *Harvard Business Review*, 35(5):113–124.

Argyris, Chris (1977) 'Double loop learning in organizations'. *Harvard Business Review*, September–October, 115–125.

Aris, A. and Bughin, J. (2005) *Managing Media Companies: Harnessing Creative Value*. Chichester: John Wiley & Sons.

Arthur, B. (1994) *Increasing Returns and Path Dependence in the Economy*. Chicago, IL: University of Michigan Press.

Auletta, K. (1991) *Three Blind Mice: How the TV Networks Lost their Way*. New York: Random House.

Auletta, K. (2004) *Media Man: Ted Turner's Improbable Empire*. New York: W.W. Norton.

Avilés JAG and Carvajal, M. (2008) 'Integrated and cross-media newsroom convergence: two models of multimedia news production — the cases of Novotécnica and La Verdad Multimedia in Spain. *Convergence*. 14(2): 221–39. doi:10.1177/1354856507087945

Avolio, B.J., Walumbwa, F.O., and Weber, T.J. (2009) 'Leadership: current theories, research, and future directions', *Annual Review of Psychology*, 60(1):421–49.

Baaji, M. and Reinmoeller, P. (2018) *Mapping a Winning Strategy: Developing and Executing a Successful Strategy in Turbulent Markets*. Bingley: Emerald Publishing.

Bahrami, H. (1992) 'The emerging flexible organization: perspectives from Silicon Valley', *California Management Review*, Summer: 33–52.

Bahrami, H. and Evans, S. (1995) 'Flexible re-cycling and high-technology entrepreneurship', *California Management Review*, 37(3): 62–98.

Balogun, J. (2001) 'Strategic change', *Management Quarterly*. January: 2–11.

Barney, J.B. (1991) 'Firm resources and sustained competitive advantage', *Journal of Management*, 17(1): 99–120.

Baltaci, A. and Balci, A. (2017) 'Complexity leadership: a theoretical perspective', *International Journal of Educational Leadership and Management*, 5(1): 30–58.

Barr, P.S., Stimpert, J.L. and Huff, A.S. (1992) 'Cognitive change, strategic action, and organizational renewal', *Strategic Management Journal*, 13: 15–36.

Barron, F.B. and Harringon, D.M. (1981) 'Creativity, intelligence, and personality', *Annual Review of Psychology*, 32: 439.

Bartlett, F.E. (1932) *Remembering*. Cambridge: Cambridge University Press.

Barwise, P. and Hammond, K. (1998) *Media*. London: Phoenix.

Bass, B.M. (1985) *Leadership and Performance Beyond Expectations*. New York: Free Press.

Bass, B.M. (1990) *Bass and Stogdill's Handbook of Leadership: A Survey of Theory and Research*. New York: Free Press.

Bass, B.M. and Avolio, B.J. (1994) *Improving Organizational Effectiveness through Transformational Leadership*. Thousand Oaks, CA: Sage.

Bass, B.M. and Steidlmeier, P. (1999) 'Ethics, character, and authentic transformational leadership behavior', *Leadership Quarterly*, 10(2): 181–217.

Baumol, W.J. (1993) *Entrepreneurship, Management and the Structure of Payoffs*. Cambridge, MA: The MIT Press.

Baumann, S. (2022) *Digital Business Ecosystems: Handbook on Digital Business Ecosystems: Strategies, Platforms, Technologies, Governance and Societal Challenges*. Edward Elgar Publishing: Cheltenham.

Bennis, W. and Biederman, P.W. (1997) *Organizing Genius*. London: Nicholas Brealey Publishing.

Bergman, J. Z., Rentsch, J. R., Small, E. E., Davenport, S. W. and Bergman, S.M. (2012) 'The shared leadership process in decision-making teams', *The Journal of Social Psychology*, 152(1): 17–42.

Bennett, N. and Lemoine, J.G. (2014) 'What VUCA really means for you', *Harvard Business Review*, 92(1), 10.

Bertelsmann Foundation European Institute for the Media (ed.) (1995) Television requires responsibility, vol. 2: *International Studies*. Gütersloh: Bertelsmann Foundation Publishers.

Bessant, J. and Tidd, J. (2007) *Innovation and Entrepreneurship*. Chichester: John Wiley & Sons.

Bettis, R.A. and Hitt, M.A. (1995) 'The new competitive landscape', *Strategic Management Journal*, 16: 7–19.

Bettman, J.R. and Weitz, B.A. (1983) 'Attributions in the board room: causal reasoning in corporate annual reports', *Administrative Science Quarterly*, 28: 165.

Bibb, P. (1993) *It Ain't as Easy as it Looks: Ted Turner's Amazing Story*. New York: Crown.

Blumler, J.G. and Nossiter, T.J. (1991) *Broadcasting Finance in Transition: A Comparative Handbook*. Oxford: Oxford University Press.

Bogner, W.C. and Barr, P.S. (2000) 'Making sense in hypercompetitive environments: a cognitive explanation of high velocity competition', *Organization Science*, (11)2: 212–26.

Bolman, J.G. and Deal, T.E. (1991) *Reframing Organizations: Artistry, Choice and Leadership*. San Francisco, CA: Jossey-Bass.

Bowman, C. and Collier, N. (2006) 'A contingency approach to resource-creation processes', *International Journal of Management Reviews*, 8(4): 191–211.

Bradley, S.P. and Nolan, R.L. (eds) (1998) *Sense and Respond: Capturing Value in the Network Era*. Boston, MA: Harvard Business School Press.

Bronson, P. (1999) *The Nudist on the Late Shift*. London: Secker & Warburg.

Brookey, R.A. (2010) *Hollywood Gamers: Digital Convergence in the Film and Video Game Industries*. Bloomington, IN: Indiana University Press.

Brown, S.L. and Eisenhardt, K.M. (1997) 'The art of continuous change: linking complexity theory and time-paced evolution in relentlessly-shifting organizations', *Administrative Science Quarterly*, 42: 1–34.

Brown, S.L. and Eisenhardt, K.M. (1998) *Competing on the Edge: Strategy as Structured Chaos*. Boston, MA: Harvard Business School Press.

Bruns, A. (2018) *Gatewatching and News Curation*. New York: Peter Lang.

Bryman, A. (1992) *Charisma and Leadership in Organization*. London: Sage.

Bryman, A., Stephens, M. and Campo, C. (1996) 'The importance of context: qualitative research and the study of leadership', *The Leadership Quarterly*, 7(3): 353.

Burgelman, R.A. (1983) 'Corporate entrepreneurship and strategic management: insights from a process study', *Management Science*, 29: 1349–64.

Burgelman, R.A. (1994) 'Fading memories: a process theory of strategic business exit in dynamic environments', *Administrative Science Quarterly*, 39: 24.

Burgelman, R.A. (2002) *Strategy is Destiny: How Strategy-Making Shapes a Company's Future.* New York: Free Press.

Burgelman, R.A. and Grove, A.S. (2012) *Strategic Dynamics: Three Key Themes. Stanford Graduate School of Business Research Paper No. 2096*. Available at: http://ssrn.com/abstract=2014454 or http://dx.doi.org/10.2139/ssrn.2014454

Burns, J.M. (1978) *Leadership*. New York: Harper & Row.

Burns, T. (1977) *The BBC: Public Institution and Private World*. London: Macmillan.

Burns, T. and Stalker, G.M. (1961/1994) *The Management of Innovation*. Oxford: Oxford University Press.

Burt, R. (1992) *Structural Holes: The Social Structure of Competition*. Cambridge, MA: Harvard University Press.

Castells, M. and Cardoso, G. (2006) *The Network Society: From Knowledge to Policy*. Washington, DC: Johns Hopkins Center for Transatlantic Relations.

Catmull, E. (2014) *Creativity Inc.: Overcoming the Unseen Forces that Stand in the Way of True Inspiration*. London: Bantam Press.

Catmull, E. (2022) 'How Pixar fosters collective creativity', in *On Creativity*. Cambridge, MA: Harvard Business Review Press

Caves, R.E. (2000) *Creative Industries: Contracts between Art and Commerce*. Cambridge, MA: Harvard University Press.

Chaffee, E.E. (1985) 'Three models of strategy', *Academy of Management Review*, 10(1): 89–98.

Chakravarthy, B.S. and Doz, Y. (1992) 'Strategy process research – focusing on corporate self-renewal', *Strategic Management Journal*, 13: 5–14.

Chan-Olmsted, S.M. (2006) *Competitive Strategy for Media Firms: Strategic and Brand Management in Changing Media Markets*. Mahwah, NJ: Lawrence Erlbaum.

Chan-Olmsted, S.M. and Chang, B.H. (2003) 'Diversification strategies of global media conglomerates: examining patterns and determinants', *Journal of Media Economics*, 16(4): 215.

Chandler, A.D. (1962) *Strategy and Structure: Chapters in the History of American Enterprise*. Boston, MA: MIT Press.

Chandler, A. (1969) Strategy and Structure: Chapters in the History of American Industrial Enterprise. Cambridge, MA: The MIT Press.

Chawla, S. and Lenka, U. (2018) 'Leadership in VUCA environment', in S. Dhir and Sushil (eds) *Flexible Strategies in VUCA*. Springer: Singapore.

Christensen, C.M. (1997) *The Innovator's Dilemma: When New Technologies Cause Great Firms to Fail*. Boston, MA: Harvard Business School Press.

Christensen, C.M. and Bower, J. (1996) 'Customer power, strategic investment, and the failure of leading firms', *Strategic Management Journal*, 17: 197–218.

Christensen, C.M. and Overdorf, M. (2000) 'Meeting the challenge of disruptive innovation', *Harvard Business Review*, March–April: 67–76.

Christensen, C.M. and Tuttle, E.G. (1999) 'Why industry leaders fail to harness disruptive technologies', *Red Herring*, May: 152–3.

Christopherson, S. and Storper, M. (1989). 'The effects of flexible specialization on industrial politics and the labor market: the motion picture industry', *Industrial and Labor Relations Review*, 42(3): 331–47.

Chua, S. and Duffy, A. (2019) 'Friend, foe or frenemy? Traditional journalism actors' changing attitudes towards peripheral players and their innovations', *Media and Communication*, 7(4): 112–22.

Coase, R. (1937) 'The nature of the firm', *Economica*, 16(4): 386.

Cohen, W.M. and Levinthal, D.A. (1990) 'Absorbtive capacity: a new perspective on learning and innovation', *Administrative Science Quarterly*, 35: 555.

Coleridge, N. (1993) *Paper Tycoons: The Latest, Greatest Newspaper Tycoons and How They Won the World*. London: Heinemann.

Collins, R. (1998) *From Satellite to Single Market*. London: Routledge.

Collins, J., Radner, H. and Preacher Collins, A. (eds) (1993) *Film Theory Goes to the Movies*. New York and London: Routledge.

Conger, J. (1989) *The Charismatic Leader: Behind the Mystique of Exceptional Leadership*. San Francisco, CA: Jossey-Bass.

Conger, J. (1999) 'Learning the language of leadership', *Human Resource Management International Digest*, March/April, 7(2): 217–28.

Conger, J.A. and Kanungo, R.N. (eds) (1988) *Charismatic Leadership: The Elusive Factor in Organizational Effectiveness*. San Francisco, CA: Jossey-Bass.

Cottle, S. (ed.) (2003) *Media Organization and Production*. London: Sage.

Coutu, D.L. (2002) 'The anxiety of learning', *Harvard Business Review*, March, 98–106.

Croteau, D. and Hoynes, W. (2001) *The Business of Media: Corporate Media and the Public Interest*. Thousand Oaks, CA: Pine Forge Press.

Cunningham, S. and Craig, D. (2019) *Social Media Entertainment*. New York: New York University Press.

Curran, J. and Seaton, J. (1981) *Power without Responsibility: The Press and Broadcasting in Britain*. London: Fontana.

Cusumano, M.A., Annabelle G. and Yoffie, D.B. (1029) *The Business of Platforms: Strategy in the Age of Digital Competition, Innovation, and Power*. New York: Harper Business.

Cyert, R.M. and March, J.G. (1963) *A Behavioral Theory of the Firm*. Englewood Cliffs, NJ: Prentice-Hall.

D'Aveni, R.A. (1994) *Managing the Dynamics of Strategic Manoeuvering*. New York: Free Press.

Daft, R.L. and Weick, K.E. (1984) 'Toward a model of organisations as interpretation systems', *Academy of Management Review*, 9(2): 284–95.

Danneels, E. (2002) 'The dynamics of product innovation and firm competences', *Strategic Management Journal*, 23: 1095.

Davenport, J. (2006) 'UK film companies: project-based organizations lacking entrepreneurship and innovativeness?', *Creativity and Innovation Management*, 15(3): 250–7.

Davis, H. and Scase, R. (2000) *Managing Creativity: The Dynamics of Work and Organization*. Buckingham: Open University Press.

Dawson, P. and Andriopoulus, C. (2021) *Managing Change, Creativity and Innovation*. London: Sage.

Day, D.V., Gronn, P. and Salans, E. (2004) 'Leadership capacity in teams', *The Leadership Quarterly*, 15: 857–80.

Day, G.S. and Schoemaker, P. (2000) 'Avoiding the pitfalls of emerging technologies', *California Management Review*, 42(2).

De Vany, A.S. and Walls, W.D. (1999) 'Uncertainty in the movie industry: does star power reduce the terror of the box office?', *Journal of Cultural Economics*, 23(4): 285–318.

Deazin, R., Glynn, M.A. and Kazanjian, R.K. (1999) 'Multilevel theorizing about creativity in organizations: a sensemaking perspective', *Academy of Management Review*, 24(2): 286–92.

DeFillippi, R.J. and Arthur, M.B. (1998) 'Paradox in project-based enterprise: the case of film making', *California Management Review*, Winter, 40(2): 125–39.

Dennis, E.D., Wharley, S. and Sheridan, J. (2006). 'Doing digital: an assessment of the top 25 US media companies and their digital strategies', *Journal of Media Business Studies*, 3(1): 33–51.

Deuze, M. (2003) 'The web and its journalisms: Considering the consequences of different types of news media online', *New Media & Society*, 5(2): 203–230.

DeVanna, M.A. and Tichy, N. (1990) 'Creating the competitive organization of the 21st century: the boundaryless corporation', *Human Resource Management*, 29: 445–71.

Dhir, S. and Sushil (2018) *Flexible Strategies in VUCA Markets*. Singapore: Springer. doi: 10.1007/978-981-10-8926-8

Diakopoulos, N. (2019) *Automating the News: How Algorithms Are Rewriting the Media*. Cambridge, MA: Harvard University Press.

Di Stefano, G., Peteraf, M. and Verona, G. (2010) 'Dynamic capabilities deconstructed: a bibliographic investigation in the origins, development, and future directions of the research domain', *Industrial and Corporate Change*, 19(4): 118–1204.

DiMaggio, P. and Powell, W. (1983) 'The iron cage revisited: institutional isomorphism and collective rationality in organizational fields', *American Sociological Review*, 48: 147–60.

Dimmick, J. and McDonald, D.G. (2003) 'The conceptualization and measurement of diversity', *Communication Research*, 30(1): 60–79.

Dixon, C. (2012) 'BuzzFeed's strategy', 24 July. Available at: http://cdixon.org/2012/07/24/buzzfeeds-strategy.

Doyle, G. (2011) 'From television to multi-platform: Less from more or more for less?', *Convergence: The International Journal of Research into New Media Technologies*, 16(4): 431–449.

Downes, L. and Mui, C. (1998) *Unleashing the Killer App: Digital Strategies for Market Dominance*. Boston, MA: Harvard Business School Press.

Doyle, G. (2002a) *Media Ownership*. London: Sage.

Doyle, G. (2002b) *Understanding Media Economics*. London: Sage.

Drazin, R. and Schoonhoven, C.B. (1996) 'Community, population, and organization effects on innovation: a multilevel perspective', *Academy of Management Journal*, 39(5): 1065–83.

Drucker, P. (1985) *Innovation and Entrepreneurship*. London: Heinemann.

Drucker, P. (1994) 'The theory of the business', *Harvard Business Review*, September–October: 95–104.

Dutton, J.E., Ashford, S.J., O'Neill, R.M., Hayes, E. and Wierba, E.E. (1997) 'Reading the wind: how middle managers assess the contest for selling issues to top managers', *Strategic Management Journal*, 18(5): 407–25.

Edmondson, A.C., and Verdin, P.J. (2017) 'Your strategy should be a hypothesis you constantly adjust'. *Harvard Business Review*, 9 November.

Eisenhardt, K.M. and Brown, S.L. (1999) 'Patching: restitching business portfolios in dynamic markets', *Harvard Business Review*, May–June: 72–82.

Eisenhardt, K.M. and Martin, J.A. (2000) 'Dynamic capabilities: what are they?', *Strategic Management Journal*, special issue, 21(10/11): 1105–21.

Eisenmann, T.R. and Bower, J.L. (2000) 'The entrepreneurial M-Form: strategic integration in global media companies', *Organization Science*, May–June, 11(3): 348–55.

Elberse, A. (2013) *Blockbusters: Hit-making, Risk-taking, and the Big Business of Entertainment*. New York: Henry Holt and Co.

Evans, P. and Wurster, T.S. (2000) *Blown to Bits: How the New Economics of Information Transform Strategy*. Boston, MA: Harvard Business School Press.

Fanta, A. and Dachwitz, I. (2020) *Google, the Media Patron. How the Digital Giant Ensnares Journalism*, 103. OBS-Arbeitsheft. Frankfurt: Otto Brenner Stiftung.

Feldman, E. (2021) 'The corporate parenting advantage, revisited', *Strategic Management Journal*, January, 114–43.

Fidler, R. (1997) *Mediamorphosis: Understanding New Media*. Thousand Oaks, CA: Pine Forge Press.

Filloux, F. (2014) 'Hard comparison: legacy media vs. digital native', *Monday Note*, 24 November. Available at: www.mondaynote.com/2014/11/24/hard-comparison-legacy-media-vs-digital-native

Fiol, C.M. and Huff, A.S. (1992) 'Maps for managers: where are we? Where do we go from here?', *Journal of Management Studies*, 29: 267–85.

First Round (n.d.) '80 percent of your culture is your founder'. Available at: http://firstround.com/article/80-of-Your-Culture-is-Your-Founder

Fiske, S.T. and Taylor, S.E. (1984) *Social Cognition*. Reading, MA: Addison-Wesley.

Fletcher, J.K. and Käufer, K. (2003) 'Shared leadership', in C.L. Pearce and J. Conger, *Shared Leadership, Reframing the Hows and Whys of Leadership*. Thousand Oaks, CA: Sage.

Flynn, F.J. and Chatman, J.A. (2004) 'Strong cultures and innovation: oxymoron or opportunity?', in M.L. Tushman and P. Anderson (eds) *Managing Strategic Innovation and Change: A Collection of Readings* (2nd edn). Oxford: Oxford University Press.

Florida, R. and Goodnight, J. (2005) 'Managing for creativity', *Harvard Business Review*, July: 124–34.

Ford, C.M. (1996) 'A theory of individual creative action in multiple social domains', *Academy of Management Review*, 21: 1112.

Ford, C.M. and Gioia, D.A. (eds) (1995) *Creative Action in Organizations: Ivory Tower Visions and Real World Voices*. Thousand Oaks, CA: Sage. pp. 1112–42.

Freeman, C. and Soete, L. (1997) *The Economics of Industrial Innovation*. Cambridge, MA: The MIT Press.
Frei, F. and Morriss, M. (2020) *Unleashed: The Unapologetic Leader's Guide to Empowering Everyone Around You*. MA: Harvard Business Review Press.
Frey, B.S. and Jegen, R. (2000) 'Motivation crowding theory: a survey of empirical evidence', *CESifo Working Paper Series*. Munich.
Fritz, B. (2012) 'Cadre of film buffs help Netflix viewers sort through the clutter', *Los Angeles Times*. Available at: http://articles.latimes.com/2012/sep/03/business/la-fi-0903-ct-netflix-taggers-20120903 (accessed 1 December 2014).
Fritz, B. (2018) *The Big Picture: The Fight for the Future of Movies* (Boston, MA: Houghton Mifflin Harcourt Publishing. p. 17.
Fulmer, W.E. (2000) *Shaping the Adaptive Organization: Landscape, Learning, and Leadership in Volatile Times*. New York: Amacom.
Gandhi, L. (2017) 'Human resource challenges in VUCA and SMAC business environment'. *ASBM Journal of Management*, 10(1): 1–5.
Gardner, W.L. and Carlson, J. D. (2015) *Authentic Leadership. International Encyclopedia of the Social & Behavioral Sciences*, 27, 245–50.
Gardner, W.M., Avolio, B.J., Luthans, F., May, D.R. and Walumbwa, F. (2005) '"Can you see the real me?" A self-based model of authentic leader and follower development', *The Leadership Quarterly*, 16(3): 343–72.
García-Avilés, J.A., Kaltenbrunner, A. and Meier, K. (2014) 'Media convergence revisited: lessons learned on newsroom integration in Austria, Germany and Spain', *Journalism Practice*, 8(5). doi: 10.1080/17512786.2014.885678
Gardner, W.L. and Carlson, J.D. (2015) 'Authentic leadership', *International Encyclopedia of the Social & Behavioral Sciences*, 27: 245–50.
Gavetti, G. and Levinthal, D. (2000) 'Looking forward and looking backward: cognitive and experiential search', *Administrative Science Quarterly*, 45: 113–37.
Georgiou, M. (1998) *Television Use in the Digital Age: A Personal Perspective on Change*. Reuters Foundation Paper No. 63. Oxford: Reuters Institute.
Gersick, C.J.G. (1991) 'Revolutionary change theories: a multilevel exploration of the punctuated equilibrium paradigm', *Academy of Management Review*, 16(1): 10–36.
Ghosh, S. (1998) 'Making business sense of the internet', *Harvard Business Review*, March–April: 127–33.
Gibson, J. (2007) 'Murdoch and meddling', *The Guardian*, 2 August: 25.
Gibson, C.B. and Birkenshaw, J. (2009) 'The antecedents, consequences, and mediating role of organizational ambidexterity', *Academy of Management Journal*, 47(2): 226.
Gil, R. and Spiller, P. (2007) 'The organizational implications of creativity: the US film industry in mid-XXth century', *California Management Review*, 50(1): 243–60.
Gilbert, C.G. (2002) 'Can competing frames co-exist? The paradox of threatened response'. Working paper from the Harvard Business School Division of Research. Boston, MA: Harvard Business School.
Gillmor, D. (2004) *We the Media: Grassroots Journalism, by the People for the People*. Sebastopol, CA: O'Reilly Media.
Gioia, D.A. and Chittipeddi, K. (1991) 'Sensemaking and sense-giving in strategic change initiation', *Strategic Management Journal*, 12: 433–48.
Gioia, D.A. and Pitre, E. (1990) 'Multiparadigm perspectives on theory building', *Academy of Management Review*, 15(4): 584–602.
Goffee, R. and Jones, G. (2000) 'Why should anyone be led by you?', *Harvard Business Review*, September–October, 78(5): 62–70.
Gomez, J. (2017) '10 keys to building successful shared universe movie franchises: a memo to studio executives', *Medium*, 13 June. Available at: https://medium.com/@Jeff_Gomez/10-keys-to-building-successful-shared-universe-movie-franchises-a9d983884ad3
Govindarajan, V. and Trimble, C. (2010) *The Other Side of Innovation: Solving the Execution Challenge*. Boston, MA: Harvard Business School Publishing.
Grove, A.S. (1983) *High Output Management*. New York, Random House.
Groysberg, B., Lee, J., Price, J. and Yo-Jud Cheng, J. (2018) 'The leader's guide to corporate culture', *Harvard Business Review*, January–February.
Gulati, R. and Garino, J. (2000) 'Getting the right mixture of bricks and clicks', *Harvard Business Review*, May–June: 107–14.

Gulati, R. and Puranam, P. (2009) 'Renewal through reorganization: the value of inconsistencies between formal and informal organization', *Organization Science*, 20: 422–40.

Gupta, A.K., Smith, K.G., and Shalley, C.E. (2006) 'The interplay between exploration and exploitation', *The Academy of Management Journal*, 49(4): 693–704.

Halek, P. and Strobl, G. (2016) 'Keeping the flow: creating opportunities based on well-structured collaboration', in Mack, O., Khare, A., Krämer, A. and Burgartz, T. (eds) *Managing in a VUCA World*. Cham, Switzerland: Springer. pp. 59–76.

Hall, R.I. (1984) 'The natural logic of management policy making: its implications for the survival of the organisation', *Management Science*, 30: 905–27.

Hambrick, D.C. (1983) 'Some tests of the effectiveness and functional attributes of Miles and Snow's strategic types', *Academy of Management Journal*, 26: 5–25.

Hamel, G. and Sampler, J. (1998) 'The e-corporation', *Fortune*, 7 December: 53–82.

Hamm, S. (1999) 'How to survive the cyber-revolution', *Business Week*, 3623: 28–35.

Hampden-Turner, C.M. (1990) *Charting the Corporate Mind: From Dilemma to Strategy*. Oxford: Blackwell.

Hannan, M.T. and Freeman, J.H. (1984) 'Structural inertia and organizational change', *American Sociological Review*, 49: 149–64.

Hastings, R. and Meyer, E. (2020) *No Rules Rules: Netflix and the Culture of Reinvention*. New York: Penguin.

He, Z. and Wong, P. (2004) 'Exploration vs. exploitation: an empirical test of the ambidexterity hypothesis', *Organization Science*, 15(4): 481–94.

Hedberg, B. (1981) 'How organisations learn and unlearn', in P. Nystrom and W. Starbuck (eds) *Handbook of Organization Design*. New York: Oxford University Press. pp. 1–27.

Helfat, C.E., Finkelsetein, S., Mtchell, W., Peteraf, M.A., Sing, H., Teece, D. J. and Winder, S.G. (2007) *Dynamic Capabilities: Understanding Strategic Change in Organisations.* Malden. MA: Blackwell Publishing.

Henderson, R.M. and Clark, K.B. (1990) 'Architectural innovation: the reconfiguration of existing product technologies and the failure of established firms', *Administrative Science Quarterly*, 35: 9–30.

Henten, A. and Oest, A. (2005) 'Copyright: rights-holders, users and innovators', *Editorial to Special Issue of Telematics and Informatics*, 22: 1–4, February–May: 1–9.

Henzler, H.A. (1998) 'Communications and media in the digital age'. Speech to mcm Forum, St Gallen, Switzerland.

Heskett, J. (2022) *Win from Within*. New York: Columbia Business School.

Hesmondhalgh, D. (2002) *The Cultural Industries*. London: Sage.

Hill, C.W. and Rothaermel, F.T. (2003) 'The performance of incumbent firms in the face of technological innovation', *Academy of Management Review*, 28(2): 257.

Hirsch, P. (1972) 'Processing fads and fashions: an organization set analysis of cultural industry system', *American Journal of Sociology*, 77(4): 639–59.

Hirsch, P.M. (2000) 'Cultural industries revisited', *Organization Science*, 11(3): 356–61.

Hitt, M.A. (1997) 'Current and future research methods in strategic management', synopsis of 1997 Research Methods Forum No. 2, Summer. Western Academy of Management Meetings. Available at: www.aom.pace.edu/edu/rms/1997_forum_strategic_management.html (accessed 6 May 2002).

Hitt, M.A., Ireland, R.D. and Hoskisson, R.E. (2001) *Strategic Management: Competitiveness and Globalization*. Cincinnati, OH: South-Western College Publishing/Thomson Learning.

Hitt, M.A., Keats, B.W. and DeMarie, S.M. (1998) 'Navigating in the new competitive landscape: building strategic flexibility and competitive advantage in the 21st century', *Academy of Management Executive*, 12(4): 22–42.

Hofstede, G. (ed.) (1980) *Culture's Consequences: International Differences in Work-related Values*. Newbury Park, CA; Sage.

House, R.J. (1977) 'A 1976 theory of charismatic leadership', in J.G. Hunt and L.L. Larson (eds) *Leadership: The Cutting Edge*. Carbondale, IL: Southern Illinois University Press.

Hu J., Erdogan, B., Jiang, K. Bauer. T. N., and Liu, S. (2017) 'Leader humility and team creativity: the role of team information sharing, psychological safety, and power distance', *Journal of Applied Psychology*, 103(3).

Huff, A.S. (1997) 'A current and future agenda for cognitive research in organisations', *Journal of Management Studies*, 6(34): 947–52.

Huff, J.O., Huff, A.S. and Thomas, H. (1992) 'Strategic renewal and the interaction of cumulative stress and inertia', *Strategic Management Journal*, 13: 55–75.

Hunt, J.G. and Conger, J.A. (1999) 'Charismatic and transformational leadership: taking stock of the present and future (Part II)', *Leadership Quarterly*, 3(10): 331–4.

Hutton, W. (2007) 'Harry Potter and the secret of success', *The Observer*, 22 August.

Huy, Q.N. (1999) 'Emotional capability, emotional intelligence and radical change', *Academy of Management Review*, 24(2): 325–45.

Jess-Cooke, C. (2009) *Film Sequels: Theory and Practice from Hollywood to Bollywood*. Edinburgh: Edinburgh University Press. p. 46.

Jenkins, H. (2006) *Convergence Culture: Where Old and New Media Collide*. New York: NYU Press. p. 113; 95–6.

Iger, R. (2019) *The Ride of a Lifetime: Lessons in Creative Leadership*. London: Bantam Press.

Ingram, M. (2013) 'Newspapers that aren't dying: four success stories and four lessons'. Available at: http://gigaom.com/2013/02/11/newspapers-that-arent-dying-four-success-stories-and-four-lessons

INMA (2022) 'How product is leading media's new growth plan'. Available at: www.inma.org/report/how-product-is-leading-medias-new-growth-path

Isabella, L.A. (1990) 'Evolving interpretations as a change unfolds: how managers construe key organizational events', *Academy of Management Journal*, 33(1): 7–14.

Jago, A. (1982) 'Leadership: perspectives in theory and research', *Management Science*, 28(3): 315–36.

Janszen, F. (2000) *The Age of Innovation*. Harlow: Pearson Education.

Jelinek, M. and Schonhoven, C.B. (1990) *The Innovation Marathon: Lessons from High Technology Firms*. Cambridge, MA: Basil Blackwell.

Jenkins, H. (2001) 'Convergence? I diverge', *Technology Review*, 104: 93–4.

Johnson, G. (1987) *Strategic Change and the Management Process*. Oxford: Basil Blackwell.

Johnson, G. (1992) 'Managing strategic change – strategy, culture and action', *Long Range Planning*, 25(1): 28–36.

Johnson, G. and Scholes, K. (1989) *Exploring Corporate Strategy: Text and Cases*. Harlow: Prentice Hall.

Jurkowitz, M. and Mitchell, A. (2013) 'Deseret news – changing two media cultures'. *Pew Research Journalism Project*, 11 February. Available at: www.journalism.org/2013/02/11/deseret-news-changing-two-media-cultures

Hess, T. (2014) 'What is a media company? A reconceptualization for the online world', *International Journal on Media Management*. 16(1) 3–8.

Kanter, R.M. (1983) *The Change Masters: Corporate Entrepreneurs at Work*. New York: Simon & Schuster.

Kanter, R.M. (1988) 'When a thousand flowers bloom: structural, collective, and social conditions for innovation in organization', *Research in Organizational Behavior*, 10: 169–211.

Kanter, R.M. (1992) *When Giants Learn to Dance* (new edn). London: International Thomson Business Press.

Kanter, R.M. (2004) *Confidence*. London: Random House Business Books.

Kanter, R.M. (2006) 'Innovation: the classic traps', *Harvard Business Review*, November: 73–83.

Katz, R.L. (1955) 'Skills of an effective administrator', *Harvard Business Review*, January–February: 33–42.

Kaufman, L. (2014) 'Vox takes melding of journalism and technology to a new level', *New York Times*, 6 April. Available at: www.nytimes.com/2014/04/07/business/media/voxcom-takes-melding-of-journalism-and-technology-to-next-level.html

Kay, J. (1993) *Foundations of Corporate Success: How Business Strategies Add Value*. Oxford: Oxford University Press.

Kellerman, B. (2004) *Bad Leadership*. Boston, MA: Harvard Business School Press.

Kelly, K. (1997) 'New rules for the new economy: twelve dependable principles for thriving in a turbulent world', *Wired*, 5.09, September.

Kueng, L. (2015) *Innovators in Digital News*. London: IB Taurus.

Knee, J.A., Greenwald, B.C. and Seave, A. (2009) *The Curse of the Mogul: What's Wrong with the World's Leading Media Companies?* New York: Portfolio.

Kotter, J.P. (1988) *The Leadership Factor*. Boston, MA: Harvard Business School Press.

Kotter, J.P. (1996) *Leading Change*. Boston, MA: Harvard Business School Press.

Kotter, J.P. and Heskett, J.L. (1992) *Corporate Culture and Performance*. New York: Free Press.

Kuhn, T.S. (1970) *The Structure of Scientific Revolutions*. Chicago, IL: University of Chicago Press.

Kunert, K.W. (1994) *Transforming Leadership: Developing People through Delegation*. London: Sage.

Küng, L. (2003) *When Old Dogs Learn New Tricks: The Launch of BBC News Online*. Case Study No. 303–119–1. Wharley End: European Case Clearing House.

Küng, L. (2004) 'What makes media firms tick? Exploring the hidden drivers of firm performance', in P.G. Picard (ed.) *Strategic Responses to Media Market Changes*. Jönköping: Jönköping International Business School.

Kueng, L. (2017) *Going Digital: A Roadmap for Organisational Transformation*. Oxford: Reuters Institute.

Kueng, L. (2020) *Hearts and Minds: Harnessing Leadership, Culture, and Talent to Really Go Digital*. Oxford: Reuters Institute.

Küng, L. (2005) 'When innovation fails to disrupt. A multi lens investigation of successful incumbent response to technological discontinuity: the launch of BBC news online'. Habilitationsschrift, University of St Gallen, Switzerland.

Küng, L. (ed.) (2006) *Leadership in the Media Industry: Changing Contexts, Emerging Challenges*. JIBS Research Reports 2006–1. Jönköping: Jönköping International Business School.

Küng, L. (2015) *Innovators in Digital News*. London: I.B. Taurus.

Küng, L. (2016) 'Leadership: overcoming overload in the media industry', in R. Picard (ed.), *What Society Needs from Media in the Age of Digital Communication*. New York and Barcelona: Social Trends Institute.

Küng, L. (2019) *Hearts and Minds: Harnessing Leadership, Culture, and Talent to Really go Digital*. Reuters Institute, University of Oxford.

Küng-Shankleman, L. (1997) 'Investigating the BBC and CNN: how culture drives strategy in broadcasting organisations'. Doctoral dissertation, University of St Gallen, Switzerland.

Küng-Shankleman, L. (2000) *Inside the BBC and CNN: Managing Media Organisations*. London and New York: Routledge.

Kuratko, D.F., Covin, J.G., Garrett, R.P., (2009) 'Corporate venturing: insights from actual performance', *Business Horizons*, 52(5): 459–67.

Lacy, S. and Simon, T. (1993) *The Economics and Regulation of United States Newspapers*. Norwood, NJ: Ablex.

Lampel, J., Lant, T. and Shamsie, J. (2000) 'Balancing act: learning from organizing practices in cultural industries', *Organization Science*, May/June, 11(3): 263–9.

Laura, S. (2012) *How the New York Times Maximizes Customer Lifetime Value*. subscribed.com/read/news-and-editorial/how-the-new-york-times-maximizes-customer-lifetime-value

Lavine, J.M. and Wackman, D.B. (1988) *Managing Media Organisations: Effective Leadership of the Media*. New York and London: Longman.

Lawrence, P.R. and Lorsch, J.W. (1967) 'Differentiation and integration in complex organisations', *Administrative Science Quarterly*, 12: 1–47.

Lawton, T. and Rajwani, T. (2011) 'Designing lobbying capabilities: managerial choices in unpredictable environments', *European Business Review*. 23(2): 167–89.

Leonard-Barton, D. (1992) 'Core capabilities and core rigidities: a paradox in managing new product development', *Strategic Management Journal*, Summer Special Issue, 13: 111–25.

Leonard-Bardon, D. (1995) *Welsprings of Knowledge*. Cambridge, MA: Harvard Business School Press.

Leroy, H., Anseel, F., Gardner, W.L. and Sels, L. (2012) 'Authentic leadership, authentic followership, basic need satisfaction, and work role performance: A cross-level study', *Journal of Management*, 41(6).

Leyroy, H., Anseel, F., Gardner, W. and Sels, L. (2015) 'Authentic leadership, authentic followership, basic need satisfaction, and work role performance: a cross-level study', *Journal of Management*, 41(6): 1677–97.

Levinthal, D.A. and March, J.G. (1993) 'The myopia of learning', *Strategic Management Journal*, 14: 95–112.

Levitt, B. and March, J.G. (1988) 'Organizational learning', *Annual Review of Sociology*, 14: 319–40.

Levitz, D. (2013) '6 principles Clark Gilbert used to transform Deseret News', 11 February. Available at: www.americanpressinstitute.org/publications/reports/white-papers/6-principles-clark-gilbert-used-transform-deseret-news

Lewin, K. (1943) 'Psychology and the process of group living', *Journal of Social Psychology*, 17: 113–31.

Lewin, K. (1947) *Field Theory in Social Science*. New York: Harper & Row.

Li, H., Li, F. and Chen, T. (1998) 'A motivational-cognitive model of creativity and the role of autonomy', *Journal of Business Research*, 92, November 2018, 179–88.

Lieberman, M. and Montgomery, D.B. (1988) 'First-mover advantages', *Strategic Management Journal*, 9: 41–8.

Lotz. A.D. (2022) Netflix and Streaming Video. Cambridge: Polity Press.

Louw, P.E. (2001) *The Media and Cultural Production*. London: Sage.

Lovelace, R.F. (1986) 'Stimulating creativity through managerial intervention', *R & D Management*, 16: 161–74.

Lomax, T. (2019) 'The franchise era: blockbust Hollywood in the 2010s ... and beyond', *Senses of Cinema*.

Lowe, G. and Noam, E. (2022) 'Is everything media? Defining the media sector and its industries in the digital environment'. Unpublished paper from the 2022 Conference of the European Media Management Association, Münich, Germany,

Lynch, R. (2021) *Strategic Management* (9th edn). London: Sage.

Mack, C. and Khare, A. (2016) 'Perspectives on a VUCA world', in O. Mack, A. Khare, Krämer, A. and Burgartz, T. (eds) *Managing in a VUCA World*. Cham, Switzerland: Springer. pp. 3–19.

Magretta, J. (2002) 'Why business models matter', *Harvard Business Review*, 80(5): 86–92.

Makadok, R. (2001) 'Toward a synthesis of the resource-based and dynamic-capability views of rent creation', *Strategic Management Journal*, 22: 387–401.

Makridakis, S. (1990) *Forecasting, Planning, and Strategy for the 21st Century*. New York: Free Press.

Malone, T. (2004) *The Future of Work: How the New Order of Business Will Shape Your Organization, Your Management Style, and Your Life*. Boston, MA: Harvard Business School Press.

Mann, N. (2015) 'The great journalism innovation problem', *Medium*, 18 December. Available at: https://medium.com/@fieldproducer/the-great-journalism-innovation-problem-ac7ba41cb77c#.ac80ocw1t

Manjoo, F. (2016) 'Tech's "Frightful 5" will dominate digital life for foreseeable future', *The New York Times*, 21 January. Available at: www.nytimes.com/2016/01/21/technology/techs-frightful-5-will-dominate-digital-life-for-foreseeable-future.html

Manning, S. (2005) 'Managing project networks as dynamic organizational forms: learning from the TV movie industry', *International Journal of Project Management*, 23: 410–14.

March, J.G. (1991) 'Exploration and exploitation in organizational learning', *Organization Science*, 2(1): 71–87.

March, J.G. and Simon, H. (1958) *Organizations*. New York: Wiley.

Marjoribanks, T. (2000) *News Corporation, Technology and the Workplace: Global Strategies, Local Change*. Cambridge: Cambridge University Press.

Martinson, J. (2014) 'Alan Rusbridger to stand down as editor in chief', *The Guardian*, 10 December. Available at: www.theguardian.com/media/2014/dec/10/alan-rusbridger-stand-down-guardian-editor-in-chief

Mauzy, J. and Harriman, R. (2003) *Creativity, Inc.: Building an Inventive Organization*. Boston, MA: Harvard Business School Press.

McChesney, R.M. (2004) *The Problem of the Media: U.S. Communication Politics in the Twentieth Century*. New York: Monthly Review Press.

McClelland, D.C. (1961) *The Achieving Society*. Princeton, NJ: Van Nostrand.

McEachern, T. and O'Keefe, B. (1997) *Re-Wiring Business: Uniting Management and the Web*. New York: John Wiley & Sons.

McGraw, K.O. and Fiala, J. (1982) 'Undermining the Zeigarnik effect: another hidden cost of reward', *Journal of Personality*, 50(1): 58–66.

McGraw, K.O. (1978) 'The detrimental effects of reward on performance: a literature review and prediction model', in M.R. Lepper and D. Green (eds), *The Hidden Costs of Rewards*. Hillsdale, NJ: Erlbaum.

Meikle, G. and Young, S. (2012) *Media Convergence: Networked Digital Media in Everyday Life*. London: Palgrave Macmillan.

Mewmarich, L. and Vera, D. (2009) 'Transformational leadership and ambidexterity in the context of an acquisition', *The Leadership Quarterly*, 20(1): 19–33.

Meyer, A.D. (1982) 'Adapting to environmental jolts', *Administrative Science Quarterly*, 27: 515–37.

Meyer, P. (2004) *The Vanishing Newspaper: Saving Journalism in the Information Age*. Columbia, MO: University of Missouri Press.

Miao, C., Humphrey, R. H. and Qian, S. (2018) 'Emotional intelligence and authentic leadership: a meta-analysis', *Leadership & Organization Development Journal*, 39: 679–90.

Mierzejewska, B. and Shaver, D. (2014) 'Key changes impacting media management research', *International Journal on Media Management*, 16(2): 47–54.

Miles, R.E. and Snow, C.C. (1986) 'Organizations: new concepts for new forms', *California Management Review*, 28: 62–73.

Miles, R.E., Snow, C.C., Mathews, J.A., Miles, G. and Coleman, H.J. (1997) 'Organizing in the knowledge age: anticipating the cellular form', *Academy of Management Executive*, 11(4): 7–20.

Miller, D. and Shamsie, J. (1996) 'The resource-based view of the firm in two environments: the Hollywood film studios from 1936–1965', *Academy of Management Journal*, 39(3): 519–43.

Milliken, F.J. (1990) 'Perceiving and interpreting environmental change: an examination of college administrators' interpretation of changing demographics', *Academy of Management Journal*, 33: 42–63.

Mintzberg, H. (1987) 'An emerging strategy of "direct" research'. *Administrative Science Quarterly*, December, 24: 582–9.

Mintzberg, H. and Westley, F. (1992) 'Cycles of organizational change', *Strategic Management Journal*, 13: 39–59.

Mintzberg, H., Ahlstrand, B. and Lampel, J. (1998) *Strategy Safari: A Guided Tour through the Wilds of Strategic Management*. New York: Free Press.

Mintzberg, H., Lampel, J., Quinn, J.B. and Ghoshal, S. (2003) *The Strategy Process: Concepts, Contexts, Cases* (global 4th edn). Harlow: Prentice Hall.

Moazed, A., and Johnson, N.L. (2016) *Modern Monopolies: What it Takes to Dominate the 21-first Century Economy*. New York: St Martin's Press.

Moran, A. with Malbon, J. (2006) *Understanding the Global TV Format*. Bristol: Intellect Books.

Morgan, G. (1986) *Images of Organization*. Thousand Oaks, CA: Sage.

Morgeson, F.P., DeRue, D.S. and Karam, E.P. (2010) 'Leadership in teams: a functional approach to understanding leadership structures and processes', *Journal of Management*, 36(1), 5–39.

Mosco, V. (1996) *The Political Economy of Communication: Rethinking and Renewal*. London: Sage.

Mumford, M.D., Zaccaro, S.J., Harding, F.D., Jacobs, T.O. and Fleishman, E.A. (2000) 'Leadership skills for a changing world: solving complex social problems', *The Leadership Quarterly*, 11(1): 11–35.

Nadella, S. (2017) *Hit Refresh*. London: William Collins.

Napoli, P.M. (2003) *Audience Economics: Media Institutions and the Audience Marketplace*. New York: Columbia University Press.

Nelson, R. (1995) 'Recent evolutionary theorizing about economic change', *Journal of Economic Literature*, 33: 48–80.

Nelson, R.R. and Winter, S.G. (1982) *An Evolutionary Theory of Economic Change*. Cambridge: Belknap.

Newman, N., Fletcher, R., Schulz, A., Simge, A. and Nielsen, R.K. (2020) 'Digital news report 2020', *Digital News Report*. Oxford: Reuters Institute for the Study of Journalism. Available at: www.digitalnewsreport.org/

Nielsen, R.K. (2018) 'The changing economic contexts of journalism', in T. Hanitzsch and K. Wahl-Jorgensen (eds) *Handbook of Journalism Studies* (2nd edn). London: Routledge. Available at: https://rasmuskleisnielsen.files.wordpress.com/2018/05/nielsen-the-changing-economic-contexts-of-journalism-v2.pdf

Nielsen, R.K. and Ganter, S.A. (2018) 'Dealing with digital intermediaries: a case study of the relations between publishers and platforms', *New Media & Society*, 20(4): 1600–17.

Noam, E. (1998) 'The market dynamics of convergence', speech to E-Screen '98 Conference, Monte Carlo, February.

Noam, E. (2018) *Managing Media and Digital Organizations*. Cham: Palgrave Macmillan.

Nohria, N. and Eccles, R. (eds) (1992) *Networks and Organizations: Structure, Form and Action*. Boston, MA: Harvard Business School Press.

Nohria, N. and Ghoshal, S. (1997) *The Differentiated Network: Organising Multi-National Organizations for Value Creation*. San Francisco, CA: Jossey-Bass.

Nohria, N. and Gulati, R. (1996) 'Is slack good or bad for innovation?', *Academy of Management Journal*, 39(5): 1245–64.

Northouse, P.G. (2004) *Leadership: Theory and Practice* (3rd edn). Thousand Oaks, CA: Sage.

Northouse, P.G. (2022) *Leadership: Theory and Practice* (9th edn). Thousand Oaks, CA: Sage.

Oldham, G.R. and Cummings, A. (1996) 'Employee creativity: personal and contextual factors at work', *Academy of Management Journal*, 39: 607.

Oliver, J. (2014) 'Dynamic capabilities and superior firm performance in the UK media industry', *Journal of Media Business Studies*, 11(2): 57–77.

Oliver, J. (2018) 'Strategic transformations in the media', *Journal of Media Business Studies*. DOI: 10.1080/16522354.2018.1546088

Oremus, W. (2014) 'BuzzFeed plagiarism, deleted posts: Jonah Peretti explains', *Slate*, August. Available at: http://slate.com/articles/technology/2014/08

Osterwalder, A. and Pigneur, Y. (2010) *Business Model Generation: A Handbook for Visionaries, Game Changers, and Challengers*. Hoboken, NJ: John Wiley & Sons.

Parry, R. (2011) *The Ascent of Media: From Gilgamesh to Google via Gutenberg*. London: Nicholas Brearley Publishing.

Pascale, R.T. and Athos, A.G. (1981) *The Art of Japanese Management*. New York: Simon & Schuster.

Pasick, A. (2015) 'The magic that makes Spotify's Discover Weekly playlist so damn good', *Quartz*, 21 December. Available at: http://qz.com/571007/the-magic-that-makes-spotifys-discover-weekly-playlists-so-damn-good

Penrose, E.T. (1959) *The Theory of the Growth of the Firm*. New York: John Wiley & Sons.

Peteraf, M.A. (1993) 'The cornerstones of competitive advantage: a resource-based view', *Strategic Management Journal*, 14: 179–90.

Peters, T. and Waterman, R.H. (1982) *In Search of Excellence: Lessons from America's Best-run Companies*. New York: Harper & Row.

Pettigrew, A. and Fenton, E. (eds) (2000) *The Innovating Organization*. London: Sage.

Pettigrew, A. and Whipp, R. (1991) *Managing Change for Competitive Success*. Oxford: Blackwell.

Pettigrew, A.M. (1979) 'On studying organizational cultures', *Administrative Science Quarterly*, 24 (December): 570–81.

Pettigrew, A.M. (1992) 'The character and significance of strategy process research', *Strategic Management Journal*, 13: 5–16.

Piaget, J. (1952) *The Origins of Intelligence in Children*. New York: International Universities Press.

Picard, R.G. (1996) 'The rise and fall of communications empires', *Journal of Media Economics*, 9(4): 23–40.

Picard, R.G. (2002a) *The Economics and Financing of Media Companies*. New York: Fordham University Press.

Picard, R.G. (2002b) 'Changing business models of online content services: their implications for multimedia and other content producers'. *The International Journal on Media Management*, 2(2): 60–6.

Picard, R.G. (ed.) (2002c) *Media Firms: Structure, Operations, and Performance*. Mahwah, NJ: Lawrence Erlbaum.

Picard, R. (2003) 'Cash cows or entrecôte: publishing companies and disruptive technologies', *Trends in Communication*, 11(2): 127–36.

Picard, R.G. (2004) *Strategic Responses to Media Market Changes*. JIBS Research Reports No. 2. Jönköping: Jönköping University.

Picard, R.G. and Lowe, G.F. (2016) 'Questioning media management scholarship: four parables about how to better develop the field', *Journal of Media Business Studies*, 13(2): 61–72.

Pooley, E. (2007) 'Exclusive: Rupert Murdoch speaks', *Time*. Available at: www.time.com/time/printout/0,8816,1638182,00.html

Porter, G. and Beyerlein, M. (2000) 'Historic roots of team theory and practice', in M.M. Beyerlein (ed.) *Work Teams: Past, Present and Future*. Dordrecht, Netherlands: Kluwer (pp. 3–24).

Porter, M.E. (1980) *Competitive Strategy: Techniques for Analyzing Industries and Competitors*. New York: Free Press.

Porter, M.E. (1985) *Competitive Advantage: Creating and Sustaining Superior Performance*. New York: Free Press.

Porter, M.E. (1996) 'What is a strategy?', *Harvard Business Review*, November–December: 61–78.

Prahalad, C.K. and Hamel, G. (1990) 'The core competence of the corporation', *Harvard Business Review*, 63(3): 79–91.

Prahalad, C.K. and Hamel, G. (eds) (1994) 'In search of new paradigms', *Strategic Management Journal*, Summer Special Issue: 5–16.

Prakash, D., Bisla, M. and Rastogi, S. (2021) 'Understanding authentic leadership style: the Satya Nadella Microsoft approach', *Open Journal of Leadership*, 10: 95–109.

Price, C.L. (2006) *Rewriting the Future for Newspaper Investors*. Dallas, TX: International Newspaper Marketing Association.

PWC (2013) 'Game changer: a new kind of value chain for entertainment and media companies'. Available at: www.pwc.com/us/en/industry/entertainment-media/publications/entertainment-providers-shift-producers.html

Quinn, J.B. (1980) *Strategies for Change: Logical Incrementalism.* Irwin, Homewood.

Quinn, J.B. (1992) *The Intelligent Enterprise.* New York: Free Press.

Rajagopalan, N. and Spreitzer, G.M. (1996) 'Toward a theory of strategic change: a multi-lens perspective and integrative framework', *Academy of Management Review*, 22(1): 48–79.

Ravid, S.A. (1999) 'Information, blockbusters and start: a study of the film industry', *Journal of Business*, 72: 463–86.

Rayport, J.F. and Svioka, J.J. (1995) 'Exploiting the virtual value chain', *Harvard Business Review*, November–December: 75–85.

Rego, A., Sousa, F., Marques, C. and Cunha, M.P. (2012) 'Authentic leadership promoting employees' psychological capital and creativity', *Journal of Business Research*, 65: 429–37.

Riepl, W. (1913) *Das Nachrichtenwesen des Altertums mit besonderer Rücksicht auf die Römer.* Leipzig: Teubner.

Ries, E. (2011) *The Lean Startup: How Constant Innovation Creates Radically Successful Businesses.* New York: Crown.

Robins, J.A. and Wiersema, M.F. (2000) 'Strategies for unstructured competitive environments: using scarce resources to create new markets', in R.K.F. Bressler, M.A. Hitt, R.D. Nixon and D. Heuskel (eds) *Winning Strategies in a Deconstructing World.* Chichester: John Wiley & Sons.

Rogers, D. (2016) *The Digital Transformation Playbook.* New York: Columbia Business School Publishing.

Rogers, E.M. (2003) *Diffusion of Innovations* (5th revised edn). New York: Simon & Schuster.

Rosenstiel, T. (1994) 'The myth of CNN: why Ted Turner's revolution is bad news', *The New Republic*, 22–29 August: 27–33.

Rosenstiel, T. (2013) '5 qualities of innovative leaders in today's media', 2 May. Available at: www.poynter.org/latest-news/the-next-journalism/212446/5-qualities-of-innovative-leaders-in-todays-media

Rousseau, D. (1985) 'Issues of level in organizational research: multi-level and cross-level perspectives', in L.L. Cummings and B.M. Straw (eds) *Research in Organizational Behavior* (7): 1–37. Greenwich, CT: JAI Press.

Royal, C. (2021) 'From boundary to bridge and beyond: the path to professionalization of product roles in journalism', August. *Journalism Studies*, 22(11):1546–65.

Sackmann, S.A. (1991) *Cultural Knowledge in Organizations: Exploring the Collective Mind.* Newbury Park, CA: Sage.

Sanchez-Runde, C.J. and Pettigrew, A.M. (2003) 'Managing dualities', in A. Pettigrew et al. (eds) *Innovative Forms of Organizing: International Perspectives.* Thousand Oaks, CA, and London: Sage.

Sanchez-Tabernero, A. and Carvajal, M. (2002) *Media Concentration in the European Market: New Trends and Challenges.* Pamplona: University of Navarra.

Sanyoura, L.E. and Anderson, A. (2022) 'Quantifying the creator economy: a large-scale analysis of patreon', *Proceedings of the International AAAI Conference on Web and Social Media*, 16(1): 829–40. Available at: https://ojs.aaai.org/index.php/ICWSM/article/view/19338

Savill, B. and Studley, J. (1999) 'Is content king? A value conundrum', *Telecommunication*, June: 26–35.

Saxenian, A. (1994) *Regional Advantage: Culture and Competition in Silicon Valley and Route 128.* Cambridge, MA: Harvard University Press.

Scase, R. (2002) 'Create harmony, not harnesses', *The Observer*, 4 August: 8.

Schatz, T. (1983) *Old Hollywood/New Hollywood: Ritual Art and Industry.* Michigan, MI: UMI Research Press.

Schatzkin, M. (2016) 'Book publishing lives in an environment shaped by larger forces and always has', 10 January. Available at: www.idealog.com/blog/book-publishing-lives-in-an-environment-shaped-by-larger-forces-and-always-has

Schein, E. (1992) *Organizational Culture and Leadership* (2nd edn). San Francisco, CA: Jossey-Bass.

Schendel, D.E. and Hofer, C.W. (eds) (1979) *Strategic Management: A New View of Business Policy and Planning.* Boston, MA: Little Brown.

Schmidt, E., Rosenberg, J. and Eagle, A. (2014) 'How Google works', slide presentation, 12 October. Available at: www.slideshare.net/ericschmidt/how-google-works-final-1

Schön, D.A. and Rein, M. (1994) *Frame Reflection: Toward the Resolution of Intractable Policy Controversies.* New York: Basic Books.

Schumpeter, J.A. (1934) *The Theory of Economic Development*. Cambridge, MA: Harvard University Press.

Schumpeter, J.A. (1942) *Capitalism, Socialism, and Democracy*. New York: Harper.

Schwartz, K.B. and Menon, K. (1985) 'Executive succession in failing firms', *The Academy of Management Journal*, 28(3): 680.

Semedo, A.S.D., Coelho, A.F.M. and Ribeiro, N.M.P. (2016) 'Effects of authentic leadership, affective commitment and job resourcefulness on employees' creativity and organizational performance', *Leadership & Organization Development Journal*, 37(8): 1038–1055.

Senge, P. (1990) *The Fifth Discipline: The Art and Practice of a Learning Organisation*. London: Random Century.

Shamsie, J. (2003) 'HBO case', in H. Mintzberg, J. Lampel, J.B. Quinn and S. Ghoshal (eds), *The Strategy Process: Concepts, Contexts, Cases*. Harlow: Pearson.

Shapiro, C. and Varian, H.R. (1999) *Information Rules: A Strategic Guide to the Network Economy*. Boston, MA: Harvard Business School Press.

Shawcross, W. (1994) *Murdoch*. New York: Touchstone.

Sherman, H. and Schultz, R. (1998) *Open Boundaries: Creating Business Innovation through Complexity*. Reading, MA: Perseus Books.

Shirky, C. (2010) 'The collapse of complex business models', 1 April. Available at: www.shirky.com/weblog/2010/04/the-collapse-of-complex-business-models

Simon, F.M. (2022) 'Uneasy bedfellows: AI in the news, platform companies and the issue of journalistic autonomy', *Digital Journalism*.

Simon, H.A. (1955) 'A behavioural model of rational choice', *Quarterly Journal of Economics*, 69: 99–118.

Sjurts, I. (2005) *Strategies in the Media Business: Fundamental Principles and Case Studies*. Wiesbaden: Gabler.

Slywotsky, A.J., Morrison, D.J. and Andelman, B. (1997) *The Profit Zone: How Strategic Business Design Will Lead You to Tomorrow's Profits*. New York: Crown.

Spar, D. (2001) *Ruling the Waves: Cycles of Discovery, Chaos, and Wealth from the Compass to the Internet*. Boston, MA: Harvard Business School Press.

Spindler, S. and van den Brul, C. (2006–7) '"Making it happen", creativity and audiences: a BBC case study', *NHK Broadcasting Studies*, 5: 29–55.

Squire, J.E. (2004) *The Movie Business Book* (3rd edn). New York: Fireside (Simon & Schuster).

Stander, F.W., Beer, L.T. de, and Stander, M.W. (2015) 'Authentic leadership as a source of optimism, trust in the organization and work engagement in the public health care sector', *SA Journal of Human Resource Management*, 13(1): 1–12.

Starbuck, W.H. (1965) 'Organizational growth and development', in J.G. March (ed.) *Handbook of Organizations*. Chicago, IL: Rand McNally. pp. 451–583. (Reprinted in *Organizational Growth and Development*, 1971. New York: Penguin Books.)

Starkey, K., Barnatt, C. and Tempest, C. (2000) 'Beyond networks and hierarchies: latent organizations in the UK television industry', *Organization Science*, 11(3): 299–305.

Staw, B.M. (1990) 'An evolutionary approach to creativity and innovation', in M.A. West and J.L. Farr (eds), *Innovation and Creativity at Work*. Chichester: John Wiley & Sons. pp. 287–308.

Sternberg, R.J., Kaufman, J.C. and Pretz, J.E. (2003) 'A propulsion model of creative leadership', *The Leadership Quarterly*, August–October, 14: 455–75.

Stewart, J.B. (2005) *Disney War: The Battle for the Magic Kingdom*. London: Simon & Schuster.

Stilson, J. (2003) 'Man with a plan', *Mediaweek*, 1 December.

Stogdill, R. (1948) 'Personal factors associated with leadership: A survey of the literature', *Journal of Psychology*, 25, 35–71.

Stogdill, R.M. (1974) *Handbook of Leadership*. New York: Free Press.

Stone, B. (2013) *The Everything Store*. London: Corgi.

Storper, M. and Christopherson, S. (1987) 'Flexible specialisation and regional industrial agglomerations: the case of the US motion picture industry', *Annals of the Association of American Geographers*, 77(1).

Sutcliffe, C. (2015) 'The two types of media acquisition and what they say about your business', *TheMediaBriefing*, 12 January. Available at: www.themediabriefing.com/article/the-two-types-of-media-acquisition-and-what-they-say-about-your-business

Tapscott, D. (1996) *The Digital Economy: Promise and Peril in the Age of Networked Intelligence*. New York: McGraw-Hill.

Teece, D.J. (2007) 'Explicating dynamic capabilities: the nature and microfoundations of (sustainable) enterprise performance', *Strategic Management Journal*, 28(13): 1319–50.

Teece, D.J., Pisano, G. and Shuen, A. (1997) 'Dynamic capabilities and strategic management', *Strategic Management Journal*, 18(7): 509–33.

Thiel, P. and Masters, B. (2014) *Zero to One: Notes on Start-Ups, or How to Build the Future*. London: Virgin Books.

Thompson, K. (2007) *The Frodo Franchise: The Lord of the Rings and Modern Hollywood*. Berkeley, CA: University of California Press. p. 6.

Tidd, J. and Bessant, J. (2018) *Managing Innovation: Integrating Technological, Market and Organizational Change* (6th ed.). Chichester: John Wiley & Sons.

Tieying, Y., Sengul, M. and Lester, R. (2008) 'Misery loves company: the spread of negative impacts resulting from an organisational crisis', *Academy of Management Review*, 33: 452–72.

Toffler, A. (1970) *The Third Wave*. London: Collins.

Towse, R. (2000) 'Creativity, incentive and reward: an economic analysis of copyright and culture in the Information Age', Ph.D. dissertation. Erasmus University, Rotterdam.

Tracey, M. (1998) *The Decline and Fall of Public Service Broadcasting*. Oxford: Oxford University Press.

Tripsas, M. and Gavetti, G. (2000) 'Capabilities, cognition, and inertia: evidence from digital imaging', *Strategic Management Journal*, Special Issue, 21 (10/11)':1147–61.

Tunstall, J. and Palmer, M. (1998) *Media Moguls*. London: Routledge.

Turner, C. (1997) 'SMEs and the evolution of the European information society: policy themes and initiatives', *European Business Journal*, 4: 47–52.

Tushman, M.L. and Anderson, P. (1986) 'Technological discontinuities and organizational environments', *Administrative Science Quarterly*, 31: 439.

Tushman, M.L. and Murmann, J. (1998) 'Dominant designs, technology cycles, and organizational outcomes', *Research in Organizational Behavior*, 20: 213.

Tushman, M., Smith, W. and Binns. A (2011) 'The ambidextrous CEO', *Harvard Business Review*, June: 74–80.

Tushman, M.L. and Nelson, R.R. (1990) 'Introduction: technology, organizations, and innovations', *Administrative Science Quarterly*, 35: 1–8.

Tushman, M.L. and O'Reilly III, C.A. (1996) *Winning Through Innovation: A Practical Guide to Leading Organization Change and Renewal*. Boston, MA: Harvard Business School Press.

Tushman, M.L. and Rosenkopf, L. (1992) 'Organizational determinants of technological change: toward a sociology of technological evolution', *Research in Organizational Behavior*, 14: 311–47.

Tushman, M.L. and Smith, W. (2002) 'Organizational technology', in J.C. Baum (ed.) *The Blackwell Companion to Organizations*. Oxford: Blackwell. pp. 386–414.

Tversky, A. and Kahneman, D. (1986) 'Rational choice and framing of decisions', *Journal of Business*, 59: 251–78.

Utterback, J.M. (1994) *Mastering the Dynamics of Innovation*. Boston, MA: Harvard Business School Press.

Van Alstyne, M.W., Parker, G.G. and Choudary, S.P. (2016) 'Pipelines, platforms, and the new rules of strategy', *Harvard Business Review*, 94(4): 54–62.

Van de Ven, A.H. (1986) 'Central problems in the management of innovation', *Management Science*, 32: 590.

Van de Ven, A.H., Venkatraman, S., Polley, D. and Garud, R. (1989) 'Processes of new business creation in different organisational settings', in A.H. Van de Ven, H. Angle and M.S. Poole (eds) *Research on the Management of Innovation*. New York: Ballinger Press. pp. 221–97.

Vanderbilt, T. (2013) 'The science behind the Netflix algorithms that decide what you'll watch next', *Wired*. Available at: www.wired.com/2013/08/qq_netflix-algorithm (accessed 1 December 2014).

Van Velsor, E. and Brittain Leslie, J. (1995) 'Why executives derail: perspectives across time and cultures', *Academy of Management Executive*, 9(4): 62–72.

Virany, B., Tushman, M.L. and Romanelli, E. (1992) 'Executive succession and organization outcomes in turbulent environments: an organisation learning approach', *Organization Science*, 3(1): 72–91.

Voci, D., Karmasin, M., Nölleke-Pzybylski, P., Altmeppen, K-D, Möller, J. and von Rimscha, B. (2019) 'What is a media company today?', *Studies in Communication and Media*, 8(1): 29–52.

Vogel, H.L. (1999) *Entertainment Industry Economics: A Guide for Financial Analysis* (4th edn). New York: Cambridge University Press.

Waldman, S. (2010) *Creative Disruption: What You Need to do to Shake up Your Business in a Digital World*. London: FT Prentice Hall.

Wallace, D. and Marer, M. (1991) 'Renegades 91', *Success Magazine*, 5 February, 38(1): 22–30.

Wallis, D. (2015) "Hearsts" – David Carey likens the media business to asymmetric warfare'. Observer.com, 15 December. Available at: http://observer.com/2015/12/hearsts-david-carey-likens-the-media-business-to-asymmetric-warfare/

Walsh, J. (1995) 'Managerial and organisational cognition: notes from a trip down memory lane', *Organisation Science*, 6: 280–321.

Walumbwa, F.O., Avolio, B.J., Gardner, W.L. and Peterson, S.J. (2008) 'Authentic leadership: development and validation of a theory-based measure', *Journal of Management*, 34(1):89–126.

Wang, C.L. and Ahmed, P.K. (2007) 'Dynamic capabilities: a review and research agenda', *International Journal of Management Reviews*, 9(1): 31–51.

Webster, J.G. and Ksiazek, T.B. (2012) *Journal of Communication*, 62: 39–56.

Weick, K.E. (1979) *The Social Psychology of Organizing* (2nd edn). Reading, MA: Addison-Wesley.

Weick, K.E. (1995) *Sensemaking in Organizations*. Thousand Oaks, CA: Sage.

Weinberger, M. (2016) 'Why Disney CEO Bob Iger told his top 400 executives to "have a love affair with technology"', *Business Insider*, 9 January. Available at: http://uk.businessinsider.com/ces-2016-disney-ceo-bob-iger-one-rule-for-technology-2016-1?r=US&IR=T

Wernerfelt, B. (1984) 'A resource-based view of the firm', *Strategic Management Journal*, 5: 171–80.

Wetlaufer, S. (2000) 'Common sense and conflict: an interview with Disney's Michael Eisner', *Harvard Business Review*, January–February: 115–24.

Whittemore, H. (1990) *CNN: The Inside Story*. Boston, MA: Little Brown.

Whittington, R. (1993) *What is Strategy and Does It Matter?* London: Routledge.

Wilding, D., Fray, P., Molitorisz, S. and McKewon, E. (2018) *The Impact of Digital Platforms on News and Journalistic Content*. University of Technology Sydney, NSW.

Wildman, S. (2006) 'Characteristics of media'. Presentation to IMMAA Meetings, San Francisco, 3 August.

Williams, R. (1974) *Television: Technology and Cultural Form*. London: Fontana.

Williamson, O.E. (1975) *Markets and Hierarchies: Analysis and Antitrust Implications*. New York: Free Press.

Wolf, M.J. (1999) *The Entertainment Economy: How Mega-Media Forces are Transforming our Lives*. New York: Times Books.

Wolff, M. (1998) *Burn Rate: How I Survived the Gold Rush Years on the Internet*. New York: Simon & Schuster.

Woodman, R.W., Sawyer, J.E. and Griffin, R.W. (1993) 'Toward a theory of organizational creativity', *Academy of Management Review*, 18(2): 293–321.

Yasai-Ardekani, M. (1986) 'Structural adaptations of environments', *Academy of Management Review*, 11(1): 9–21.

Yoffie, D.B. (ed.) (1997) *Competing in the Age of Digital Convergence*. Boston, MA: Harvard Business School Press.

Young, J.S. and Simon, W.L. (2005) *Icon Steve Jobs: The Greatest Second Act in the History of Business*. New York: John Wiley & Sons.

Yukl, G. (1999) *Journal of Applied Psychology*, 103(3), The Leadership Quarterly, 10(2), 285–305.

Yukl, G. (2002) *Leadership in Organizations* (5th international edn). Englewood Cliffs, NJ: Prentice-Hall.

Zaccaro, S. J., Rittman, A. L. and Marks, M.A. (2001) 'Team leadership', *The Leadership Quarterly*, 12: 451–83.

Zollo, M. and Winter, S.G. (2002) 'Deliberate learning and the evolution of dynamic capabilities', *Organization Science*, 13: 339–51.

Zook, C. and Allen, J. G. (2010) *Profit from the Core: A Return to Growth in Turbulent Times* (2nd edn). Cambridge, MA: Harvard Business School Press.

INDEX